AUTHENTIC LEADERSHIP

Robert W. Terry

Foreword by Harlan Cleveland

AUTHENTIC
LEADERSHIP

Courage in Action

Jossey-Bass Publishers · San Francisco

Substantial discounts on bulk quantities of Jossey-Bass books are available to corporations, professional associations, and other organizations. For details and discount information, contact the special sales department at Jossey-Bass Inc., Publishers. (415) 433-1740; Fax (415) 433-0499.

For international orders, please contact your local Paramount Publishing International office.

Manufactured in the United States of America. Nearly all Jossey-Bass books and jackets are printed on recycled paper that contains at least 50 percent recycled waste, including 10 percent postconsumer waste. Many of our materials are also printed with vegetable-based ink; during the printing process these inks emit fewer volatile organic compounds (VOCs) than petroleum-based inks. VOCs contribute to the formation of smog.

Library of Congress Cataloging-in-Publication Data

Terry, Robert W.
    Authentic leadership : courage in action / Robert W. Terry.
      p.   cm.—(A Joint publication in the Jossey-Bass public administration series, the Jossey-Bass nonprofit sector series, and the Jossey-Bass management series)
    Includes bibliographical references and index.
    ISBN 1-55542-547-X (acid-free paper)
    1. Leadership.   I. Title.   II. Series: The Jossey-Bass public administration series.   III. Series: The Jossey-Bass nonprofit sector series.   IV. Series: The Jossey-Bass management series.
HD57.7.T46   1993
658.4′092—dc20   93-17060
                                                 CIP

Credits are on page 316.

FIRST EDITION
HB Printing   10 9 8 7 6 5 4 3   *Code 9350*

A joint publication in

the Jossey-Bass Public Administration Series,

the Jossey-Bass Nonprofit Sector Series,

and

the Jossey-Bass Management Series

CONTENTS

FOREWORD

When I came to Minnesota in 1980 to become the first dean of the University of Minnesota's Hubert H. Humphrey Institute of Public Affairs, there was no established field for the study of leadership. By its nature, such a field would have to be a creative mix of art and science, of instinct and reason. To help fill the vacuum, we decided early on to pioneer in leadership studies.

We created a sudden "five-foot shelf" of readings, ranging from works by Aristotle and Lao-Tzu to Jean Monnet's insightful *Memoirs* and the soon-to-be-published *Leadership* by historian James MacGregor Burns. We started a midcareer course and called it "Reflective Leadership." (Don't you mean "effective"? we were often asked that first year. But we thought effectiveness in public affairs was a function of reflective thought even more than of action skills—and I still do.) We carved out a special place in our new program for women in leadership, whose sometimes differing skills and aptitudes have enormously widened the talent pool for the generalist role in leadership functions.

But who could lead such a venture? No one had yet figured out just how to "teach" leadership. I frequently faced in those early days the dubious query, can leadership be taught?—to which I could only offer an equally dubious riposte: "I'm not sure. All I know from experience is that leadership can be learned."

We searched among people with experience as positional leaders in government and business, learning that the correlation between position and wisdom is not necessarily positive. We talked to thoughtful academics who seemed to lack the inclination for action.

Then we got lucky. Robert W. Terry had put the University of Chicago's unusual Ph.D. in Social Ethics to use by serving as a consultant in the defense of diversity. This driving, outgoing, yet thinking man was neither an orthodox leader nor an orthodox professor; indeed, he seemed remarkably disinterested in power or tenure. But he shared the dream of a Reflective Leadership Center.

To hire a man with a personality so extroverted and a mind so fascinated with theory-building was risky, a counterintuitive shot in the dark. We would be introducing into the university setting a free spirit bound to stir up his students, make some of his academic colleagues restive, and baffle his university overseers. But Bob Terry made the dream come true. He also kept reflecting on what he was trying to do, and the result is this unusual book. In *Authentic Leadership: Courage in Action,* Terry reviews six major ways of thinking about leadership and suggests a seventh way which is influenced by all the others but proposes a new synthesis.

As educator, leader, or philosopher, Bob Terry defies being pigeonholed. The inadequacy of conventional categories bedevils any effort to describe him.

If I present him as a general theorist of leadership, you would not visualize a large, energetic, cheerful, phrase-making lecturer, a highly successful group facilitator, or a racism opponent who once wrote a book (*For Whites Only*) that sold more than a quarter of a million copies.

If I say he was educated in theology and social ethics, that wouldn't suggest he developed, in the eighties, a practical way to deliver leadership education to executives—although it might explain why he stuck with the title "Reflective Leadership" to describe what he was doing.

This practitioner of public affairs, veteran of many conflicts about race, gender, sexual orientation, and national origin, is motivated (as the book you are holding well illustrates) not only to generalize from his own experience, but also to learn from combining and analyzing what other theorists have written. Yet he sees beyond them to propose a fresh perspective on bringing people together in organizations to make something different happen.

This author grapples courageously with the concept of courage and related notions about fear and violence, sacrifice and scapegoating, imitation and exposure. His comments are deeply influenced by psychology, anthropology, and spirituality—much more deeply than is yet the comfortable norm in the burgeoning literature of leadership.

Bob Terry delights in paradox and irony, in conflict as well as reconciliation. He sees leadership as a remedy to we-they polarities; as an antidote to imitating, and thus, becoming, what we fear; and as the instrument, in John Gardner's recent words, of "wholeness incorporating diversity" (1992).

His is a trailblazing way of thinking about the common good to be found in diversity. It helps explain why leadership, which Woodrow Wilson called "an exalted function," should be as profoundly disturbing to those who study it as it is to those who practice it for better or for worse.

Not every leader will find the time or feel the urge to think hard about leadership, the get-it-all-together function. Not every leader will summon the courage to think hard, for example, about courage. But the premise of this book, and its promise too, is that hard thinking occurs somewhere near the center of the human experience called leadership—and that for leaders, to propel ourselves "beyond the comfort zone" is the beginning of wisdom.

Bob Terry is well beyond the comfort zone in this revealing, often self-revealing, book. Because it combines such a personal touch with so rational a congeries of categories, his readers will find him hard to ignore and impossible to forget. Leaders and readers—

and especially those who are both—have reason to be grateful for
this example of authenticity in action.

Minneapolis, Minnesota   Harlan Cleveland
June 1993   *President*
                                  World Academy of Art and Science

                            Professor Emeritus and former Dean
                             Hubert H. Humphrey Institute
                                      of Public Affairs
                                 University of Minnesota

PREFACE

These are momentous and difficult times. The end of the Cold War, the new cooperative agreements in Western Europe and the opening of Eastern Europe, the reunification of Germany, and the waning of apartheid in South Africa have all contributed to a new, deep belief that fundamental global transformation is within our grasp. Yet as I write, dozens of nations are engaged in armed conflict, civil war, and even genocide. Old enmities in the Middle East continue to smolder and flare, yet negotiators are, at last, meeting to discuss peace. Hope and joy mingle routinely with fear and desperation. Every day, events amaze us with their irony.

The dichotomies produced by international events are paralleled in feelings about families, communities, organizations, and cities across the United States. In one study, two-thirds of U.S. citizens said the country was in decline (*St. Paul Pioneer Press,* 1992). As we examine U.S. education, health care, religion, business, and labor, we increasingly criticize our nation's capacity to be sufficiently strong ethically, politically, socially, and economically to secure a hope-filled future.

Yet in the midst of this traumatic doubt, reform is in the air. The worst urban unrest in recent U.S. history raises the possibility that we will rethink urban policy. The quality movement challenges members of all organizations to think deeply and candidly about customers, service, and managerial philosophy. Ideas for school reform are debated all over the country. The old wrestles with the new as all of us struggle to build viable and humane futures. Ecological sanity and global and cultural diversity emerge as Gordian knots that our economic, political, social, and cultural changes must untie.

The world is crying out for leadership. In both the crises that affect the future of the globe and the urgent everyday issues that confront every family and village, the time is at hand to pause, to step back and ask ourselves, *What is leadership and what is expected of us as leaders?*

To ask these questions, however, is to challenge the adequacy of prevailing leadership perspectives. How comforting it would be to believe that some expert knows a simple formula for leadership and can offer a sure way for leaders to define and solve problems. Yet leadership experts differ profoundly, offering conflicting theories about the nature of effective leadership. Some theorists say the essence of leadership is vision. Others say it is empowering followers. Still others offer leaders specific management skills, on the premise that even if we cannot diagnose the problem and have experts fix it, perhaps we can manage it.

In addition to offering a puzzling array of theories, the field of leadership studies raises many exceedingly complicated and provocative questions. Beyond the tantalizing fundamental question—namely, what is leadership—there arise such questions as, What is courage? Is it inherent in leadership? What is vision? How crucial is vision to leadership? What is the relationship between ethics and leadership? How do leaders deal with ethical relativism? Is there any connection between spirituality and leadership? What is effective leadership action? What strategies and skills are essential to leadership?

Genesis of the Book

I came to write *Authentic Leadership* for a number of personal reasons, all of which have also influenced the purpose and shape of this book. As the director of the Reflective Leadership Center at the Hubert H. Humphrey Institute of Public Affairs at the University of Minnesota, I faced daily choices over what to teach about leadership and how to teach it. I also found that the methods we use to teach leadership reveal as much about our understanding of leadership as our leadership theories do.

As a theorist, I seek to understand how seemingly disparate ideas can be related to one another. As a social ethicist, I believe that the degree to which we as leaders are aware of the true and the real in ourselves and in the world is a predictor of the efficacy and authenticity of our action.

I am a generalist in a world of specialists. My ideas on leadership have evolved from the seminars I have led in such diverse fields as agriculture, business, government, and the arts and from my personal interest in issues of color, gender, sexual orientation, social class, and physical disability. These ideas have not been developed behind academic walls but in the world of history, community, and organizations. It is my belief that only cross-disciplinary inquiry can elicit the profound insights that pertain to the comprehensive questions of leadership.

Finally, my personal experiences and tastes of power and pain as I have participated in the struggle against racism both propel and anchor my view of leadership. While presenting leadership theory and practice, this book also reports a personal odyssey of reflective action.

Scope and Treatment

In *Authentic Leadership: Courage in Action,* I propose that leadership depends on an ability to frame issues correctly—that is, to answer the question, What is *really* going on? Leadership also depends on an ability to call forth authentic action in response to the issues it identifies. In order to describe how leadership frames issues accurately and embodies and promotes authenticity, I have found it essential to develop a new leadership theory and practice that incorporate the authenticity, the ethical sensibility, and the spirituality needed by leaders if their work is to be relevant to today's problems. Within that view of leadership, my purpose is to accomplish two broad goals, set in the context of three dichotomies. These goals and context will result in a comprehensive framework for leadership.

The two goals are (1) to build a perspective of leadership that offers a unique orientation yet also embraces the diverse viewpoints within other current leadership studies and (2) to construct a practical set of tools and guides that leaders can use to enhance their everyday leadership action.

This study is undergirded by the three polarities: *theory* and *practice*, the *one* and the *many*, and the *true* and the *real*. Each term in each dichotomy must be addressed separately if we are to understand the richness inherent in reflective action and hence, in leadership.

One of the reasons leadership theory often fails to work consistently or to be inclusive is that it starts from the wrong premise. My premise is that leadership is a subset of *action*. This theoretical shift carries enormous consequences for consideration of courage, vision, ethics, and spirituality as they relate to leadership. In addition to a starting point, a comprehensive view of leadership must propose a central organizing principle. What idea or notion can unite theory and practice, the one and the many, and the true and the real? What principle can appreciate the richness and diversity of other leadership theories, be both forever open and self-correcting, and be grounded in action? I propose that this principle is *authenticity*. It is the union of authenticity and action that forms the basis of my definition of leadership.

Leadership theories face the constant danger of ethnocentrism. To be truly comprehensive, any leadership theory must meet the test of local applicability in diverse cultural, geographic, political, economic, and social settings. Because I am a white, male, urban, straight, middle-aged U.S. citizen, my theory of authentic leadership inevitably contains pitfalls of perspective deriving from these facts about my background. To avoid as many of these solipsistic traps as possible, I have subjected my leadership theories to cultural review by diverse groups around the United States and the world.

Audience

Authentic Leadership is a book for those who facilitate, administer, and teach leadership programs, whether in communities, educational institutions, organizations, or government. It offers a comprehensive perspective and practical teaching ideas and tools. Examples ground the theory; theory offers fresh insights on old problems.

It is a book for reflective activists. In other words, I have tried to write it for those who live in both the practical and the theoretical worlds. Since leadership thrives when both divergent and convergent thinking are applied to issues, this book is written for those who like to think both divergently—challenging old thought forms by extending boundaries and making new connections—and convergently—synthesizing diversity into new structures and proposing new unified directions.

Authentic Leadership will appeal to those who want to explore the idea that leadership comes to a situation with no sure answers and a profound sense of the inauthentic. It will also be a valuable resource for people seeking skills not usually taught in current leadership programs.

Overview of the Contents

Part One offers six views of leadership. Chapter One begins by examining the global demand for leadership in a time of great hope and great fear. It discusses the history of the leadership concept and presents a method for defining a coherent field of study. The next two chapters propose a new and inclusive typology of the six existing schools of leadership. Chapter Two describes three traditional views of leadership: personal, team, and positional/functional; Chapter Three presents three provocative views: political, visionary, and ethical. These perspectives are arranged analytically, rather than historically, so that the main issues raised by one perspective are answered by the next. All six schools point toward a necessary seventh view.

The issues raised by the six schools of leadership become part of the Action Wheel of leadership described in Part Two. The Action Wheel, introduced in Chapter Four, defines six features always present in any human action: existence, resources, structure, power, mission, and meaning. Chapter Five illustrates how leaders use the Action Wheel to frame issues and understand what is really going on. In Chapter Six, I turn from action to authenticity, action's ever-present partner. Authenticity and the reasons it is necessary to leadership are defined and clarified to create the outline of authentic action leadership.

Key aspects of leadership are examined in Part Three. In Chapter Seven, I discuss leadership and ethics, to show why authentic leadership requires sound ethics. I define six ethical principles that correspond to the Action Wheel and can be universally recognized. Chapter Eight delves into the meaning of leadership vision. Following the Action Wheel, I identify six metaphors that are frequently used to shape our ideas and attitudes about life. Whether or not we are consciously aware of them, these metaphors also influence our public policies. Used inauthentically, they can appear to justify inauthentic beliefs, such as racism. In Chapter Nine, I delineate authentic and inauthentic uses of power. I propose one answer to the question, What expressions of power are appropriate for leadership? Chapter Ten revisits the six schools of leadership to demonstrate how they function together within a comprehensive framework and how they are still incomplete without one further view of leadership.

In Part Four, I describe a seventh view of leadership. Chapter Eleven presents six criteria for recognizing authentic leadership. In Chapter Twelve I discuss the need for leaders to take responsibility for conquering fear. Leadership courage and the leadership commons, the places where leadership can safely engage others, are also defined. Finally, in Chapter Thirteen, I discuss leadership, spirituality, and hope, revealing leadership's source of strength and authenticity and its potential for guiding us out of fear into hope.

Part Five comprises three resources that describe practical skills for authentic action leadership. Resource A illustrates how leadership frames issues of conflict, Resource B looks at authentic action and "system savvy," and Resource C reviews the issue of a leader's personal skills and character and the extent to which abilities and aptitudes can be formed.

Purpose

This book proposes a philosophy of leadership and a philosophy of life. It is neither dispassionate (although it is analytical) nor value- and policy-neutral (although it presents diverse views). Rather, the theory developed here not only focuses on particular aspects of leadership action but also suggests directions for such action.

I have attempted here to help leaders frame issues, understand legitimate and illegitimate uses of power, assess competing visions, and articulate a global ethic. Above all, I want to inspire leaders to find the courage to face their fears and build a more authentic world.

Mendota Heights, Minnesota   Robert W. Terry
June 1993

To my wife, Cathy,
and my new blended family,
especially my son Steven,
who is beginning his journey
into Authentic Leadership.

ACKNOWLEDGMENTS

This book has been under way for ten years. The greatest acknowledgment is to all of you who on a regular basis asked the most embarrassing questions: So how far along are you on the book? When do you expect it to be published?

Many people greatly assisted in the development of the themes that are included in this book. They include my colleagues at the Humphrey Institute: Sharon Anderson, Carrie Bassett, Charles Bates, John Bryson, Darryl Bussler, Harlan Cleveland, Barbara Crosby, Marcia Cushmore, Tom Fiutak, Nora Hall, Pam Hudson, Rick Jackson, Pat Kowalski, Linda McFarland, Shari Meerschaert, David O'Fallon, Geri Perrault, John Schneeweis, and Bill Swenson.

I am grateful for the support from my colleagues in the Minnesota Extension Service. They include Donna Rae Scheffert and Jerry Miller. The physical layout of the Action Wheel was developed by Donna Rae Scheffert and other extension colleagues, including Janet Ayres, David Boothe, Clair Hein, Stu Hunting, and William Kimball.

Support and encouragement also came from Jan Arnow, Carol Bonasaro, Ralph Brauer, George Calledine, Lisa Carlson, Bruce Gibb, Fran Holden, Joyce Kaser, Scott Marquardt, Keith Morton, Magaly Mossman, Louise Ninneman, Ted Paynther, Greg Peterson, Reola Phelps, John . Poupart, Bill Scheurer, George Shapiro, Jerry Shaw, Cynthia Stover, Doug Wallace, and Reg Wilson.

I want to personally thank Lee Bolman for his thoughtful questions, which enhanced the substance of the book. Copyeditor Elspeth MacHattie greatly strengthened the clarity and orderly presentation of arguments in this text. Lasell Whipple, project editor, and Alan Shrader, senior acquisitions editor, also sustained me with their continued encouragement.

Finally, thanks to the participants in the Reflective Leadership Center as well as the graduates of the Rocky Program of the University of Colorado, Denver, for their continued support and encouragement.

R.W.T.

THE AUTHOR

Robert W. Terry is president of the Terry Group. For eleven years, he served as the first director of the Reflective Leadership Center at the Hubert H. Humphrey Institute of Public Affairs at the University of Minnesota.

He received his B.S. degree (1959) in rural sociology from Cornell University and his B.D. degree (1964) in church and society from Colgate Rochester Divinity School. He was awarded his M.A. and Ph.D. degrees (1973) in ethics and public policy by the University of Chicago. For outstanding work with students at the University of Minnesota, he was given the Gordon L. Starr award in 1984.

Terry's research, teaching, and writing have centered on leadership, quality, and diversity. He is especially concerned about the connections between these three organizational initiatives, which are usually treated as separate issues. In 1970, Terry wrote *For Whites Only*, which sold over 250,000 copies. Through his articulation of a self-conscious examination of whiteness, he has been considered one of the pioneers in the fight against racism.

AUTHENTIC
LEADERSHIP

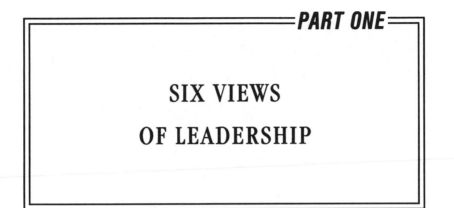

PART ONE

SIX VIEWS
OF LEADERSHIP

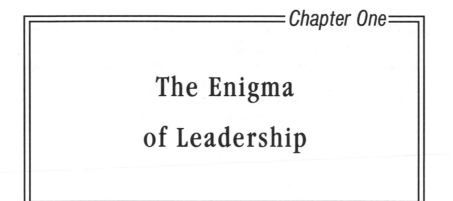

Chapter One

The Enigma

of Leadership

Just the other day the enigma slipped through my door again. An academic colleague walked into my office and announced, "We want to start a leadership program, and we want your advice."

Leadership is a hot item today. New leadership programs sprout up everywhere. Books, articles, seminars, and workshops abound. Chambers of commerce, corporations, educational systems, the military, consulting firms, and foundations are all creating or relabeling programs to emphasize leadership. Like the latest diet fad, the current vogue for leadership study risks producing merely isolated techniques or gimmicks, lucrative training programs, revised labels for old content, or even worse, charismatic demagogues who tout quick societal or organizational fixes.

John Case (1987) expresses what many of us know from experience: what can't be taught in leadership is good judgment. Other leadership advice is appropriate only in some situations. For example, says Case, the advice that leaders must have a vision may work for some, but it did not work for Nolan Bushnell, founder of

Chuck E Cheese's and Pizza Time Theaters. Even though his vision was strong his company was "short on customers" (p. 20). Likewise, the advice to strengthen others by sharing power and information worked for Jan Carlzon, president and chief executive officer of Scandinavian Airlines System, but did not work for Donald Burr, founder of People Express Airlines. Case concludes, "The real trouble with the theorists of leadership . . . is that yesterday's leaders may be today's goats even though they are still the same people with the same virtues. Steven Jobs, founder of Apple Computer, Inc., created a new industry with his vision of inexpensive, easy to use computers . . . then, pffft" (p. 20). Jack Falvey (1988), writing in the *Wall Street Journal* and noting that General Motors had "invested three million dollars plus on a program called 'Leadership Now,' " observed that GM would "soon discover that it cannot spend its way to instant leadership" (p. A22).

Compounding the leadership enigma is public attention to certain leaders' lives. Reporters probe for what they define as weak spots in the personal armor of political candidates; columnists ask who measures up to what they believe is leadership caliber. With surgical precision, commentators dissect everyone from presidential contenders to local school board officials in an effort to lay bare inner motives. We scrutinize leaders; we ignore leadership. We confuse those in positions of leadership with the process and content of leadership. As James MacGregor Burns (1978) remarks, "Leadership is one of the most observed and least understood phenomena on earth" (p. 2).

Our frenetic interest in leadership often seems unfocused and hastily conceived, like my colleague's grand designs about starting a leadership program. When I tried to understand exactly what my visitor had in mind, I discovered that the first item on her agenda was leadership skills. "Which leadership skills?" I asked. Puzzled, she replied, "You know, leadership skills!" Having been down this road before, I had to tell her that I knew of no such bundle of leadership skills. What counts as a leadership skill depends on the definition of leadership. When I asked for her definition of leadership, she had no ready answer; nor is she an isolated example.

As I travel across the country, consulting with leadership

program directors and visiting with program participants, I find the same story repeated. Despite increasing attention to leadership education, there is little sustained systematic thinking about leadership itself. Program designers and advocates seem confident in their knowledge of leadership until pressed to define it. Then, the supposed clarity disappears like water on a hot griddle. As a result, leadership courses sit precariously on unexamined foundations. Challenge the foundations and the edifaces crumble. What Burns (1984) said nearly a decade ago is still true: "The vast and diverse empirical work in leadership will continue here and abroad, but it may swell rather than flower in the absence of continued central theoretical work of broad proportions and yet rigorous quality. . . . What we need is not only more and better general theorists of leadership in the various disciplines but also a place for them to study, to interact, to think and to write. What we need is an Institute for Advanced Study of Leadership, [to address] the dire challenges to moral and political leadership in the coming decade and the next century" (p. viii). Indeed, the rapid rise of leadership education appears to be in inverse relationship to a comprehensive understanding of leadership itself, and the field of leadership studies often appears in disarray. We can discuss the personal habits, bank balances, medical histories, and family secrets of public leaders in at times embarrassing detail. Yet, observes Burns (1978), "We fail to grasp the essence of leadership that is relevant to the modern age and hence we cannot agree even on the standards by which to measure, recruit, and reject it" (pp. 1-2).

Yet the history and current state of leadership studies is also charged with excitement. One only has to skim *Stogdill's Handbook of Leadership* (Bass, 1981) or review *Measures of Leadership* (Clark and Clark, 1990), sponsored by the Center for Creative Leadership in North Carolina, to sense the explosion of leadership research. The conflicts and ferment of debate in leadership studies signal that the times offer us an opportunity to break new ground and set promising directions for leadership thinking and practice. My task is to search for convergence among these studies, without destroying their diversity. Unity should give us access to diversity; it should never seek to make diversity irrelevant.

The Enigma of the World

Leadership studies demand theoretical acumen; leadership in the world calls for practical wisdom. It is one thing to understand leadership; it is quite another to live it. However, the world of thought and the world of action are similar in that both are puzzles and both invite our inquiry and simultaneously resist it.

Today, we have the hope of world transformation—the falling of the Berlin Wall, the restructuring of the former Soviet Union, the changes in Eastern Europe, Somalia, and South Africa. Talk of a new world order and peace dividends inspires rejoicing and confidence in the future.

Yet our hope is tempered by threats of civil wars and the reemergence of unbridled nationalism, anti-Semitism, genocide, and racism. The wished-for peaceful future rests on a shaky foundation. Appearance and reality blur as we search desperately to know what is really going on and to chart a fitting response. Diversity is an unyielding fact of our time. Individuals differ by history, experience, personality, class, gender, community, society, and culture, and this diversity can cut in two directions. If quickened by fear, it divides; if quickened by hope, it unites. Can the many and the one find each other, offering both diversity and unity at the same time? Is global and communal pluralism possible? Reconciliation on any level seems far off when we view savage hostilities over such basic needs as food and land and over ingrained cultural interests. Seemingly intractable conflicts stand in enigmatic contrast to the joy and celebration of liberation and freedom as the peoples of the globe search desperately for a less dangerous and unpredictable world.

John Chancellor (1990), reflecting on the U.S. predicament during this time of "peril and promise," defines himself as a "frightened optimist" (p. 12) who is both angry and frustrated:

> My anger is caused by our borrowing from foreigners
> to maintain what seems to me a sham prosperity; by
> the failure of the federal government to address Amer-
> ica's indebtedness in an honest way; by the loss of our
> competitive position in the world; by the scandalous
> performance of the country's educational system; by

the decay of our inner-cities; by the beggaring of America's children; and perhaps, most of all, by the infuriating custom of our political leaders to avoid difficult decisions. My frustration is caused by the realization that millions of Americans underestimate the enormous strength of the United States [and] by the fact that many appear to have given up the fight [p. 11].

Hope and fear, the abilities to see the good and the bad, may be the inescapable twin companions of rapid change, setting a context for leadership practice in which we all take the stance of frightened optimists.

The Challenge to Rethink Leadership

Profound ambiguities in the world and in leadership studies challenge those of us engaged in leadership theory and practice to rethink leadership. To do so, we must transcend both leadership as expertise and leadership as management. We must be willing to engage the three polarities that are the context for any reflective examination of leadership. These polarities are the theoretical and the practical, the true and the real, and unity and diversity (or the one and the many). As I suggested in the Preface, we cannot have good practice without coherent theory, we cannot exploit the gifts of diversity without unity, and we cannot fully explain the real in the form of actual events without contemplating the true in the form of potentially universal precepts.

Theory and Practice

Rethinking leadership challenges us to attend to two leadership phenomena: the formal world of leadership studies and the practical world of leadership in action. Throughout this book, I propose a theoretical framework of leadership that is also a practicable guide for leaders themselves, because, if I know and do not do, there is no leadership. If I do without knowing, there is no leadership. Of what value is a theory that is not workable in the world, or work in the world that is not grounded and informed by thought? Theory and practice mutually educate and directly challenge one another. We need to inquire what drives thought into practice: logic, courage, conditions of personal urgency? What sustains reflective action? On what does leadership base hope, courage, and logic? What quickens us to be authentic amid rampant inauthenticity, to search for the common ground amid conflicts?

Unity and Diversity

In both studies of leadership and everyday leadership, we are persistently made aware of and struggle with diversity and unity. Even superficial reading in leadership studies reveals perspectives profoundly at odds with each other. Some theorists believe that leadership is inherently unethical; others, inherently ethical. Some view leadership as clearly distinct from management and expertise; others view the difference as at best blurred and, on reflection, not important. Some believe leadership can be taught; others say it is caught. Some rest their definition of leadership on traits, others on situations, organizations, or politics. Diversity in leadership studies is a fact. The question is, can we rethink leadership and construct a unified and comprehensive perspective that values these differences?

Active leadership confronts diversity at every turn. International conflicts torment political leaders; national conflicts threaten to destroy fragile liberation movements in South Africa and Eastern Europe. Within the United States, as Chancellor (1990) pointed out, we are immersed in issues with no clear definitions or solutions. Is there any permanence in a time when change, propelled by technology and political events, confounds common sense? On what foundation do we construct an ethic? Is a global, national, or local ethic even conceptually possible?

These issues were driven home to me recently when I was invited to offer a cultural diversity seminar to individuals committed to advancing people of color in higher education. After outlining six different perspectives on racism (see Chapter Eight), I was attacked for not dealing with the real issue. "What was that?" I asked. "Racism," was the terse reply. As the challenge continued, it became clear that the angry participant himself was using one of the perspectives I had outlined. Thus, an advocate of diversity in practice did not want to explore a diversity in viewpoints. He believed he knew what was true and real.

Is everybody a fundamentalist on something? Are there absolutes that mediate what is true and real or is knowledge really opinion—no better or worse than anyone else's opinion? Are we, then, forever caught in our own perspectives, with no real capacity for, let alone interest in, transcending *our* cultural ethnocentrism, *our* paradigms, *our* frameworks, and *our* metaphors? Yet, in contrast to this relativism, we see Eastern youngsters gorging on Western culture, wearing jeans and listening to Western music and television. Likewise, we see people in the West seeking spiritual healing from gurus in India and Pakistan, searching out cultural roots in Africa, and otherwise creating identities out of cultures other than their own.

Leadership's challenge is to reach across boundaries and to confront superficial unity in order to tap the richness of deep diversity, actions that, in turn, will lead to the discovery of a deeper unity.

The True and the Real

Not only does leadership face the challenge of unity and diversity, whether in study or in the world of action, it confronts the problem of discovering what is really going on, then living the answer. What is true and real? What is abstract and what is concrete? These questions apply to leadership itself. Some theorists say that Hitler was not a leader. Others believe such a claim is nonsense. By what criteria should we judge "real" leadership? Why does vision work in one place but not in another? Why is empowerment touted by some theorists as essential, only to be found inadequate by others?

Moreover, what is true and real in the world? Mitroff and Bennis (1989), in their provocative book *The Unreality Industry*, perceive an almost demonic turning away from reality in high-technology societies. They suggest that "the fundamental dialectic for our times is between reality and unreality, especially now that we have the power to influence and create both," and they seriously question which "side of the dialectic will win out, the ability of man to face directly and honestly the complex realities he's capable of creating, or the ability of man to turn away from reality and to invest his energy increasingly in the denial of reality?" (p. 89). The reason we are inventing "substitute realities," say Mitroff and Bennis, is that the world has become so complex that "no one person or institution [can] fully understand or control it. . . . If men cannot control the realities with which they are faced, then they will invent unrealities over which they can maintain the illusion of control." Mitroff and Bennis point out that "unreality is a big business. For example, by some estimates, public relations, i.e., the deliberate manufacturing of slanted information, accounts for up to 70 percent of what passes for news and information in our society. The end consequence is a society less and less able to face its true problems directly, honestly, and intelligently" (p. 6). If what Mitroff and Bennis say is true, then the problems of diversity are compounded daily. Not only are there conflicting perspectives on what is true but denial and ignorance, fostered by unrealities, distort those perspectives, falsely inviting us to make them real.

The enigma of the world requires our most serious intellectual efforts. For what is at stake in probing the enigma and overcoming its challenges is nothing less than our ability to leave a legacy of a world that is better than the one we inherited.

The Task of Defining Leadership

At the time Burns called for a center for advanced leadership studies, a small group of us at the University of Minnesota's Hubert H. Humphrey Institute of Public Affairs began meeting to address the question, What is leadership? We found that two University of Minnesota home economics professors, Margery Brown (professor emeritus) and Beatrice Paolucci, had developed a framework to aid them in defining home economics as a practical science. This framework outlined four possible avenues for defining a field: (1) survey current writers, researchers, and practitioners to identify present operational definitions; (2) philosophically compare several conflicting definitions presently vying for intellectual attention; (3) philosophically dissect one component of a definition in great detail, such as the mission of the field; and (4) conduct a thorough philosophical analysis to provide a definition (and its essential parts in as much detail as time will allow). The definition must have its history in the roots of the field and be a reasoned presentation of what the field *ought* to be if it is intellectually and morally defensible (Brown and Paolucci, 1979, p. v).

Some of these avenues had already been traveled by those attempting to define leadership, with, at best, modest and mixed results. For example, *Stogdill's Handbook of Leadership*, edited by Bernard Bass (1981), illustrates the survey approach. Its value lies in its inclusiveness: over 3,000 books and articles are categorized and summarized. However, its strategy of drawing an all-inclusive definition from the diverse studies results in a statement that sheds little light on the depth and richness of the studies: "Leadership is an interaction between members of a group. Leaders are agents of change, persons whose acts affect other people more than other people's acts affect them. *Leadership occurs when one group member modifies the motivation or competencies of others in the group* [emphasis added]. Research in the 1970's often expressed this as the directing of attention of other members to goals and the paths to achieve them. It should be clear that with this definition, any member of the group can exhibit some amount of leadership" (p. 16). In this definition, the relationship of leaders to followers is left vague, leadership is not distinguished from power, and the justification of leaders' goals remains unexamined.

The comparative and dissection approaches to defining a field are pursued in *Leadership: Multidisciplinary Perspectives*, edited by Barbara Kellerman (1984). This book sheds new light on leadership studies by venturing beyond traditional academic boundaries. Yet Kellerman is cautious about claiming intellectual progress. She argues that leadership studies have suffered from a "lack of a common language. . . . First, the major terms have never been defined so they are clear to all who would employ them. Second and more important, the individual disciplines, because they eventually focus on their own questions and conceptualizations, are simply too narrowly based to undertake a broad enough investigation." Kellerman concludes from this that "leadership is a subject that demands an interdisciplinary approach" (pp. x–xi).

As we in the research group reviewed sources such as Bass and Kellerman, we became intrigued by Brown and Paolucci's fourth analytical avenue—that of examining historical roots and stating what the field *ought* to be. Performing a historical search was relatively easy. (The result of that investigation is presented in the next section of this chapter.) The task of determining what leadership ought to be if it is "intellectually and morally defensible" as a discipline became the essence of the remainder of this book.

History of the Concept of Leadership

The research group began by examining the history of the term *leadership*. The second edition of the *Oxford English Dictionary* (OED) credits Foublanque with introducing the word in 1834, in a now familiar political context, when he wrote, "Is the leadership of the House to be conservatively settled by placing the minority in office?" Subsequent examples confirm that the first meaning of leadership was positional leadership. It was equated with a title or office. A secondary meaning focused on generalized traits of leaders—their ability to lead. By the 1930s, the word leadership had expanded to include the idea of *influence*.

Our current ideas about leadership have been shaped not only by the ways this word was used over the past 150 years but also by other, much older, words. For example, Edward C. Pinkerton (1982) documents a host of English words such as *captain, capital,* and *headman* derived from Latin *caput,* meaning *head.* Even in medieval times, capital meant *goods, property, principle.* "Etymologically," Pinkerton says, "the word principle means 'of the prince, of the first man.' Similarly, capital means 'of the chief, of the head man.' One may assume that the accumulated wealth that capital stands for was originally property that belonged to the chief or prince as representative of the tribe" (p. 57). Wealth becomes social position, which becomes a highly visible form of leadership.

Another of our ideas about leadership stems from the Greek noun *agogos.* It is derived from the verb *agein,* which English-speaking translators have long chosen to render as *to lead* or *to drive. Agogos,* therefore, is translated as *leader.* The related Latin verb *ago, agere* is translated "to drive, to lead; to set in motion; to do, to act, to perform; to manage" (Pinkerton, p. 3). *Demagogue* comes from Greek *demos* (the common people) plus *agogos.* In ancient Athens, a *demagogos* was a leader of the people or of a popular faction (Pinkerton, p. 1). Today, *Webster's Seventh New Collegiate Dictionary* defines a demagogue as a "leader who makes use of popular prejudices or false claims and promises to gain power." These unfavorable meanings were already gaining ground in Athens during the Peloponnesian wars of the fifth century B.C., and they have long influenced our view of what leaders can be and do.

A shortened form of *agogos* leads to a third notion about leadership. According to Pinkerton, "a variant of agos shows up as part of the Greek word *strategos,* 'leader of an army,' . . . formed on *stratos* 'army,' and *egos* equivalent to *agos,* 'leader, captain'" (p. 2). The English words *strategy* and *strategem,* which are derived from this root, brought into our language the idea that leadership requires a combination of skills, vision, and situational adaptability.

If there is one dominant connection in these definitions, it is action. They spring from doing, practicing, and being involved in life. They are also linked to valued capital, the common people, position, and role. They connote processes, guidance, journey, shepherding, and strategy. They embody power, drive, command, and influence, and they evoke images of eminence, prominence, importance, and value. However, as the research group worked its way deeper into a review of leadership studies, the clarity of these insights diminished, for if leadership was action, what *kind* of action was it?

An Intellectually and Morally Defensible Definition

The historical review opened a pathway but charted no sure course. Direction came from Brown and Paolucci's suggestion that a definition of a field be intellectually and morally defensible. The intellectual aspect was obvious to the group. We had not really understood, however, that an ethical defense was intrinsic to a definition of leadership. Yet, as we labored, that requirement became the essence of our work, and it generated a disconcerting result. What began as dispassionate inquiry emerged as a personal statement about our own passion and involvement in everyday life. We struggled in six areas.

First, as I have described, we were challenged by the enigmatic quality of leadership to explore the sources of the term's meanings. The focus on action that we identified became the ground on which to build a modern definition of leadership.

Second, we had to recognize current manifestations of leadership, both in its history and its practice. Diversity was not to be underplayed but acknowledged and embraced.

Third, the enigma surrounding the concept and practice of leadership invited ordering. However, was it possible to articulate a structure that included many options but did not sacrifice their integrity? Or were we better advised to rejoice in the richness of diversity and to give up the search for convergence?

Fourth, the inquiry itself called forth both personal and communal involvement. We felt a kinship with other reflective practitioners and a challenge to tap our own leadership experiences.

Fifth, the enigma of leadership posed tough questions about leadership's purposes. Does leadership have particular ends or is it a means to any number of ends? Is purpose intrinsic or extrinsic to leadership? Is purpose intrinsic or extrinsic to human action? As we pressed these issues, we found ourselves examining our own motives. What was leadership's real interest to us? As the group moved back and forth between abstract analyses of leadership and personal examples, we realized that purpose, which for us included a lively sense of the future, was not something from which we could totally distance ourselves. We were beginning to see the shape of a normative definition.

And sixth, we arrived at our normative definition when we realized that exploration of the enigma demanded an exploration of the meaning and value of human life itself. For if leadership is a subset of human action, then an inquiry into leadership had to be an inquiry into the total human condition and into ourselves as human beings. Leadership was not to be reduced to techniques, quick fixes, or heroics. It was to be viewed, we came to believe, as a particular mode of engagement with life, requiring a lifelong commitment to growing toward human fulfillment. Since we, as human beings, could not study engagement with life impersonally, we became the study's subject. We became the enigma.

Summary

In this age when we face multitudinous local, national, and global challenges that inspire both hope and fear, we need more than ever to arrive at a comprehensive theory of leadership that is also a practical guide for leaders. We need to embrace many leadership perspectives in a new unity to use all our knowledge. And we need to face the true and real. In my view, this means that our leadership must provide authentic action.

To study leadership is to study what others have said and then to study ourselves. In the next two chapters, I will review existing leadership studies for the perspectives that enrich our understanding and provoke our analysis and our imagination. Both the seeming disarray and the ferment in the field of leadership studies open opportunities for fresh inquiry and insight. Chapter Two will examine three traditional views of leadership. Chapter Three will explore three more provocative perspectives. Then I will turn to the study of ourselves.

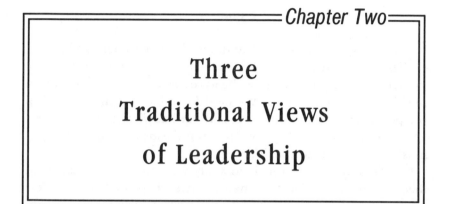

Three
Traditional Views
of Leadership

Personal leadership, team leadership, and positional/functional leadership are three traditional leadership perspectives that provide many insights into the roles leaders play. I will examine key questions about each perspective and define the elements that should be considered in any discussion of what leadership is and how it can be taught.

Personal Leadership

Someone once gave me a card that said, "ENFP Spoken Here." With puckish delight, the person put it on my desk in the place where others would keep an official-looking plaque bearing their name and title. The letters refer to my personality type on the Myers-Briggs Type Indicator: Extroverted, Intuitive, Feeling, Perceptive. To the person who gave me the card, "ENFP Spoken Here" said more about who I was than "Robert Terry, Director." It also demonstrated the still-powerful attraction of what may be the oldest face of leadership—personal theory, or as it is often called, trait theory. I prefer the term *personal theory* because I find that this school of thought attributes both certain inherent traits and acquired skills to leaders. It is the focus on the "leadership" characteristics of separate individuals that sets this school of leadership study apart from the others.

Bass (1981) observes that "the study of leadership is an ancient art." Plato, Caesar, and Plutarch all discuss leadership. "The Chinese classics are filled with advice to the country's leaders. The ancient Egyptians . . . demanded of their leader the qualities of authority, discrimination, and just behavior. An analysis of Greek concepts of leadership as exemplified by different leaders in Homer's *Iliad* identified: (1) justice and judgment—Agamemnon, (2) wisdom and council—Nestor, (3) shrewdness and cunning—Odysseus, and (4) valor and action—Achilles" (p. 5). As Bass points out, early "theorists sought to identify different types of leadership and to relate them to the functional demands of society. In addition, they sought to account for the emergence of leadership either by examining the *qualities of the leader* or the *elements* of the situation" (pp. 5–6; emphasis added).

As that sign on my desk testified, personal theory has a strong, persistent appeal. When we see Susie rallying other little kids to build a playhouse, it is hard to avoid ascribing some inborn capacity to her. Because young children have not had enough experience to have learned leadership skills, the conclusion that we almost automatically make is that any propensity to lead is an inborn talent.

Personal theory's attractiveness also arises from our fascination with the lives of individuals who seem to shape history. All of us have puzzled over what intangible qualities make great leaders. Eleanor Roosevelt said of Hubert Humphrey, "He has the spark of greatness." Like moths we are attracted to the flame the leadership spark kindles as we try to understand why certain people seem effortlessly to rise to positions of leadership the way others seem destined to win Olympic medals or Pulitzer Prizes. Some theorists have found leadership to be an innate set of qualities that only a few individuals have. Others offer a more inclusive theory that contends everyone has the potential to lead even though individuals will lead differently, depending on their personalities.

Exclusive Personal Theory

The most deterministic example of the exclusive approach that I have found is Jon Karlsson's *Inheritance of Creative Intelligence* (1978). Karlsson suggests that some day it may "be possible to demonstrate a concentration of certain genes in selected groups of people such as mathematicians and scientists and political leaders or in members of the clergy" (p. 156). He is optimistic that, once these genes are identified, genetic engineering can produce positive results for the human community, and he is puzzled that some creative persons are not picked as leaders. Nevertheless, he caps his argument by noting the human "tendency to think of people as falling into recognizable categories such as leader types, business types or criminal types." He suggests that "perhaps some analysis is now possible with biological bases for such divisions" (p. 160). This biological argument is often the undeclared partner in the heroic view of history. Biology makes the leaders; the leaders make history. It is a neat and appealing way of answering the enigma of leadership. Baffled by the ease with which Susie leads the other children on the playground, we shrug our shoulders and say, "She's a natural leader."

A less biologically based assessment of personal traits is found in Bass's summary (1981) of hundreds of leadership studies: "If the order of frequency of factors is significant, it would appear that successful leadership involves certain skills and capabilities—interpersonal, technical, administrative and intellectual—enabling leaders to be of value to their group or organization. These skills allow them to maintain satisfactory levels of group cohesiveness, drive and productivity. They are further assisted in execution of the above functions if they possess a high degree of task motivation, personal integrity, communicative ability and the like" (p. 90).

Charisma is a personal characteristic that is seen as a great leadership gift by some and as the root of demagogy by others. Daniel Goleman (1990) suggests charisma is one of the "traits that help leaders to the top [but] can prove disastrous later . . . when charismatic leaders . . . reveal personality flaws that mattered relatively little when they had less power. . . . The difference between good and bad leaders often comes down to the distinction between healthy and unhealthy narcissism. A healthy narcissist knows what he's good at and knows to take advice about what he's not so good at. [Healthy narcissists'] self confidence is the basis of their charisma. By contrast, unhealthy narcissists combine an almost grandiose sense of certainty with a disdain for subordinates" (Sec. 3, Part 2, p. 25).

The exclusive approach identifies a range of qualities as leadership characteristics, qualities that not everyone possesses. According to this school of thought, the ones who have these qualities are destined to lead, and the rest of us must be content to follow.

Inclusive Personal Theory

Because the rigidity of the exclusive theory leaves some people feeling inadequate or left out, the everyone-can-be-a-leader approach of the inclusive personal theory is more popular today. The best example of the inclusive perspective is the theory and use of the Myers-Briggs Type Indicator (MBTI). Quoting St. Paul's dictum that we are "many members in one body" but with "gifts differing" (Romans 12:4, 6), and basing the core of her argument on Swiss psychoanalyst Carl Jung's personality theory, Isabel Briggs Myers contends that we are born with personality preferences. Our lives, then, are dramas of personality development within basic type categories.

One reason that the Myers-Briggs instrument and approach are so well received today is that they recognize everyone's capacity to lead. Everyone's personality is assured significant recognition. Yet this affirmation of differences creates a curious problem. We need other people, and yet the idea that opposites attract and easily do well together is flawed. As a modern adage puts it, Opposites attract only for the first two marriages. Often, opposites irritate us, because we usually want others to behave according to our standards, to conform to our ideas about coping with a lousy boss, raising a family, being a good neighbor, making decisions, or analyzing situations. From the Myers-Briggs point of view, the best strategy is to treat others according to type. Yet, just as cultures can become chauvinistic about *their* languages, so individuals can become myopic about *their* types. We face the dilemma of cooperating with others while simultaneously appreciating the variety of their gifts.

Personal Theory and Determinism

Was there really some strange, yet identical, twist in the DNA of such diverse personalities as Harriet Tubman, Marie Curie, Abraham Lincoln, Mahatma Gandhi, Martin Luther King, Jr., and Boris Yeltsin that made them leaders? Suppose some Nobel-Prize-winning genius does succeed in unraveling the genetic code for leadership, what do we do? Clone a whole society of leaders? Institute special privileges for those who pass genetic muster?

And how do we define the characteristics some leadership studies believe are essential? Intelligence, for example, appears on many lists of leadership characteristics, yet what is intelligence? Howard Gardner's "pluralistic view of the mind" (1987) challenges standard IQ tests (p. 188). Drawing on recent brain research, Gardner distinguishes not one but seven intelligences: linguistic, logical-mathematical, spatial, musical, bodily-kinesthetic, interpersonal, and intrapersonal (pp. 188–189). If Gardner is right, the trait net must be wide indeed.

In addition, even the inclusive theory is reductionist in its applications. Can human personalities be reduced to simple combinations of traits? Is "ENFP Spoken Here" a sufficient description of me or someone else? What are the consequences for leadership education? If personal theory is right, the task for leadership education is to develop tools to isolate and identify appropriate characteristics, to administer tests to everyone, and to develop nurturing educational experiences that will enhance the development of those traits.

Although it is legitimate and even helpful for us to use the MBTI or some other instrument to identify personal characteristics, we must also recall how racists and sexists have turned biological characteristics into justifications for vicious forms of oppression. We must be wary of any argument for leadership that is based primarily on innate qualities (see Higham, 1978). Personal theory can contribute to an understanding of human action but it cannot comprehend that action's full complexity.

Ultimately, we must ask, Is not determinism self-contradictory? If freedom is self-reflection—that is, our genetic capacity to identify and then work to transcend our genetic limitations—then accepting inborn limits denies inborn potential. It would be foolish to ignore inborn characteristics. Yet history is full of examples of people who succeeded because they transcended limitations, in both body and thought.

Team Leadership

For team leadership theorists, leadership is not so much a matter of possessing the right personal characteristics as a matter of being able to develop teams of others. These theorists focus on devising effective ways of training people to lead in groups. In this view, anyone can acquire the ability to understand and master a situation if he or she has been educated in specific leadership skills and has learned how to match a selection of those skills to the appropriate situations. We all know people who fail to adjust to the situation; the boss who cannot get it through her head that the Amalgamated Widget account cannot be handled like the Universal Synthetic Properties account; the coach who doesn't notice that Jack doesn't respond well to the yelling that motivates Eric; the city council member who loses an election because he fails to see that his constituents no longer support increased development. Team theorists approach such leadership problems in one of two ways, structured or unstructured.

Structured Team Theory

The structured approach to team leadership is exemplified by Paul Hersey and Kenneth Blanchard, widely sought-after consultants and trainers in industry who are closely identified with the term *situational leadership*. In such books as Blanchard's *Leadership and the One Minute Manager* (1985, coauthored with Patricia Zigarmi and Drew Zigarmi) and Hersey's *The Situational Leader* (1984), the two have argued that leaders need to modify their styles to match the needs of those they lead. Both believe leaders can be trained to diagnose situations and act appropriately.

The simplicity of this leadership model is a major part of its appeal. Working within the context of an organization's overall goals, leaders provide resources to match various situations' requirements. These leadership actions reverse traditional leadership behavior. Traditionally, subordinates work for the boss; here, the boss's task is to produce results by working for the subordinates. The "secret" of team leadership, say the theorists, is to diagnose the followers' performance level, match leadership style to that level in order to improve performance, and contract with the followers to sustain performance. Blanchard, Zigarmi, and Zigarmi identify four levels of performance: competence, commitment, confidence, and motivation (p. 49)—and four strategies a leader must master in order to function well—directing, coaching, supporting, and delegating (p. 46). In contrast to Myers-Briggs adherents who believe in giving different strokes to different folks, this model suggests different strokes for the same folks depending upon the situation. Differing personality types are not an issue, because leadership is not personal, it is interactional. And all can learn the appropriate leadership skills.

The drawback to structured team theory is that it does not address activities that transcend particular circumstances. A general in the military, for example, might use situational leadership to motivate his or her unit commanders to accomplish an objective, but would need different tools and abilities to understand and act on the wider responsibilities of being a general. The reach of leadership is far greater than acting to achieve a specific result in a particular setting. Situational leadership appears to be another word for management. There is no question that situational sensitivity is crucial to a leader, but it is an insufficient base for a comprehensive view of leadership.

Unstructured Team Theory

Unstructured team theory is grounded in small-group research. Those who study group dynamics have found that the wide variety of tasks involved in any group activity cause leadership to shift from person to person, depending upon the task at hand. For example, John might lead as he initiates a definition of the group task, Alice might assume leadership as she offers a piece of information, and Alan might lead as he undertakes to include everyone in the discussion. In this view of team functions, all can lead the group, and likewise, all can block its effective functioning.

This leadership perspective is harder to teach than situational leadership because it is more dynamic, unstructured, and complex. However, different researchers have formulated lists of the skills they believe are required, and their findings do overlap, sharing a common cluster of items (see Johnson and Johnson, 1975, p. 5). The implications for leadership education are quite clear. If leadership requires the mastery of these sets of task and maintenance skills, then we should train people in them. Practice, feedback, and more practice would be the dominant pedagogical method.

Positional/Functional Leadership

The personal and team approaches are too simplistic to be comprehensive views of leadership, but simplicity is a seductive siren for individuals exploring the leadership enigma. When the wily Odysseus sailed within range of the Sirens' songs, he had his men tie him to the mast so he could hear the songs without leaping overboard in pursuit of them. Similarly, we need to hear what is good in each school of leadership, while arming ourselves against simple acceptance.

As an antidote to the allure of personal and team leadership, we can listen to Lewis Thomas (1984), who has eloquently pondered our role upon this planet and who reminds us that "our deepest folly is the notion that we are in charge of the place, that we own it and can somehow run it. We are beginning to treat the Earth as some sort of domesticated household pet, living in an environment invented by us, part kitchen garden, part park, part zoo. It is an idea we must rid ourselves of soon, for it is not so. It is the other way around. We are not separate beings, we are a living part of the Earth's life; owned and operated by the Earth, probably specialized for functions on its behalf, that we have not yet glimpsed" (p. 36).

The positional/functional theorists, many of whom have connections with large public and private institutions, view leadership much as Thomas views human beings. Leadership is only a part of a larger political, social, and economic environment. Leaders emerge through a process analogous to natural selection. They are shaped by the demands of particular conditions and are judged by their ability to maximize institutional or national adaptability.

Positional Theory

A leadership study sponsored by the U.S. Army finds that the focus of leadership literature has undergone "a shift in emphasis from the small group to the organization as the unit under analysis; and from the personality of the individual leader to the job requirements (i.e., behavioral demands) of the leadership role. The literature also suggests that there are important differences in the activities of appointed leaders (or managers) at different levels in the organization" (Clement and Ayres, 1976, p. 3). In today's world of complex international forces and huge bureaucracies, the personal and team approaches to leadership can seem myopic. Working in a giant multinational corporation, for example, a graduate of the team school might make the false assumption that the Hersey-Blanchard skills of directing, coaching, supporting, and delegating are all that are required, no matter what position he or she might hold. This hopeful leader may find out too late that the Peter Principle— everyone rises to his or her own level of incompetence—is alive and well. Successful prior performance may mean only lower-level success. Positions at a higher level typically require skills not demanded by previous positions.

Recognizing this problem, Clement and Ayres outlined a comprehensive organizational approach in which they isolated nine dimensions that every bureaucracy had to address in order to function well: communication, human relations, counseling, supervision, technical assistance, management science, decision making, planning, and ethics. Plotting these nine activities against the military hierarchy—lieutenants through generals—the authors developed an organizational leadership matrix that illustrates, for example, what a lieutenant has to do in regard to ethics that differs from what a captain, colonel, or general has to do. Lieutenants are expected to recognize the need to be punctual, discreet, fair, and honest in dealing with people. Generals are expected to articulate organizational value systems, focus on organizational integrity, and develop ethical frameworks consistent with governmental goals and policies.

Using this matrix, military leaders could identify role expectations, assess performance prior to promotion to a higher position, and defeat the Peter Principle. The beauty of the matrix is that it can be applied to any large bureaucracy. For example, as an experiment, a team that I was on applied the matrix to an urban public school. Once the team had replaced the nomenclature of the military hierarchy with that of the academic hierarchy, we had to change only about ten words on the matrix!

The elegance of a positional approach has also proven attractive to other theorists. Gary Yukl (1981) acknowledges the "ferment and confusion" in the leadership field, but sees the beginnings of order in the chaos. He offers an integrated model that relates personal, situational, and organizational factors. His work represents a masterful and comprehensive review of the literature and relates diverse parts to the whole. However, he limits his view of leadership to managerial leadership and does not discuss leadership's nature. He believes that "leadership research should be designed to provide information relevant to the entire range of definitions, so that over time it will be possible to compare the utility of different conceptualizations and arrive at some consensus on the matter" (p. 5). But we need research on the nature of leadership itself, rather than endless studies within an ill-defined field. Yukl tries to order parts into a whole. Perhaps we need a new whole, so we can grasp what parts are appropriate to include.

At first glance, it might appear that Warren Bennis and Burt Nanus (1985) are out to explore a total theory of leadership. However, the main data for their study comes from interviews with ninety CEOs, over half of whom were from Fortune 500 companies. In other words, Bennis and Nanus study positional leaders, defining the skills and competencies of the highest leaders in bureaucracies. In effect, they fill in the content in one column of boxes on the military's organizational matrix. "The important thing to keep in mind . . . is that nothing serves an organization better—especially during the time of agonizing doubts and uncertainties—than leadership that knows what it wants, communicates those intentions, positions itself correctly, and empowers its workforce" (p. 86). Even Nanus's newest book, *Visionary Leadership* (1992), proposes strategies for positional leaders to marry vision to organizational strategic planning.

Certainly it is no accident that researchers like Bennis and Nanus tie leadership directly to position. As we saw earlier, the history of people's thoughts on leadership shows a similar bias. Moreover, nearly all the leadership books in the business market today are targeted toward heads of organizations or aspiring heads. For example, Kouzes and Posner's provocative *The Leadership Challenge* (1990) outlines "how to get extraordinary things done in organizations." The authors find that leaders "challenged the process, inspired a shared vision, enabled others to act, modeled the way, encouraged the heart" (p. 8). However, all the people studied were heads of organizations or divisions. Thus, even though the insights are valuable, the implied theory is positional rather than comprehensive.

Each of the following authors also studies headship, and even this partial list shows the importance of this school in the leadership literature: Burns, *On Being a Leader* (1989); Cribbin, *Leadership* (1981); Crosby, *Leading: The Art of Becoming an Executive* (1990); Bothwell, *The Art of Leadership* (1983); Cohen and March, *Leadership and Ambiguity: The American College President* (1986); Conger, *The Charismatic Leader* (1989). Even Wes Roberts's entertaining *Leadership Secrets of Attila the Hun* (1985) and Kenneth Blanchard and Norman Vincent Peale's brief study of ethical management (1988) report from the positional perspective. In none of these volumes is there a discussion of leading from the middle, the bottom, or the outside.

The hundreds of chamber of commerce–sponsored leadership programs sprouting across the country are primarily designed to equip young adults to fill positions on voluntary, nonprofit boards of directors. All too often, these programs highlight the operation of each sector of the community and avoid serious grappling with the topic of leadership itself. (Of course, there are exceptions, such as the Leadership St. Louis and Leadership Philadelphia programs.) Positional people are interested in positional leadership. What is of little interest to them is leadership from the streets or from communities.

Functional Theory

In contrast to the positional model, in which leadership development involves promotion up through the ranks, the functional view is more attentive to the leadership demanded by cultural change. One of the most articulate proponents of this view is Michael Maccoby, author of *The Gamesman* (1976) and *The Leader* (1981). For Maccoby, leadership is a function of a system. As the system changes, so do the requirements and definitions of leadership. Leadership becomes the process of guaranteeing that an organization or a society will adapt to new economic and technological environments. Unlike the leadership theorists who apply predetermined traits or skills to different contexts, Maccoby sees contexts shaping the form of leadership.

For example, Maccoby identifies four different U.S. work ethics in the country's social evolution: the Protestant, or Puritan, ethic; the craft ethic; the entrepreneurial ethic; and the career ethic (1981, p. 24). Each of these ethics has produced a different model of leadership. At the present, Maccoby says, "Different social characters and work ethics exist side by side (or in confusion and conflict) as the economy changes unevenly in different parts of the country. The newest ethic invariably fits a social character adaptive to the leading edge of technology, whereas older ethics fit less industrialized parts of the country or the mature and declining industries. By reviewing leadership and the work-ethic in American history, we can see why models that have served in the past no longer bring out the best in a new social character in the United States or other advanced industrial democracies" (1981, p. 24).

The key word in Maccoby's description is *adaptive*. Leadership is determined by external events and so must evolve. People caught in the flux of social forces must adapt to survive. Because technology shapes our current environment, we need leaders who can cope imaginatively with the economic and organizational retrenchments and expansions new technologies create. As species survive by adapting, so do systems—and so must those who depend upon systems. Maccoby recommends that leaders intensify their study of history, biography, and philosophy.

Confronting the question of whether these adaptive functional leaders need a vision, Maccoby declares that "one man's Utopia might be another's prison." Nevertheless, he believes that in today's society, where "young people fear to hope," leaders can engage our spirit "by showing that rational improvement is possible in the economy, at the work place, and through multilateral negotiations to control armaments. This requires creating the structures and processes that further human and economic development, that involve people in solving problems equitably, understanding themselves and the universe, in a spirit of disciplined play and informed benevolence" (1981, pp. 236–237).

For Maccoby, then, truth is what works; good ethics is what contributes to effective system functioning and survival. This emphasis on system change allows Maccoby and other functional theorists to focus on a wider perspective than do proponents of the positional approach. Yet the functionalists' point of view still raises many questions: Is adaptability the most appropriate organizing principle for human engagement with the world? Isn't vision more important than either the functional or positional theorists suggest? Is culture more creative and complex than they imply? Most of all, by emphasizing what "works"—in either a positional or functional context—have they opened the door to a dangerously relativistic ethic? Mussolini made the trains run on time, but did he exemplify what leadership is all about? The next schools of thought I will discuss address these issues.

Summary

Each of the approaches to leadership discussed in this chapter studies an important aspect of leadership. Some people do have gifts for heading activities. Others have gifts for influencing people or for leading from within or by example. Leadership education can encourage these talents. The ability to lead teams, or be a leader within a team, is essential in any cooperative undertaking. The necessary skills are being identified, are teachable, and should also be a part of leadership education. We could not continue to evolve as a society without leaders who can adapt to our systems' functional requirements; our organizations could not flourish without leaders who can master positional leadership skills. A comprehensive theory of leadership will recognize the value in these three diverse perspectives and will accept the value from all of them, thereby lessening the weaknesses and dangers each perspective possesses when applied in isolation.

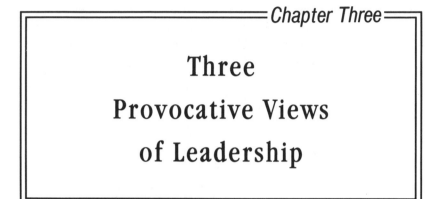

Chapter Three

Three Provocative Views of Leadership

Harlan Cleveland, former dean of the Humphrey Institute, had a twinkle in his eye. This man who has advised presidents and negotiated with foreign leaders was about to confound an audience eager to hear his views about leadership. Instead of offering them an attractive menu of team skills or a magic formula for running an organization, he would tell them that true leaders are followers. Although I have seen him do this often, I never tire of it, because, by challenging conventional wisdom, Cleveland forces his audience to think more deeply about the leadership enigma. The three leadership views I am about to discuss also challenge conventional wisdom. By focusing on power, vision, and ethics, these views address especially thorny leadership issues and invite us to probe the enigma in a new vein.

Political Leadership

According to a number of theorists, leadership is political: that is, it is a subset of power. This power may be either *power over* or *power with.* Either way, political leadership does not adapt to change but initiates change, focusing either on accomplishing the will of the leader (power over) or the will of the followers (power with).

Power-over Theory

Barbara Kellerman (1984) believes that some management theorists, and most Americans for that matter, have a deep ambivalence about whether power over others is intrinsically good or bad. "We long for, and at the same time resist, strong leadership," she says. Yet sooner or later we produce "those who persist in defining public goals, and instructing on exactly how to reach them" (p. 64). For Kellerman, power over is ethically neutral and absolutely essential for change. Her leader "is the one who makes things happen that would not happen otherwise" (p. 70). The focus is on the leader's making a difference, not on the quality of that difference.

Kellerman also states that "leaders, in contrast to heads, are accorded their authority spontaneously by group members" (pp. 70–71). "There seem to be good reasons to believe," she says, that "the stratification of political authority, power, and influence may be *by nature* intrinsic to human social existence" (p. 84). In other words, "We follow by instinct" (p. 83). The leaders we follow by instinct persuade, influence by example, act as revolutionaries, master circumstances, interpret a sense of community, and participate in class struggle (pp. 71–72).

Kellerman admits Burns might be correct in his belief that some leaders touch a deep aspect of human consciousness and offer possibilities for profound change. However, she does not agree that such leadership is inherently ethical; rather, it can elevate or debase (p. 80). Yet she suggests an ethical view of leadership when she rejects authoritarian leaders as too repressive and extraordinary leaders as too rare. She believes that we in the U.S. must generate political leaders who are skilled integrators, who keep their eyes on long-range goals rather than short-term rewards, and who mobilize us on our own, shared behalf. Only those leaders who accomplish all these objectives can make a positive, substantial, and lasting difference for the entire nation.

Kellerman's work is provocative because she wrestles with one of leadership's most profound paradoxes. We are drawn to the simple answer that leadership is a matter of biological determinism and ethical neutrality, but we also long for choice and ideals in our lives.

F. G. Bailey (1989) is a more overt power-over theorist, who unhesitatingly declares that "leadership belongs to a larger category, domination or the exercise of power" (p. 7). Like Kellerman, Bailey finds that leadership is set apart from other forms of domination, such as master/slave or boss/subordinate, by the intrinsic motivation of people to follow leaders. The followers' "attachment to the leader is direct and is its own reward" (p. 8). However, Bailey also finds, and accepts, that leadership must be inherently unethical as it seeks to control followers:

No leader can survive as a leader without deceiving others. . . . Leadership, in one of its aspects, is the art of cutting into [the] chaos [caused by a messy and complicated reality] and imposing a simplified definition on the situation, that is, making people act as if the simplified picture were the reality. This cannot be done in any honest, open, reasoned, dispassionate, and scientific fashion. The leader must be partisan. He must use rhetoric. He must be ruthless, be ready to subvert values while appearing to support them, and be clever enough to move the discourse up to a level where opportunism can be successfully hidden behind a screen of sermonizing about the eternal verities. Leadership is a form of cultivating ignorance, of stopping doubts, and stifling questions [pp. ix, 2].

Effective political leadership must "go beyond the ethical constraints of [the leader's] own society" (p. 10), because "the real world . . . continually throws up something new" that must somehow be dealt with (p. 175). To achieve change, power must reach beyond structural constraints, thereby violating cultural norms or ethical standards. It is not that power *should* be over structure in some ethical sense—it just is.

Although the duplicity of leadership cannot be altered, Bailey suggests that there is solace in knowing the truth about leadership. This truth may even "urge compassion for those intrepid and (sad to say) indispensable people who allow their souls to be corrupted by the exercise of power" (p. xiii). Indeed, the leader need not desire villainy, but "he must have the imagination (and—a paradox—the moral courage) to set himself above and beyond the established values and beliefs if it is necessary to do so in order to attain his ends" (p. 174). There is also solace in knowing there are inhibitors to political deception: normative standards, political rivals, and "mature cynicism," which "subscribes to principles that are derived from basic material, social, and spiritual needs but mistrusts (until given grounds to do otherwise) those in authority who make a parade of their own virtues." Mature cynics tolerate the games. They mobilize only to restrain "serious defilements" (pp. 171–172).

Power-with Theory

Other theorists emphasize that leadership empowers followers to accomplish important community needs. This power-with perspective lies at the heart of efforts by political or social movements, community organizers, and citizen renewal projects to mobilize people to define and secure their own agendas. Central to this view is a suspicion of, even a distaste for, formal authority. Local grassroots people are authentic; public officials are at best questionable.

A contemporary advocate of this view is Harry C. Boyte, author of *The Backyard Revolution* (1980), *Free Spaces* (1986; coauthored with Sara Evans), *Community Is Possible* (1984), and *Commonwealth: A Return to Citizen Politics* (1989). Boyte, a student of Saul Alinsky, unabashedly admires Alinsky's approach of helping people help themselves through building "mass power organizations." "Only through such groups," says Boyte, "could people who are accustomed to humiliation and defeat all their lives experience a new self-respect and gain hope" (1984, p. 30). According to Boyte, Alinsky maintained that organizations were most effective when operating on a basis of power rather than idealism. "They had to know their opponents, use the establishment's rules against them, ridicule, embarrass, and do whatever else was necessary—with non-violent and reasonably legal limits, and the experience of the group taking action—to win" (1984, p. 130).

Like many contemporary community organizers, Boyte was shaped dramatically by the Civil Rights Movement. As a teenager, he worked for Dr. Martin Luther King, Jr., on the staff of the Southern Christian Leadership Conference, and saw King's " 'dream' come alive in countless small towns across the South. . . . Communities began to believe that they might in fact control their futures, they also achieved . . . what King called the 'new sense of somebody-ness' which he believed was the Civil Rights Movement's greatest achievement" (1984, p. 12).

Yet Boyte recognizes a deep element of ambiguity in his ideal of devolving "authority to those closer to home and to institutions grounded in the life of actual textured communities" (1984, p. 213). He notes that "appeals to the heritage of the American people can take on very different meanings, depending on the social position and nature of the group making the appeal" (1984, p. 216). Populism has tended to have white, Christian, and male meanings, as it did during the presidential campaigns of George Wallace.

For Boyte, King democratized and broadened populism. The Civil Rights Movement not only attacked and sought to transform unjust institutions and organizations, "it was also a school for citizenship" (1984, p. 217). Thus, in the power-with perspective, empowerment stems from a collective sense of community and stands against unconnected individualism. "People 'learn to do it for themselves,' and politicians' work is to do people's work," as community activist Sonia Hernandez put it (Boyte, 1984, p. 218).

In Boyte's work focusing on the idea of commonwealth, the theme remains the same: "When citizen groups take the initiative in the public debate, assuming a responsibility for public goods in which everyone has a stake, they may link their own concerns and interests with those of a broader society in ways that have transformative effect" (1989, p. 143).

Ronald Heifetz and Riley Sinder (1988) offer a challenging extension of the power-with school when they challenge the view that says leadership is "(1), providing vision or taking stands, and (2), interacting effectively when managing power and authority in order to generate sufficient organizational and political alignment to realize the leader's intentions" (p. 181). According to Heifetz and Sinder, this view encourages dependency and weakens individuals' ability to face, define, and solve problems for themselves. If leaders try to exercise power over and attempt to solve problems themselves, then their leadership is inauthentic and nonproductive because "no leader can consistently provide constituents with solutions, security, or meaning. Perhaps all that a leader can reliably provide, given such expectations, is failed expectations" (p. 183).

To illustrate the need for power-with approaches to problems, Heifetz and Sinder construct a typology of leadership problems. Heifetz is a psychiatrist, and the typology, therefore, uses examples from medical practice. A type 1 problem is a straightforward, mechanical dilemma which merely requires some expertise to "get it fixed." The patient has realistic expectations that his or her difficulties can be cured by the doctor without much effort on the part of the patient (p. 185). In a type 2 situation, such as heart disease, "the doctor can offer some remedies, but no cures. . . . The patient can be restored to more or less full operating capacity, but only if he takes responsibility for his health by making appropriate life adjustments" (p. 185).

A type 3 situation involves chronic disability or impending death. Typically, everyone involved, including the patient, concentrates on finding solutions to the disease, but this response diverts the patient's attention from the work at hand (p. 186). What is that work? The patient must face the harsh realities that go beyond the condition. He or she must make the most out of life, prepare family and friends for the eventual death, and complete important tasks. Heifetz and Sinder argue that only the patient and his or her family can do this (the hospice movement helps), not the doctor. Although physicians may have to change their styles depending on the situation, "the basic stance of the physicians—to help the patient do his work—will remain constant" (p. 187). Similarly, public policy solutions generally require "adjustments in the community's attitudes and actions. Who else but those with stakes in the situation can make the necessary adjustments?" (pp. 187–188).

The implications for leadership are that the leader needs "technical know-how" and "the improvisational flexibility and insight to manage others in doing work on frustrating situations where the definition of the problem, let alone the solution, is not clear" (p. 190). In these type 2 and type 3 situations, leadership must go "beyond or against the expectations. . . . In other words, a person is rarely, if ever, authorized to exercise leadership" (p. 194).

In addition, Heifetz and Sinder state that the person exercising leadership does not necessarily know what to do. In fact, "the need for leadership arises precisely because there are many highly problematic situations in which no one knows what to do. If the directions were clear, the solution available through technical expertise, then the authority in that field would suffice; one could presumably bring him in, or elect him" (p. 195). Rather than provide answers, true leaders mobilize the group's resources, serving as catalysts rather than problem solvers.

The difference between Boyte and Heifetz and Sinder is that for Boyte, leadership provides resources for people to do their own work, while for Heifetz and Sinder, it provides resources for people to do both their own and "real" work. Heifetz and Sinder usually see the people as the final judge of what is best. Yet, when work must be evaluated for its appropriateness, an extrinsic set of standards arises. This distinction between real work and other kinds of work can lure Heifetz and Sinder into the power-over school. It can also open a deeper line of inquiry into authenticity.

When a group of people engage in mass hysteria, groupthink, or "avoidance" of any sort, and someone outside the group diagnoses this avoidance, has not a new authorization process emerged, in which an outside expert becomes the ultimate reality tester? Is leadership a psychiatric intervention to challenge followers to deal with real work? Furthermore, the concept of *real* work is loaded with ethical overtones that suggest this work is a duty, not a choice. When psychiatric authority becomes power over, that authority would seem to be acknowledging an implicit ethic and an implicit claim of authenticity. At the least, psychiatric or other professional authority would seem to bear an implicit responsibility to be accountable to the values of the profession in question.

The power-with approach is not limited to grass-roots and community leadership. It is also taking hold within those organizations that foster *empowerment* and *participatory management*.

Peter Block (1987) exemplifies the thinking of organizational theorists who believe empowerment can resolve many workplace problems. Block argues that "if we wish to replace bureaucracy with entrepreneurial spirit, helplessness with empowerment, then we have to take a hard look at organizational politics. Politics is the exchange of power and so goes hand in hand with empowerment." Block believes that "the process of organizational politics as we know it, works against people taking responsibility. We empower ourselves by discovering a positive way of being political. . . . We must be powerful advocates for our units in a way that does not alienate those around and above us (p. xiii).

Although empowerment is a popular concept within modern management circles, a word of caution is in order. Managers or positional leaders who say to followers, "I'm going to empower you," send shudders to the core of power-with theorists. Beware, they say, of anyone coming to empower you. Most likely, they intend only to delegate tasks. Delegation is a positional leadership activity that transfers responsibility and/or authority to others. Empowerment is claimed by the individual or group that will exercise the power. Empowerment is not given but taken.

Both power-over and power-with theorists see power as the ultimate end, and the ultimate judge, of true leadership. But power for what? This vexing question shapes the visionary and ethical leadership perspectives.

Visionary Leadership

Power may be crucial for leadership, but is it all that matters? Power uninformed by vision merely diffuses energy. Vision directs human action by assessing current trends and pointing people toward a desirable future. A truly visionary leader teaches, providing insight so that people understand both the future's possible content and the process by which that content is predicted and/or created.

Content Visionary Theory

Harlan Cleveland, who believes true leaders are followers, is a prime example of a content visionary. Like Gardner (1989), Cleveland believes that leadership is widespread in the world. His vision of a million or so emerging leaders in the United States led him to found the Humphrey Institute's Reflective Leadership Center in 1981. His goal was to convene leadership practitioners and theorists to think about critical policies generated by new social trends. Participants identified different scenarios for the future and were challenged to act on their visions (Cleveland, 1980).

Vision is called for by many leadership theorists. It figures in Boyte's perception (1984) of Martin Luther King, Jr., and to some extent in Kellerman's concept of power (1984). The visionary is one of the Myers-Briggs temperament types, and the ability to create and transmit a vision can be an ingredient in situational theory. Cleveland and like-minded theorists, however, see vision as the *essence* of leadership, not merely one ingredient.

Vision is the heart of leadership because vision transcends political interests, testing the outer limits of the vested views that lock people into parochial perspectives, limit creativity, and prevent the emergence of new cultural and political realities. Vision designs new synergies. Vision challenges everyday, taken-for-granted assumptions by offering new directions and articulating what people feel but lack words to say. Vision speaks the unspeakable, challenges the unchallengeable, and defends the undefendable. Cleveland (1985) reflects that "the art of executive leadership is above all a taste for paradox, a talent for ambiguity, the capacity to hold contradictory propositions comfortably in a mind that relishes complexity" (pp. xv–xvi).

Cleveland's belief that the true leader is in reality a follower represents his own most basic paradox. He points out that the major changes of our times were not generated by established leaders. They "boiled up from people (and new leaders) who had not previously been heard from" (p. 42). After the people find the answer,

> Then the experts and pundits and pollsters and labor leaders and lawyers and doctors and business executives and foundation officers and judges and professors and public executives, many of them chronically afflicted with hardening of the categories, catch up in jerky arthritic moves with all deliberate speed. The press serves as a gatekeeper, moving all this informa-

tion from its specialized sources to the general public, where it is then circulated through informal, but powerful, interpersonal networks. And only then, when the policy decision is long since made and the experts have finally done the programming, written the editorials, raised the money, painted the directional signposts, and staged the appropriate media event, the publicity heroes and heroines come forth, the ones *People* magazine thinks are our leaders, to climb aboard the train as it gathers momentum and announce for all to hear the new direction of march—speaking by television from the safety of the caboose [p. 43].

Futurists are often leadership visionaries. Naisbitt's *Megatrends* (1982) and the work of the World Future Society (for example, *The Futurist: A Journal of Forecasts, Trends and Ideas About the Future*) are just two very public examples. In the past, the leadership skill the futurists taught was trend analysis—X leads to Y. Now, after many false predictions, they concentrate on the skill of crafting scenarios. Many chambers of commerce or other city organizations hire futurists to draft three or more scenarios as community options.

Scenarios are superior to trend analysis because they cluster a series of interdependent variables into an image or story. Citizens and communities, and businesses and nonprofits, can view and compare multiple possibilities derived from multiple interactions of variables. Shell International assembles a team whose only responsibility is to develop two global scenarios. Senior management then positions the organization, in large measure, in light of those two story lines. (To learn more about scenario writing, see Schwartz's *The Art of the Long View*, 1991.)

Process Visionary Theory

A second set of visionary theorists takes a slightly different view. Using Thomas Kuhn's pioneering work *The Structure of Scientific Revolutions* (1970) as their departure point, most believe the world and its organizations are in the midst of a fundamental paradigm shift. Joel Barker (1985b), an international consultant who has made his reputation by helping organizations understand paradigm thinking, states that a paradigm "tells you that there is a game, what the game is, and how to play it successfully." It is "a set of rules and regulations that (1) describes boundaries, and (2) tells you what to do to be successful within those boundaries. . . . A paradigm shift then is a change to a new game and a new set of rules" (p. 13; see also Barker, 1992). For Barker, leadership lives between paradigms, taking people from the more comfortable to the less comfortable, from the familiar to the unfamiliar. As the new reality emerges, leadership opens our eyes to the new world that is manifesting itself.

Innovation Associates take a similar tack. Their work and the efforts of others in this school are summarized by John Adams (1984, 1986). These theorists blend philosophy, theology, organizational theory, intuition, and educational methodology to cast light on our current transitional era. David Nicoll suggests that the process visionary approach is based on the idea that paradigms are analogous to tribal stories that tell how the world came to be and how the tribe fits into the world. The story provides a context within which people can function meaningfully. Today, our global and national "tribes" are between stories and, therefore, confused. As we develop a new story, we must alter much of what we think, feel, and do. What our grandchildren will accept as fact, we are in the process of discovering and creating. It is important for us to recognize we are facing a change that matters (Adams, 1984, p. 4).

For Charles Keifer and Peter Senge, the transformation is so dramatic that organizations must experience *metanoia,* or fundamental change. If organizations fail to become metanoic organizations, they cease to compete. In a metanoic organization, five beliefs constitute the core and "form a coherent organizational philosophy": "a deep sense of vision or purposefulness; alignment around that vision; empowering people; structural integrity; and the balance of reason and intuition" (Adams, 1984, p. 70). In Keifer and Senge's view, leaders are responsible for that vision or purpose. But these leaders are teachers, not controllers. Indeed, "Most [metanoic leaders] don't even think it's possible to control an organization from the top." Therefore, these leaders "recognize that they must continually work to overcome the authoritarian mentality, because it is inimical to the spirit of equality and responsibility they seek" (Adams, 1984, p. 78).

Senge (1990) also views the common notion that reality can be broken into small parts for problem solving as antithetical to vision. Instead, he says, we should "build 'learning organizations,' organizations where people continually expand their capacity to create the results they truly desire, where new and expansive patterns of thinking are nurtured, where collective aspiration is set free" (p. 3).

When I attended Keifer and Senge's three-day leadership and mastery seminar, I and the other participants practiced envisioning the future, and then we claimed it by imagining we were already living it. To test our intuitive powers, we engaged in an eye-opening activity. We were placed in groups of eight to ten people, most of them strangers. After someone said the name of someone no one else knew, someone else was asked to intuit something about this mystery person. When the responses were recorded and tallied, we were amazed to find that all the groups had averaged 80 to 90 percent accuracy. Intuition can clearly be a solid, even necessary, mode of knowing.

Noël Tichy and Mary Anne Devanna (1986) are process vision advocates who picture organizational transformation as a drama with three acts: "Act 1—recognizing the need for revitalization; Act 2—creating a new vision; Act 3—institutionalizing change" (p. 6). Vision is central to their total work, and they show how vision operates even in large bureaucracies.

Finally, Kenneth Callahan (1990) invokes process vision when he suggests that church leadership is a journey in which mission teams of pastors and laity focus on four leadership tasks:

1. Helping persons rediscover power in their own lives and destinies
2. Constructing new communities of reconciliation, wholeness, caring, and justice—in the name of Christ
3. Creating a new theological direction and specific, shared purposes

4. Launching and leading intentional missional
teams to meet specific, concrete human hurts and
hopes—both societal and individual—in the world
[p. 139].

Because Callahan has an explicitly Christian and thus value-
directed perspective, he bridges the visionary and ethical perspectives. However, his primary focus is process vision. The ethical or
theological content of a vision is secondary.

To those of us who find our own times clouded and confused, visionary leadership offers a possibility that we can come to
grips with the larger forces that mold us. Yet the visionary approach, too, is incomplete, for although it requires ethical reflection, it does not claim that ethics is inherent in leadership.

This lack of attention to ethics per se is troubling. To challenge his seminar audiences to avoid "paradigm paralysis," Joel
Barker flashes a motto on the screen: "If you think it's impossible,
get out of the way of those who are doing it." He uses this motto
for a positive reason; however, meaning left unexamined is dangerous. Six million Jews could not possibly be eliminated systematically, yet it was done. Are we to get out of the way of those whose
visions are nightmares, or to get in their way? Vision separated from
ethics can lead to tyranny. Therefore, I must press on to the last of
the six leadership perspectives.

Ethical Leadership

For too many people who study, teach, and practice leadership,
ethics seems an afterthought, something they attend to only as a
formality. Yet almost everyone that I ask believes that there is such
a thing as unethical leadership. This is not to say that people who
study leadership do not think ethics is important as a subject. However, they often do not see ethics as integral to an exploration of
leadership. The theorists who do focus on ethics fall into two broad
categories: those who believe that leadership is intrinsically ethical
(and therefore not leadership when it is unethical), and those who
see ethics as an extrinsic standard by which the highest forms of
leadership are identified.

Intrinsic Ethical Theory

To begin to understand the unique perspective of those who believe that ethics is the essence of leadership, we can listen to Rost's *rejection* (1991) of the ethical school of thought: "My view . . . is that these scholars have confused the nature of leadership with the practice of morally good leadership. . . . In trying very hard to attain some conceptual clarity as to the nature of leadership, it is very important that we not confuse what leadership is with what leadership should be" (p. 166).

Who are these "confused" scholars, and what do they see that Rost does not? David Campbell (1984) offers one of the most succinct ethical definitions of leadership when he says that leadership is "any action that focuses resources toward a beneficial end" (p. xv). Beneficial ends might include profits, lower taxes, better health care, the elimination of war, more love in the world, beauty, happiness, and personal serenity (p. xv).

Christopher Hodgkinson (1983), working from an organizational orientation, finds that leadership involves an inherently valuative artistic process. The organization is like an artist's canvas and leadership styles are like paint; therefore, "values impinge upon and are intertwined in every phase of the administrative process." Because values are involved, conflict is generated, and the subsequent tensions "between individual and organization in the one direction and between organization and environment in the other . . . ensure that administration is a difficult art and one which can be at once the noblest, the oldest and the basest of the professions" (pp. 3–4).

Robert Greenleaf (1977), the author of *Servant Leadership*, adds an ethical perspective to his visionary view when he states: "The failure (or refusal) of a leader to foresee may be viewed as an *ethical* failure because a serious ethical compromise today is sometimes the result of a failure to make the effort at an earlier date to foresee today's events and take the right action when there was freedom for initiative to act" (p. 26). For Greenleaf, foreseeing the unforeseeable and having the courage to act on that knowledge appropriately are the keys to leadership.

Similarly, Max De Pree's *Leadership Is an Art* (1989) and

Leadership Jazz (1992) reach beyond a positional perspective to address ethical demands on leadership. Both positional leadership and "roving" leadership (which is spread throughout the corporation) "must take a role in developing, expressing, and defending civility and values" (p. 17).

Although Robert Tucker (1981) views leadership as value neutral, he recognizes that this is a break with the historical legacy of political leadership. It is Plato's view that leadership "is an activity with utility for the polis, the activity of giving direction to the community of citizens in the management of their common affairs, especially with a view to the training and improvement of their souls" (p. 3). In contrast, Burns, in his pioneering study *Leadership* (1978), sees no escape from the normative task. For Burns, leadership is a subset of power, yet an ethical stance is also essential to leadership. True leadership is exercised "when persons with certain motives and purposes mobilize, in competition or conflict with others, institutional, political, psychological, and other resources, so as to arouse, engage, and satisfy the motives of followers. This is done in order to realize goals mutually held by *both* leaders and followers. . . . Naked power, on the other hand, admits of no competition or conflict—there is no engagement" (p. 18).

Burns's critics see his position as a difficult one to defend, because it raises the thorny question, Who decides what is ethical? Burns's answer to this question centers on three dimensions of leadership: the character of the leader-follower relationship, the substance of the vision of human need, and the level of moral reasoning.

The test of the leader-follower relationship is how the leader uses power. Someone who imposes his or her will on another is a tyrant. In contrast, a leader presupposes and affirms follower independence, engaging in a dialogical relationship that will necessarily result in conflict. The follower must be able to resist, debate, and voluntarily follow. Only then is the one who uses power a leader. In other words, Burns views empowerment as a critical aspect of leadership, because anything less oppresses people. Yet Burns sees leadership as more than empowering or visionary. For him, the logical next question is, How does one judge which act or vision is appropriate? Despots have visions, and mobs experience empowerment; neither vision nor empowerment guarantees ethical action.

Thus, for Burns, leadership must also meet human needs. But this ethic raises a further ethical problem. How does a leader adjudicate between one person's perceived need for a Mercedes and another's need for food and shelter? Burns's answer incorporates Maslow's hierarchy of human needs, in which physiological needs form the base of a hierarchy that progresses upward "to safety needs (including the desire for freedom from fear and insecurity and harm), to the need for affection and belongingness (including the sense of being involved and accepted in a group), to the need for esteem, and to other needs higher in the pyramid or ladder. Once [one need is] alleviated, the next pressing need . . . becomes the priority" (p. 66). Leadership takes individuals to a higher level on the needs scale, but that does not mean leadership takes individuals to the top. A leader must not get too far in front of the followers, suggests Burns, or the leader will cease communicating with those followers.

Finally, in Burns's view, leadership raises the followers' level of moral reasoning. This part of his definition also creates difficult questions for Burns: Whose criteria shape the moral reasoning? What about cultural diversity? Is there any universal set of ethical principles?

The heart of Burns's view of ethics in leadership lies in his developmental conception of change among followers. Most, if not all, developmental schemes are inherently ethical. By that I mean that lower development is less valued than higher, both quantitatively and qualitatively. Each higher level in a hierarchy seeks to include and expand that from which it came. Therefore, Burns finds his answer in the work of moral development theorist Lawrence Kohlberg. Burns observes that Kohlberg used information from several cultures to identify six stages of moral development among individuals. These progressive stages range from a preadolescent level—in which the individual "is orientated toward punishment, defers to superior power, and sees proper actions as those that satisfy [mainly personal] needs"—through "conventional" stages, up to "postconventional" stages. In the postconventional stages, individuals have "greater awareness of the role of procedural rules in group and individual norms. These rules and values are shared by *a social transaction or contract for overall utility:* 'the greatest good for the greatest number.'" In the final stage, the focus is on general ethical principles that Kohlberg calls "logical, comprehensive, universal, and consistent." These principles are "liberty, equality, dignity, justice, and human rights" (p. 73). (For a thorough analysis of Kohlberg's framework, see Munsey, 1980.) Leadership raises the stage of moral discourse; tyranny lowers it.

Burns's analysis does not suggest that leaders are ethically perfect. It does mean, however, that leadership helps followers move one ethical level above where the leader finds them. The Boston racial conflicts over busing—described by Lukas (1986)—offer a negative example of this process. Applying Burns's criteria, we would fault Boston leaders because they did not offer leadership that "operates at need and value levels higher than those of the potential follower" (Burns, 1978, p. 42). Instead, they appealed to fears and prejudices, thereby eroding any hope of community reconciliation and hope, and also failing to be true leaders.

This emphasis on meeting people's needs and elevating their moral reasoning fuels Burns's main distinction (1978) between two kinds of leadership: transactional and transforming. Transactional leadership "occurs when one person takes the initiative in making contact with others for the purpose of an exchange of valued things" (p. 19). Transactions can be trades or bargains for votes, goods, or psychological benefits. The market is one in which each party knows the rules, is informed about the ends and means, and makes a deal. In contrast, transforming leadership "occurs when one or more persons *engage* with others in such a way that leaders and followers raise one another to higher levels of motivation and morality." Such leadership "ultimately becomes *moral* in that it raises the level of human conduct. . . . Naked power-wielding can be neither transactional nor transforming; only leadership can be" (p. 20).

In this way, Burns puts an ethical stamp on leadership itself. While other perspectives may imply or infer an ethical interest, Burns argues for the centrality of ethical reasoning and behavior in leadership theory and practice.

The distinction between transactional and transforming

leadership is widely used in the leadership literature, yet often, the ethical argument gets lost. Tichy and Devanna (1986), for example, rely on Burns's transforming/transactional distinction, but I do not sense that they see leadership as inherently ethical. To a large extent, Burns pioneered the ethical view of leadership, and for a number of years, he stood alone as its advocate.

From the ethical perspective, leadership skills would have to include reaching an ethical understanding of oneself and the world, clarifying ethical principles, practicing analysis of ethical cases, and creating and employing leadership strategies that encourage people to seek higher levels of ethical reasoning.

Extrinsic Ethical Theory

Janet Hagberg's *Real Power* (1984) offers a six-stage model of leadership that is an extrinsic evaluative framework. Briefly, the six levels are (1) leads by force, inspires fear; (2) leads by seduction and deals, inspires dependency; (3) leads by personal persuasion, inspires a winning attitude; (4) leads by modeling integrity, inspires hope; (5) leads by empowering others, inspires love and service; and (6) leads by being wise, inspires inner peace. Level 1 is mainly coercive; level 2 opts for trade-offs and deals; and level 3 is rooted in charisma. But the particular value of Hagberg's analysis lies in her forthright and provocative suggestions for leadership beyond the third level of power.

Level 4 leaders are "mostly concerned with doing the . . . fair or just thing in the long run." They lead because "they have become deserving of the trust that followers have in them, and they are honest with their followers, even if it is painful for them all" (p. 161). Stage 5 leaders are "servant leaders" who empower others, drawing out their best. Their vision transcends self and is "rooted in love, justice and peace for all" (p. 161). Stage 6 leaders are rarely found because most do not aspire to leadership of any kind. "They are so truly selfless that if they were to engage as leaders, it would be simply as the result of genuinely living their life purposes and acting on the wisdom that dwells so deeply within" (p. 166). Hagberg implies that we would not, or should not, recognize these leaders if they are to be truly effective. They seem to be personifications of the leadership enigma.

John Heider's *The Tao of Leadership* (1985) takes Hagberg's view further. For Heider, the Tao of Lao-Tzu, itself profoundly ethical, transcends ethics. It directs us toward the spiritual, toward a new communion that enhances and goes beyond ethics. In this view, "specific actions are less important than the leader's clarity or consciousness. That is why there are no exercises or formulas to ensure successful leadership" (p. 75).

Henri Nouwen's book *In the Name of Jesus* (1989) reflects on a Christian view of leadership and asks, "What makes the temptation of power so seemingly irresistible? Maybe it is that power offers an easy substitute for the hard task of love. It seems easier to be God than to love God, easier to control people than to love people, easier to own life than to love life" (p. 59).

Other authors also reflect this view of leadership as a spiritual presence. Autry's *Love and Profit: The Art of Caring Leadership* (1991) and Covey's *The Seven Habits of Highly Effective People* (1989) and *Principle-Centered Leadership* (1991) carry this perspective forward. An even more challenging work is *Managing as a Performing Art,* by Peter Vaill (1991), who moves us into spirituality and opens a window onto the realm of hope and courage.

Yet the ethical school overall is fraught with difficulties. Most reflectors on leadership are comfortable thinking of "ethical" and "unethical" as modifiers of leadership. Hitler, the often used example, was clearly a leader, they say, but an unethical one. Therefore, to argue that leadership is inherently ethical confounds common sense and observation. Moreover, what is ethical in one culture may be unethical in another. There is no universally accepted ethic that can be manifested in leadership. Relativism is reality, say the opponents of the inherently ethical view. Relativism is also a political defense against lock-step thinking and behavior. Beware the carriers of absolute truth, say the relativists. To force one view is only to lay bare one's own ethnocentrism.

A second weakness in the ethical perspective is its tendency to avoid the question, Why are people unethical? A comprehensive view of human behavior must face this perplexing problem. Does not leadership theory have to transcend ethics and ask the hard questions about evil and hope, cynicism and faith, good people producing bad effects, and evil resulting in good?

Summary

I began my quest for a definition of leadership by reviewing the history of the term. That history suggested that action is the common factor in all views of leadership. I presented an overview of six schools of leadership theory and the two subsets of each school:

- Personal leadership theory: (1) exclusive, (2) inclusive
- Team leadership theory: (1) structured, (2) unstructured
- Positional/functional leadership theory: (1) positional, (2) functional
- Political leadership theory: (1) power over, (2) power with
- Visionary leadership theory: (1) content, (2) process
- Ethical leadership theory: (1) intrinsic, (2) extrinsic

Not only is each school distinct in focus and definition, but each school requires that a leader learn and use different skills.

More importantly, both the three traditional views of leadership and the three provocative views implicitly call for a comprehensive and profound view of leadership that goes beyond single schools of thought to explore the depths and heights of the human condition, including the human potential for spirituality.

This analysis sets the stage for the development of a theory of leadership that will also be a theory for leaders to use in practice. Leadership understood as authentic action will acknowledge, access, and embrace all six existing perspectives and reveal a seventh view. I will also propose models that leaders can use as they face the complexities of "reading" the world and determining what ought to be done. My view of leadership will thus point in two directions—back through the six leadership theories and forward into the world of human action.

Any one narrow view of leadership should be suspect. Beware of counterfeit leadership. What then would authentic leadership be and do? This question orders the remainder of this book.

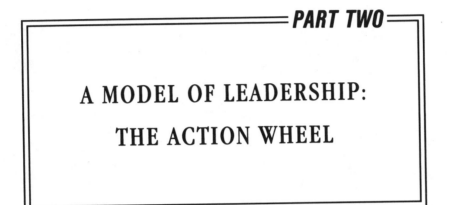

PART TWO

A MODEL OF LEADERSHIP:
THE ACTION WHEEL

Chapter Four

Leadership in Human Action: The Model

The human universes of *action* and *authenticity* embrace and position all the other parts of my leadership model. In Chapters Four and Five, I will build the action framework of leadership by defining the generic features of action; in the remaining chapters, I will link authenticity to action both conceptually and experientially.

The Argument for Action

Why is action the human universe within which leadership must exist? First, the concept of action appears in our historical sources for the terms *lead, leader,* and *leadership,* suggesting that leadership has always been considered action, even if that connotation was unexamined and intuitive.

Second, when action is viewed as the universe that contains leadership, it is possible to move beyond the conceptual dilemmas raised by Burns's work. When leadership springs from power, as Burns proposes, then it is an impossible struggle to make purpose

also central to leadership. When leadership dwells within action, leadership can easily exhibit both power and purpose.

Third, action as a framework clarifies some persisting puzzles in leadership studies. For example, What is the relationship between leadership, management, and expertise? What is followership? How does leadership connect to ethics, vision, courage, and hope? And, What leadership perspective and skills are appropriate in what circumstances?

Fourth, action is conceptually broad enough to embrace the six perspectives described in Chapters Two and Three, critique them, and build on them, while remaining a unique perspective in its own right.

Moreover, as a term, *action* is experientially neutral enough that it does not alienate the other perspectives. *Showing up* and *engaging* are the minimum requirements for leadership as a subset of action. Persons can show up and engage; alternative theories can show up and engage; organizations, nations, states, cultures can show up and engage. Any conceptual or actual entity can function within the action model. Action has, of course, often been more narrowly defined than I will define it. Physiologists discuss involuntary action—a blink of the eye or a heartbeat. Behaviorists focus on stimulus and response, and operant conditioning. Communalists such as Aristotle locate human action in political communities, restricting it to citizens. Existentialists and voluntarists such as Jean-Paul Sartre and Hannah Arendt find will and decision making to be the impetus for action. Other theorists, such as Rollo May, highlight direction and transcendental mission as action's *sine qua non*. The term has a history of diverse definitions, and the Action Model will embrace them all.

The Need for Model Building

What do picking up a pencil and combating racism have in common? Very little if we concentrate on the sequence of moves in each act; a great deal if we isolate and compare the parts of each action. By searching for the generic features of all human actions—that is, features implicit in everything we do, from blinking to securing

world peace—it is possible to connect all actions structurally in an Action Model, without sacrificing individual significance.

At the outset of this task, however, I am reminded of May's discussion (1958) of theory builders who act out an "edifice complex." Even more unnerving is the following parable told by Kierkegaard:

> A thinker erects an immense building, a system, a system which embraces the whole of existence and world history, etc.—and if we contemplate his personal life, we discover to our astonishment this terrible and ludicrous fact, that he himself personally does not live in this immense high-vaulted palace, but in a barn along side of it, or in a dog kennel, or at the most in the porter's lodge. If one were to take the liberty of calling his attention to this by a single word, he would be offended. For he has no fear of being under a delusion, if only he can get the system completed . . . by means of the delusion [Oden, 1978, p. 21].

Moreover, self-delusion may lurk in the nature of language itself and in the relationship between concepts and reality. A long-standing debate rages in philosophy between objectivists and subjectivists. Objectivists separate subject from object. For them, categories of thought correspond to and represent real-world properties. There is a direct fit between the language about the world and the world itself. In contrast, subjectivists view categories of thought as embodied in experience, thereby connecting subject and object. Rather than attending to correspondence, they focus on imagination, figure and ground, and perception.

Nevertheless, there is at least a tenuous agreement among many critical thinkers that a "both and" strategy can undergird theory construction. Lakoff (1987) identifies four points of agreement as a tentative launch point for theorizing: "a commitment to the existence of the real world, a recognition that reality places constraints on concepts, a conception of truth that goes beyond mere internal coherence, and a commitment to the existence of stable knowledge of the world" (p. xv).

Does the debate about categories, the mind, and the world matter? Lakoff (1987) again supplies an answer.

> It matters for our understanding of who we are as human beings and for all that follows from that understanding. The capacity to reason is usually taken as defining what human beings are as distinguishing us from other things that are alive. If we understand reason as being disembodied, then our bodies are only incidental to what we are. If we understand reason as mechanical—the sort of thing a computer can do—then we will devalue human intelligence as computers get more efficient. If we understand rationality as the capacity to mirror the world external to human beings, then we will devalue those aspects of the mind that can do infinitely more than that. If we understand reason as merely literal, we will devalue art [p. xvi].

In many ways, Lakoff's "experiential realism," as he labels his approach, informs my work. The generic features of action will emerge from lived experience and in turn inform it. However, I also propose to weave a line of argument between and beyond the subjectivism-objectivism debate. Both have insights; both err. Each, alone, ends in intellectual stalemates that neither alone can handle. Objectivists fail to appreciate the richness of language; subjectivists fall prey to the traps of cultural relativism. In order to construct a comprehensive framework of leadership, I believe we need an approach that deeply appreciates metaphorical thinking, imagination, creativity, and diversity, but that is also able to ground and justify a universal framework of action, a global and personal nonrelativistic ethic, and a spiritual basis for hope.

Criteria for the Generic Features of Action

My approach to identifying the generic features of action builds on several philosophical predecessors: Aristotle (McKeon, 1941), who distinguished four causes of action (final, formal, efficient, and material); sociologist Talcott Parsons (1967), who identified four functional prerequisites in his theory of action (patterned maintenance, goal attainment, integration, and adaption); and philosopher Alan Gewirth (1982), who distinguished two generic features of action (purposiveness and freedom).

I propose that there are seven standards to judge the features of action that will become a model for leadership. First, the features must be the *minimum* ones necessary to account for action. In other words, Occam's razor applies: entities ought not to be multiplied unnecessarily. Second, the features must be *distinctive* enough to be analytically separable. They must point to different aspects of action, ones that are not collapsible into each other. Third, the features must be *inclusive*. They must embrace a large number of particular actions without losing their own distinctiveness. Fourth, the features must be relatively easy to *identify* when a leader is analyzing any particular action. Fifth, the features must be capable of being connected and related to each other and *assembled* into a whole. Sixth, the distinguishing and connecting of the generic features and the use of the theory must *generate insight* about some critical aspect of an action.

And seventh, the theory of action, with the generic features in place, must be able to *ground, inform,* and *enrich* both our understanding of leadership and our engagement as leaders.

Before I define the seven generic features, let me briefly revisit Lakoff's argument about the status of categories as concepts. In an effort to avoid the either/or of the subjectivist versus objectivist debate, I am proposing a both/and solution. My seven generic categories do not correspond to reality with the fit of a surgeon's glove. Nor can they. The definitions blur at the boundaries because they come from reflection upon experience, not from "pure" thought. They are enmeshed in life because they clarify life experiences. My orientation is not theory to practice. Instead, I begin with action, calling it into review, teasing out its essential features, and then testing in real situations those features, which came from real situations. The features and the frame in which I assemble them provide, I believe, both theoretical and experiential support for informed reflective leadership engagement in the full panoply of life experience, because the generic features of action are implicit in *all* action.

What then are these generic features that are minimal in number, analytically distinguishable, inclusive, readily applicable to real life, connected to each other, productive of insight, and essential for understanding leadership theory and practice?

Generic Features of Action

The seven generic features of human action are:

- Fulfillment: an *embodiment* term, denoting that *into which* human action moves
- Meaning: a *significance* term, justifying that *for which* human action moves
- Mission: a *direction* term, identifying that *toward which* human action moves
- Power: an *energy* term, signifying that *by which* human action moves
- Structure: an *organizing* term, denoting that *through which* human action moves
- Resources: a *material* term, connoting that *with which* human action moves
- Existence: a *limiting and possibility* term, outlining that *from which* human action moves

I will examine mission, power, structure, and resources, before turning to existence, meaning, and fulfillment.

Mission

Any aspect of an action that refers to its direction—its *toward which*—constitutes mission. All such terms as *purpose, expectation, aim, vision, goal, intention, objective,* and *desire* point toward an action's mission. Although many authors distinguish between these terms, at the generic level, all the terms indicate the toward which of action. Mission is the primary concern of the visionary leadership theorists.

Power

Power is the actual expenditure of energy. In contrast, a potential for energy is a resource, just as, in the material realm, coal in the ground is a resource, coal when it is burnt is power. Power is the decision, commitment, passion, and volition that energizes mission. It can be intense or relaxed, strong or weak, wild or calm. Power is the *by which* of human action. Mission apart from power languishes as an unfulfilled expectation. Power is the primary concern of the political leadership theorists.

Structure

Structure is the *through which* of action—the plans, institutional arrangements, maps, forms, and processes that order and funnel power toward mission accomplishment. Without structure, energized mission has nowhere to go. Positional/functional theorists focus on structural concerns.

Resources

Anything that is useful, measurable, and needed to accomplish the mission meets the criteria for a resource. Resources are the *with which* of action, and without them, action languishes. Team leadership theorists are focused on the resource feature of action.

Existence

Existence is the ground and the setting of action. It is the *from which* of action, and it both limits and makes possible any action. Resources are one product of existence, but existence is also the ecological and historical setting of action. Without existence, an action is disconnected from its particularity, or uniqueness, and its past. Existence is the aspect of action that personal leadership theorists attend to.

Meaning

Meaning is the why of action—the *for which* we act. The particular values, reasons, and rationalizations that justify a particular action constitute its meaning. However, any general list of values is simply a resource; a value or a reason must be specific to an action in order to possess meaning. Meaning evaluates, recommends, justifies, and makes sense of life. Meaning is the context of action, just as existence is the setting of action. Meaning is the primary concern of the ethical leadership theorists.

Spirituality is a subset of meaning yet transcends meaning. Triggered by some limit or possibility—death, birth, suffering—spirituality inhabits the intersection of meaning and existence. It raises the ultimate challenge of life, asking individuals to engage life without ultimate answers. Spirituality calls for faith-based action, and it bridges meaning and fulfillment.

Fulfillment

Fulfillment is the completed act, the *into which* meaning, mission, power, structure, resources, and existence converge at any given time and place. Thinking, doing, and being converge in fulfillment. If the mission is to write a poem, the produced poem is fulfillment. If the mission is to murder someone, the actual murder is fulfillment. Some actions produce objects separate from the actor, such as a poem. Some actions, such as speaking, are integral to the actor while acting. Some actions are virtual, such as imagination; some are actual, such as walking. Fulfillment, we should note, does not imply *ethical* action. It is any completed act. The seventh view of leadership is grounded in fulfillment, with its focus on courage, authenticity, and hope.

Every human act reveals these seven generic features, all the time, every time. These features are explicitly or implicitly present whether the action has happened, is happening, or will happen. The features are present, even if the actor is unaware of them.

Overview of the Uses of Generic Features

Six of the seven generic features have both descriptive and constructive uses. Describing these features answers the questions: What went on? What is going on? What will go on? Used constructively, features perform an action audit: Has mission been sufficiently attended to and understood? Has each of the other essential elements of the anticipated action been understood?

Earlier, I stated that the essential leadership question is, What is really going on? With the generic features before us, we have what I believe are the essential generic questions every leader should ask about an ongoing event in order to ensure an adequate answer to that one overriding question of what is going on. The generic questions are:

> What is the history of this event or situation? (Existence)
> What are the central resources? (Resources)
> What are the plans and processes? (Structure)
> What is the stakeholders' level of commitment? (Power)
> What is the mission (Mission)
> What is at stake? (Meaning)
> What is the event in its completed action? (Fulfillment)

If any of these seven questions are left unanswered the resulting picture of the event is distorted.

The questions can evaluate completed, ongoing, or future events. Using the questions prospectively is most complicated because the questions seem to demand predictions. However, the role of the questions when we are anticipating an action is to say that there will be meaning, mission, and power issues in the anticipated action, just as there are in present and past actions. For example, suppose you were called upon to give a speech on your leadership program. With your knowledge of the generic features of action, you could predict that the speech, to be complete, would consist of at least seven parts:

- The history of the leadership program (existence)—where it came from, its limits and possibilities
- The members and materials of the leadership program (resources)—what is available to be mobilized and used
- The organization of your leadership program (structure)—how the formal and informal relationships are ordered and operate

- The pivotal decision makers and overall vitality of the leadership program (power)—who is actually driving the organization and her, his, or their commitment
- The direction of the leadership program (mission)—the overall vision and particular goals
- The value and significance of the leadership program (meaning)—the justification of the whole operation
- The speech, either delivered or to be delivered (fulfillment)

Thus, in applying the action model, two steps are involved. First, identify the action to be analyzed—making a speech, organizing a committee, thinking about the causes of poverty, or carrying out any other need or desire. And second, ask the seven leadership questions about the action. The remainder of this chapter will pursue a fuller development and justification of the generic features. Readers for whom the preceding discussion of the features of action is sufficient may want to skip ahead at this point to the next chapter, where the features will be put into the context of a particular process.

Generic Features: An In-depth View

Each generic feature can, of course, be defined with ever-increasing complexity. Yet the art and science of taxonomy is neither arbitrary nor whimsical. It is only through complex categorizing that we can say, for example, that a book is clearly different from a dog, and that a dog-eared book, while related in appearance to a dog's floppy ear, is yet distinct from a dog's ear. So, with a caution born from recognizing the dangers as well as the necessity of definitions, I will proceed to a deeper examination of the seven generic features of action.

Existence: A Limiting and Possibility Term, That from Which Human Action Moves

The concept of existence has had a long and embattled philosophical history, and the question of its meaning has always been at the heart of philosophical controversy. Barrett (1958) highlights what is at stake: "That existence is not a genuine predicate has been one of the more entrenched dogmas of Positivism and Analytic philosophy. . . . For the Positivist, existence is not a concept because it is too empty, thin and therefore ultimately meaningless; for Kierkegaard, my existence is not a concept because it is too dense, rich, and concrete to be represented adequately in any mental picture. My existence is not a mental representation but a fact in which I am plunged up to the ears, and indeed over the head" (p. 264).

Barrett comments that what matters is not whether we rig our language so that *exists* is a permissible predicate (and language can be rigged either way), but what we make of existence—whether we give it its due as a primal and irreducible fact, or somehow convert it into a shadowy stand-in for essence (p. 265). *"So far as he logicizes, man tends to forget existence,"* says Barrett. *"It happens, however, that he must first exist in order to logicize"* [emphasis added] (p. 264).

In my view, existence is the setting from which human action occurs, that part of life that is a given. It is the historical and ecological legacy that defines limits and cradles possibilities. It includes inherited artifacts, rituals, and routines that may or may not be consciously valued. It is also language, that part of existence that offers the resource with which we interpret experience and imbue events with value and significance.

Existence is the foundation of becoming—life from death, being from nonbeing. It is the inherent potential capacity of resources and also the ultimate check, the final restraint. Existence is neither good nor bad; it just is. It identifies the particular and the unique in any act, while also identifying the inescapable setting of all action. Existence is the basis of all answers prior to reflection. It defines our reality, it tells us what is safe and what we should fear.

In times of historical calm and continuity, there are few existential issues. Patterns of the past are sure predictors of the future and go largely unquestioned. However, let baffling things happen to us, and we work diligently to make those things intelligible. In times of transition, "when one age is dying and the new one not yet born, and the individual is either homeless and lost or achieves a new self-consciousness" (May, Angel, and Ellenberger, 1958, pp. 17–18), the problem of existence becomes the catalyst for a search for new meaning.

Meaning: A Significance Term,
That for Which Human Action Moves

Meaning is what imbues action with significance, and justifies or rationalizes action. It answers the *why* or *for which* of action. Meaning is public, it involves values, it is shared through common symbols, and it makes dialogue possible.

One way that staff at the Reflective Leadership Center have found to dramatize public meaning is to have participants play *BAFA' BAFA'* (Shirts, 1977). In this simulation game, players organize two very different cultures, alpha and beta. Each culture has its own rules, power arrangements, and set of cultural assumptions. Alpha is a warm, friendly, maternal society; beta is competitive and egalitarian. Persons in the alpha culture visit beta and vice versa. Their task is to try to understand the other culture by living within it for a short time. Within twenty minutes, alphas become thoroughly alpha, betas become thoroughly beta, and each group thinks the other group thoroughly odd. Confronted with each other, they struggle mightily to bridge a chasm of difference.

BAFA' BAFA' simulates the crisis of meaning that occurs when the everyday symbols and signs used to make sense of life and draw significance from events are shorn away. The game creates culture shock and shows that when a situation is familiar, inherited meaning is assumed. Let the situation be novel and our innate need to create meaning is triggered. Thus, we both rehearse old meanings and create new meanings throughout our lives. At its best, this activity is the process of scientific advance, of invention and creativity. At its worst, it is the process of stereotyping and of maintaining prejudice and bigotry.

Consider this example: if we are driving down a road in the United States and we see two solid yellow lines down the center of the street, what do they mean? Neither side can cross over. What is the meaning of a dotted line on our side and a solid line on the other side? We can pass, the other side cannot. What is the meaning of question marks down the center of the street? One respondent to this exercise retorted, "Questionable area!" This was a great response. She took the potential of *question mark* (existence) from her language pool (resource) and applied it to the novel situation. An explanation in terms of what we already know is one response to novelty. Another response is to invent a whole new theory to explain the novelty. *New*, of course, always means new to some degree. Individuals remain rooted in existence, even as they discover $E = mc^2$, DNA, or plate tectonics. To put it another way, we do not walk forward into the future. We back into the future, looking over our shoulders. As long as nothing unusual appears, we are unperturbed. It is the new or anomalous that demands our attention, invites our imagination, and triggers our significance-making ability.

Another respondent who was asked the meaning of the question marks hypothesized that drugs from a police raid had made their way to transportation department workers, and the question marks were the result. What a fertile imagination, and what stereotyping of road workers. Suppose, in the next day's paper, we saw the headline "Fraternity Brothers Admit Road Marking Damage." For many of us that would explain the question marks. A stereotype and/or a fact would be confirmed. However, what if the very next day's paper reported that the damage was not a fraternity prank? Now we are back to square one, but with two quandaries. First, Where did the question marks come from and what do they mean? And second, How did fraternity brothers enter the story initially?

Meaning is difficult to inspect directly. Clarity of our sense of self and our sense-making processes partially evaporates when we employ traditional empirical investigation methods. Subjectively, however, meaning is discernible by contrast, when one family of meanings bumps into another. That is why *BAFA' BAFA'* is such a valuable teaching tool. Other cultural analysis approaches for uncovering meaning include examination of orienting metaphors, parables, morality tales, art, humor, and values.

Metaphors. In high school, I was taught by English teachers to put metaphors in my writing to enrich it, and I was taught by chemistry teachers to take metaphors out of my writing so that I might be precise. As I now know, both sets of teachers were misguided in thinking that metaphors could be added to or subtracted from language. What philosophers of language now believe is that metaphors constitute language itself, and they devote much effort to analyzing metaphoric use. As Clancy (1989) observes, "it is important to realize that metaphor is an integral part of our thought process. We use metaphor much as we breathe; we cannot avoid its use or its consequences. As Wittgenstein puts it, we cannot escape the web of language; and it is an inherent human limitation, tantamount to not being able to jump out of one's skin. As Heidegger said: 'Language is the house of Being. Man dwells in this house.' I should add that this house is built on and of metaphor" (p. 13).

"The essence of metaphor," write Lakoff and Johnson (1980), "is understanding and expressing one kind of thing or experience in terms of another" (p. 289). Metaphors may be orientational: for example, up, down, front, back, here, there. They may be ontological, describing some aspect of reality as if it had properties of another aspect—for example, "time is money." If the context is shared, the metaphor will readily open a new perspective, but if the context is not shared, the metaphor will not work. Lakoff and Johnson give a wonderful example of the importance of shared context: "Please sit in the apple-juice seat. In isolation, this sentence has no meaning at all, since the expression 'apple-juice seat' is not a conventional way of referring to any kind of object. But the sentence makes perfect sense in the context in which it was uttered. An overnight guest came down to breakfast. There were four place settings, three with orange juice and one with apple juice. It was clear what the apple-juice seat was. And even the next morning when there was no apple juice, it was still clear which seat was the apple-juice seat" (p. 12).

Parables. Parables also offer depths of insight not easily achieved by factual language. Consider the wisdom the following parable conveys. Søren Kierkegaard, who was noted for his penetrating stories, wrote the parable to answer this question: "When the task is becoming one's self, to what shall we compare the individual who does not even recognize that he has or is a self?"

> It is related of a peasant who came bare footed to the
> capital, and had made so much money that he could

buy himself a pair of shoes and stockings and still have enough left over to get drunk on—it is related that as he was trying in his drunken state to find his way home, he lay down in the middle of the highway and fell asleep. Then along came a wagon, and the driver shouted to him to move or he would run over his legs. The drunken peasant awoke, looked at his legs, and since by reason of the shoes and stockings he didn't recognize them, he said to the driver, 'Drive on, they are not my legs' [Oden, 1978, p. 19].

Morality Tales. For Reich (1987), culturally significant meaning is found in myth-based morality tales. He finds these tales in the background of political discourse, where they "inform our sense of what our society is about, what it is for. . . . They shape our collective judgments. They anchor our political understandings." Reich defines a *mythology* as a "culture's device for interpreting its reality and acting on it" (pp. 5-8), and he identifies four such myths in the U.S.: "Mob at the Gate," "Triumphant Individual," "Benevolent Community," and "Rot at the Top."

Art. Eaton (1988) defines aesthetics as "delight taken in intrinsic features of objects or events that are traditionally considered worthy of sustained attention or reflection" (p. 9). Kupfer (1984) suggests that aesthetics informs everyday life—sexuality, sport, decision making, death—and is not the "exclusive province of museums and concert halls" (p. 1). Art enriches life, it does not flatten or dull the experience of life.

For both Eaton and Kupfer, art or any aesthetic expression both transmits meaning and invites inspection of meaning.

Humor. Humor can be a powerful conduit to meaning. It is a way to convey otherwise unsayable truths about human existence. Like art, it reveals meaning by juxtaposing the obvious with the novel. Also like art, it frees the imagination through its ability to tear down boundaries and stereotypes.

Values. At the heart of meaning lie our values. They determine the significance of our actions. They rationalize and/or justify why we act. Our ethical principles are the final appeal, the last stop in our argument—when each of us says, in effect, "I did it because it is right, because it is good, because it is the fitting thing to do."

Metaphors, parables, morality tales, art, humor, and values open paths for understanding human discourse. They relativize thought and quicken the necessity for real dialogue. When we mediate reality through metaphors, parables, morality tales, art, humor, and values, then we introduce humility into any conversation about meaning. We replace a claim of absolute certainty with a search for mutuality of perspectives, shared meaning, and shared understanding.

If leadership is a subset of human action, then leadership must attend to meaning rehearsal and meaning creation. If leadership is to discern what is true and real, what is actual and what is virtual, then leadership must be open to others' interpretations of events. Leadership, therefore, is inherently dialogical. It encourages the bumping of one perspective with another. It reaches for shared meaning among diverse meanings, shared value among conflicting values. It seeks to reveal what is happening and what ought to happen, and does so within the givenness of existence.

The relationship of meaning to existence raises a fundamental question. Existence triggers questions of meaning; meaning surrounds existence. Thus, there is an open horizon as we struggle over these ultimate questions. Spirituality lives and moves at the intersection of meaning and existence. It asks about the grounds for hope, the antidote to despair and cynicism, the ultimate meaning of life and death, the meaning of tragic moments of suffering, and the grounds for responsibility and obligation. In other words, spirituality, at this stage of my argument, is understood as a wider context of meaning. Thus, I am suggesting that spirituality transcends both meaning and existence, inspiring fulfillment. This last point will be addressed in more detail in Chapter Thirteen. Moreover, spirituality, as I understand it, is not a doctrine but rather a quest and an experience, as we search for hope that life is sustainable and credible, significant, and worthy of living.

Mission: A Direction Term, That Toward Which Human Action Moves

Mission directs our attention toward a future state of affairs. As long as we are considering that toward which we want to move, we are considering the mission of our action. Missions can be personal, organizational, or societal. They can be in conflict or alignment with each other. My son's mission to play basketball may conflict with my mission to have him clean his room, and both may conflict with his fraternity's expectation that he will do a work project at the fraternity house.

Societies often express broad missions through their positional leaders. President Reagan was noted for stating missions with great aplomb, as in this example: "I have always believed that this land was placed here between two great oceans by some divine plan. It was placed here by a special kind of people—people who had the courage to uproot themselves and leave heart and homeland and come to what in the beginning was the most undeveloped wilderness possible . . . and that destiny can build a land that will be for all mankind a shining city on a hill" (Thompson, 1982, p. 1). Yet even such broad missions—meant to align individuals around a shared meaning—will face opposition from some. Even a shining city on a hill does not capture everyone's dream nor reflect the experience of U.S. citizens who have seen their hopes dulled by racism, sexism, and class divisions.

Missions can be *mini* or *mega*. Mini-missions are those millions of toward whiches that direct our everyday activities: I'm going to get up, I'm going to get dressed, I'm going to go to the store. Many of these mini-missions are so habitual that we give them scant attention. But they are nevertheless present, guiding and directing.

Leadership has little interest in these mini-missions; instead, it focuses on mega-missions. Mega-missions can be personal, organizational, or societal. The difference resides in their scope and seriousness to the actor. Personally, my mission may be to enter therapy, change jobs, commit fraud. Organizationally, a mission may be to achieve 'next day delivery' or to gouge the public. Likewise, a national vision could be Reagan's "city on a hill." All are significant in scope and seriousness. They all reach outward and expand the focus of activity; they all require energy and commitment.

However, it may be that leaders are not necessarily conscious of their real missions—especially the mega ones—but through personal and communal reflection, therapy, or feedback, or by bumping against alternative views, we can bring them to consciousness and acknowledge and own them.

Missions are also not necessarily ethical. When Martin Luther King, Jr., said, "I have a dream," he invited us into a vivid future of equality and justice and let us taste of its potential. He invited us to claim a hope as our own and to help fulfill it. However, this scenario could just as well apply to Hitler. The vivid images of the future he professed invited people to claim his vision as their own, align with it, and fulfill it in their everyday lives. Later, in my discussion of authenticity and ethics, I will offer criteria to assess different visions of the future. The important point here is that, as a generic feature, mission is descriptive, not normative. Mission clarity is crucial to organizational effectiveness, strategic planning, and organizational development. Mission, to be energy giving, must be concise, clear, trusted as real, shared, and believed to be doable. Yet, as a generic feature, mission can be vague, unclear, misleading, private, or utopian.

Power: An Energy Term, That by Which Human Action Moves

There is no action without power. Mission and meaning are not enough. Existence only sets the stage. If there is no energy and commitment to drive action, nothing happens.

What is power? As a theorist and teacher, I have continually found power the most thorny of the seven generic features to define and explain. I think this is due to our strong preconceived ideas and feelings about power. Terrifying experiences are often related to our ideas about power. We have only to recall experiencing an earthquake, flood, forest fire, or tornado to understand how helpless power can make us feel. Power also connotes historical wrongs. The massacre at Wounded Knee is just one of many tragic abuses of power. It was no accident that the authors of the U.S. Constitution, worried lest power be concentrated in the hands of the few, divided the federal government into three branches, and specified appropriate checks and balances. We are painfully aware of the abuse of power in everything from the apartheid imposed by South African ruling whites to the murders under the regime of former Ugandan president Idi Amin. Amnesty International reports are filled with cases of torture, murder, and victimization by those in authority in countries throughout the world. In our own country, the poor, people of color, women, gays and lesbians, Jews, and dissenters have been subject to sad abuses.

Yet despite our worry about power, we are drawn to it, intrigued by it. Television programs that glamorize power or vividly depict its abuses garner high ratings. We are lured toward the rich and famous. The stories and scandals of royalty tantalize our imagination. We seek to be more powerful, and we rank ourselves by our relative power. There is an ambivalence in us about power, and it runs deep. I often ask participants at the Reflective Leadership Center how many of them think they are powerful. One or two hands sheepishly go up. Like fire, power draws and repels us at the same time. It can even be argued that we in the United States have an antileadership attitude that guarantees resistance to any person who emerges too strongly. He or she will be turned out of office or discounted as power hungry. I am amused by radicals who want to organize the "powerless." My suggestion is that they meet at a cemetery! The only people who are completely powerless are the dead. But it is hard for us to admit our power, because we are so aware of its negative potential.

Power has also bedeviled political scientists, even though it is their special subject. Some view power as a quantity, a zero sum, with only so much to go around; others view power as a relationship and an expansive positive sum. For some, power is control-led, it is accomplishing our will. For others, it is liberation, accomplishing our will in spite of others. For still other political theorists, power is self-directed, without regard to another. We can empower ourselves without being over or under someone else. All these connotations, experiences, and opinions of power are what make it so difficult to clarify power as a generic feature of action.

I mentioned earlier that Burns views leadership as a subset of power. An examination of the serious theoretical difficulties that I believe this view causes will also supply some insights into the meaning of power. Burns (1978) argues that "the two essentials of power are motive and resource. The two are interrelated. Lacking motive, resource diminishes; lacking resource, motive lies idle. Lacking either one, power collapses" (p. 12). In my terms, Burns's view of power is tied to the mission and resources features of action. He describes the "power process" as one in which "power holders . . . , possessing certain motives and goals, have the capacity to secure changes in the behavior of a respondent . . . , human or animal, and in the environment, by utilizing resources in their power base, including factors of skill, relative to the targets of their power-wielding and necessary to secure such changes" (p. 13).

Moreover, power wielders are to be distinguished from leaders. Power wielders seek to accomplish their own will, whether or not it is the will of others. Leaders seek to meet the will of both leaders and followers. "To control *things*—tools, mineral resources, money, energy—is an act of power, not leadership, for things have no motives. Power wielders may treat people as things. Leaders may not. All leaders are actual or potential power holders, but not all power holders are leaders" (p. 18).

Burns articulates the power-with perspective; however, this definition also perpetuates the ambivalence about power. Power wielders are problematic; leaders are honorific. Thus, power itself takes on a negative cast. Yet, in Burns's view, leadership is a subset of power. Furthermore, under this definition, leadership cannot easily embrace coercive acts by positional leaders. But are there no cases where power can legitimately coerce people against their will? Was President Kennedy not a leader when he dispatched troops to Selma, Alabama, to enforce the Civil Rights Act? Did he not clearly coerce some for the benefit of others? When power is defined too narrowly, the definition not only limits power but also limits leadership.

Yet power, generically understood as a feature of action, is neither good nor bad, authentic or inauthentic. Like the other features of action, it just is.

To his credit, Burns seeks to transcend his own analytical dilemma, and his intuition about power takes a positive direction when he points out that "forty years ago Bertrand Russell called power the fundamental concept in social science, 'in the same sense in which Energy is a fundamental concept in physics.' This is a compelling metaphor; it suggests that the source of power may lie in immense reserves of the wants and needs of the wielders and objects of power, just as the winds and the tides, oil and coal, the atom and the sun, have been harnessed to supply physical energy" (p. 12). Energy is the clue we have been seeking. By focusing on energy, we can differentiate power from the other features of action. We can show that power is only one, not the, essential embodiment of human action. (Astin and Leland, 1991, also agree that energy, rather than control, best frames power.)

What is power? *It is the actual expenditure of energy.* This expenditure may be either literal or metaphorical. Energy is the visible aspect of the life force in nature, animals, and human beings; it is also the invisible spirit behind *commitment*, that uniquely human dimension of power.

Commitment is the activity of making and keeping decisions over time. It releases and focuses energy. It can be expressed as personal or as collective will. For example, suppose we had to conduct a power audit in a family, a school, an organization, or even in your personal life. First, we would check for energy level. Is the atmosphere lively, intense, flowing, and engaged, or is it flat, dull, and stifled? Is morale up or down? Is motivation high or low? Is there anger, joy, delight, whimsy, playfulness, hostility, frustration, or isolation? Is there a collective sense of participation and involvement? Second, we would identify the critical stakeholders: teachers and students, administrators and suppliers, parents and children, elected officials and citizens, or others. What is their energy level, their stake, their extent of commitment? Third, we would check people's capacity to make and keep decisions over time. Power involves making *and* keeping decisions. Every morning, I listen to public radio, assess the news reports, and make thoughtful decisions about U.S. domestic and foreign policy. Who cares? No one, because I can make the decisions but I can't carry them out. Conversely, there are those who have the authority to keep decisions but not make them. We have power when we can both make and keep decisions.

Power can also be a bluff or be rooted in our perception of others. We give power to others when we believe they can and would make us keep decisions if they were challenged to do so. Furthermore, power is not a one-shot activity. Instead, it expands and contracts over time. When John says he made a decision and kept it in 1981, that is less likely to represent power than to be an accident.

Thus, power is dynamic, flowing, and changing over time. To be even more fully articulated, power can be examined under six themes. First, power requires a prevailing sense that our own energy, whether individual or collective, is legitimate and appropriate. We are entitled to express power simply because we are alive. Second, power requires a deep sense of personal or collective self-determination. This sense relates to our decision to commit or not to commit. Third, power involves outward expression. Commitment takes many forms, not all of which are ethical, including persuading, bargaining, coercing, manipulating, exploiting, dominating, and rebelling. (For a fuller examination of these phenomena, see Chapter Eight.) Fourth, power translates into institutional forms such as reflection, debate, voting, and consensus making. Fifth, power requires current political information and skills in order to assess and engage in a current context. And sixth, power depends on retrospective ownership of past actions. Over the years, both our small and our momentous decisions are laid down like the layers of rock we sometimes see exposed by earthquakes or bulldozers. These early decisions limit our capacity to commit. All too often, we rely on past experience to say a thing cannot be done, only to be overrun by those doing it. However, our past actions can also offer new opportunities to commit.

In summary, power is an essential part of action and of leadership. It is not the primary aspect; it is one of seven. It is that by which action moves.

Structure: A Form and Process Term, That Through Which Human Action Moves

There is no action without structure. Structure funnels power and creates and/or distributes resources. It provides the forms and processes of action.

The act of bringing a spy to trial in a democracy provides an especially clear view of structure's relationship to action. Spy cases present a serious problem for democracies. Trials must be held in public, yet these public trials reveal the very state secrets the spy is on trial for stealing. How, then, can a nation try a spy yet preserve its secrets? The mission in this instance is clear, the commitment is in place, but without a specific structure there would be no action.

The structural solution to the public trial dilemma was developed by John Martin, chief of the Internal Security Section of the U.S. Justice Department. Rules of evidence required public access to court proceedings; therefore, Martin proposed a redefinition of the rules (a change now legitimated by law). Under the new rules, each juror is given a document containing the secret—for example, the configuration of a classified piece of equipment on a fighter plane. When the prosecutor wants to discuss that secret, he or she instructs the jury to examine a particular page in the document of secrets. Thus, the jury knows the secret, but the public record shows only the page reference. A structural solution solved a sticky political dilemma.

Structure, like power, is ubiquitous. It is neither good nor bad; it just is. Research methodology in the sciences is structure bound. Protocols in an oncology ward must be observed in order to generate accurate and comparable data. The rules of a game structure its outcome. A budget, a blueprint, a room arrangement, a decision-making process, and an assembly line are all structural features of action.

Structure makes everyday tasks easily doable. We all have sets of habitual structures. Drinking black coffee at breakfast, wearing color-coordinated clothes, paying monthly bills, observing seniority promotion processes, negotiating with upper management, following Robert's *Rules of Order* are all examples of our use of structures. We know what it means to be a dutiful parent by driving the kids to hockey practice or emptying the garbage. We are clear about tasks and rules within organizational and community settings.

Structure regulates conflicting schedules, provides a basis for planning, and provides predictability. Even a dynamic rendering of human life that stresses innovation, creativity, intuition, and perhaps chaos presupposes a minimal structure. Recent studies about chaos, for example, report a paradoxical conclusion. While seeming to be order's antithesis, chaos has describable patterns (Gleick, 1987).

Structures may be tight or loose, rigid or flexible, effective or ineffective. Organizational theorist Henry Mintzberg (1979), for example, defines the structure of an organization simply as "the sum total of the ways in which it divides its labor into distinct tasks and then receives coordination among them" (p. 2). He identifies five typical structural configurations for organizations: simple structure, machine bureaucracy, professional bureaucracy, divisionalized form, and adhocracy (p. 301).

Yet we are also aware that set procedures do not always work. Informal processes may be operating (sometimes intentionally) at odds with the formal arrangements. For example, positional leaders often set up kitchen cabinet decision-making procedures to circumvent formal structural constraints and speed decisions that might otherwise get bogged down in bureaucratic procedures, or informal networking may temporarily replace due process rules for job promotion. It is, of course, these kinds of nonstated, but nevertheless real, institutional procedures that often perpetuate privileges for some and penalize others. It is for this reason that laws mandating formal processes get tougher, in order to ensure fairness and to correct structural inequities.

Structures may have unintended effects as well. The Racketeer-Influenced and Corrupt Organizations Act, a law to fight organized crime, is currently being used by lawyers and the courts to try any pattern-of-practice crime, such as antiabortion demonstrations that intimidate women seeking abortions. The building of high-rise low-income housing in Chicago to solve the problem of adequate shelter also created high-crime districts and speeded the deterioration of housing stock.

Building structures requires imagination. Suppose you wanted to generate money (resources) to help the poor but were reluctant to propose a coercive tax. A colleague of mine has proposed that cities initiate "Round Up." The idea is simple and doable. If you were at a check-out counter and your bill was $39.22, the cashier would ask you, "Do you want to round up?" If you said yes, you would pay $40. The electronic cash register would total the

$.88 difference with other round-up amounts, and periodically, the accumulated monies would be presented to an ethically impeccable body for distribution to various service organizations. The "tax" is voluntary; the amount of money generated could be enormous, and the technology is available.

Leadership attends to structure by both proposing and building forms and processes that carry missions forward. Leadership evaluates whether structures are having their intended effects. Without structure, there is no action. It is the through which of action.

Resources: A Material Term, That with Which Human Action Moves

Resources are the materials used in action. To be a resource, material must meet six criteria. First, someone must recognize it as potentially usable. Second, it must be selected for the mission at hand. Third, it must be able to be put to use. Fourth, it must be manageable. Processes must be available to use or transform it for desired outcomes. Fifth, it must be an artifact that can be quantified; that is, it must have a life apart from its creator. And sixth, it must be potentially and/or actually available.

To make this definition more vivid, I distinguish resources from *stuff*. Stuff and resources are similar. They both meet five of the six criteria, but they are different on one point. Resources are wanted; stuff is not wanted. I have resources; you have stuff! Parents have resources; children have stuff—so when children go away to camp parents often throw out their stuff.

Thus, in a particular context, chairs, tables, lawn mowers, ideas, and books of blueprints may or may not be resources. If my mission does not require that I have a chair, the chair is not a resource. However, if my mission is cutting the lawn, then a lawn mower is a resource. When a resource ceases to be a resource, it returns to existence, the source of all resources and the location of stuff. Leadership depends on resources; there is no action without them.

Fulfillment: An Embodiment Term, That into Which Human Action Moves

Fulfillment is the completed human act, the point when what was once the future becomes embodied in the present. Fulfillment is the completed act lodged in the stream of other acts, other anticipations, other conditions, yet it is a happening here and now, not then and there. Every act of fulfillment defines boundaries. Images, dreams, and wishes have no sharp boundaries; they blend into each other and are virtual rather than actual. Fulfillment incarnates and sharpens edges, forces resolution, and embodies values. It is that into which human action moves.

Fulfillment is a critical category for leadership. Leadership, as a subset of action, is action. It is real in actual time and space. It holds together meaning, mission, power, structure, and resources in existence. It unites thinking, being, and doing.

The seven features of action are always present, even if one or more of them is problematic. For example, institutional reform can change particular organizational structures. Laws mandating equal opportunity employment invalidate informal hiring processes. However, we should not conclude that, while the hiring system is being restructured, there is no structure in operation. There is always some form and process, even if it is dysfunctional. Likewise, even when the mission is confusion, some mission is always directing the action, even if that mission is simply to get through until tomorrow. As generic features, mission, existence, resources, power, structure, and meaning are always implicit in an action, whether or not they are being attended to and whether or not they are well expressed and functioning as expected.

Fulfillment happens. It is not always desirable, good, or beautiful. It can be messy, unethical, or totally destructive. The old adage, "not to act is to act," reflects this omnipresence of action as a generic feature of human beings showing up.

Applying the Features of Action

Prior to exploring the generic features of action, I recommended seven leadership questions. Those questions are designed to increase our ability to distinguish among the features of action in real-life situations. The key is to treat the leadership questions as constants within the Action Wheel, and allow the real world—as it must—to be fluid.

In order to practice identifying the generic features of a particular action, readers can build a house in their minds. What is involved? It is relatively easy to generate the list of what we would need: building materials, blueprints, carpenters, building permits, and so on. But what is a blueprint—a mission or a structure? Are carpenters a resource or power? Is money a resource or power? Identifying the features of action can also jog our memories about aspects of an issue we may have forgotten. What aspect of building a house is existence? What aspect is meaning?

Here is a practical exercise. Identify the action feature that describes each of the following aspects of house building:

1. Budget
2. Building permit
3. Enforcement of zoning codes
4. Home, security, family warmth, friendliness
5. Completed home
6. Cement blocks
7. Perimeter foundation in place
8. Rental property
9. Cash
10. History of house building

The answers are:

1. A budget is structure, the form the house will take.
2. A building permit is structure when we are obeying the law that requires a permit; it is power when enforced; it is a resource when we have the paper in hand.
3. The enforcement of zoning codes is power—specifically, coercing.
4. The ideas of home, security, and so forth are meaning, the significance of and justification for the house.
5. The completed home is fulfillment.
6. The cement blocks, when sitting in a pile, are a resource.
7. The perimeter foundation, cement blocks stacked and cemented together, is a structure.
8. The concept of rental property is meaning, another possible reason why the house is being built.

9.   Cash is a resource, a necessary, valued ingredient.
10.   The history of house building is existence, the rich reserves of
      knowledge from all house building.

Cash is often a confusing aspect in this example. Most of us want to equate money and power. In this model, they are distinguished. Can someone be rich and not be powerful? Yes, that person can be a professional basketball player! Conversely, can someone be poor and powerful? Yes, if certain conditions are met—if a person or group has clear values, a tightly focused mission, and a commitment in place and is well organized. These conditions can make individuals and social movements highly effective even when they are up against richer and better-known persons and richer and larger organizations.

Suppose we decide that the mission is "to build a house." What then is the meaning? The meaning would be why we want the house. And suppose our answer is that it is a place for children to be raised in warmth and security. This statement of meaning can now be turned into a mission. Instead of saying we're going to build a house, we can say that the mission is "to establish a home." What then is the meaning? The meaning answers the question of why we want a home and not just a house. Thus, by looking at the kind of questions we are raising, we will know whether we are focusing on meaning, mission, power, structure, resources, or existence. Mission answers the question toward what, meaning answers the question why.

Summary

Viewing leadership as a subset of action gives leadership equal access to all the features of action, both as categories for investigation and as modes of action that leadership can fulfill. The seven generic features of action—meaning, mission, power, structure, resources, existence, and fulfillment—are the components of the Action Wheel. These features are found in every human action. In themselves, they are value neutral, neither good nor bad. However, knowing that every action has meaning of some sort requires leadership to seek out that meaning. Knowing that every action has

resources of some sort requires leadership to identify those resources. Every feature can be and should be identified. It is in this
way that leadership discovers what is really going on.

In the next chapter, I will develop the framework of the
Action Wheel, placing these features of action into a pattern that
orders them and also generates insight.

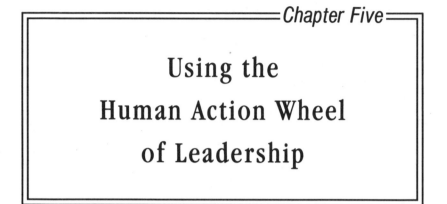

=Chapter Five=

Using the
Human Action Wheel
of Leadership

Leadership requires more than a general view or "guestimate" of what is going on. The leadership question is, What is *really* going on? Therefore, the ability to frame an issue correctly is essential to leadership. For as we frame issues, so too will we solve them.

Heifetz and Sinder's three-part leadership typology (1988; described in Chapter Three) presented a continuum of possible responses using a medical analogy. Clearly understood problems and their solutions will respond to a technical approach in which little is required of the patient. When the treatment for the disease is less certain, the patient will have increased interaction with the doctor and must also work to change behavior. In the third scenario, patient and doctor together must figure out what is wrong and how to cope with it or prepare for the known outcome. For Heifetz and Sinder, this is the premier leadership scenario.

I agree that it is possible and useful to distinguish the technical, managerial, and leadership actions along a continuum of increasing difficulty of problem recognition and solution. Leadership is providing resources to people to do real work, Heifetz and Sinder argue. I agree with that also, although I would call real work *authentic action.* What troubles me is that Heifetz and Sinder's theory offers little guidance beyond defining leadership's mission. Heifetz and Sinder seem to say "trust the process," but I believe that results in dependence on a skilled authority figure. Yet where do we go from here? If we live in a world of no answers and no authority figures to solve problems for us, we can easily flounder and tumble headlong into despair.

Therefore, I propose an issue- or action-framing tool which I call the *Action Wheel* (see Figure 5.1). By using the Action Wheel, we can dissect human action fulfillment into six component parts. Then, if we want to redirect our attention and shift the action outcome to a new possibility of fulfillment, we can know what we are doing and why we are doing it. I will illustrate how the tool functions for each of six generic features. I will also discuss the form and process of the Action Wheel; that is, the wheel's structure. The formal relationships among the generic features are important to an understanding of all human action and of the issues that action raises. The chapter will conclude with suggestions for teaching the action-framing tool to potential and practicing leaders.

Formal Relationships of Features of Action

Effective theory seeks to connect the parts of a particular model in ways that generate new insights, perhaps even wisdom. In the case of the Action Wheel, my objective is to connect the parts in ways that improve our ability to understand key issues. I have also been guided by two hypotheses. The first one is that *all human action is structured the same—in every act, in every situation.* In other words, the generic features of action are related to each other in a particular and a universal form, which is displayed in the inner wheel in Figure 5.1. Let us name this part of the whole Action Wheel the Diagnostic Wheel.

The Diagnostic Wheel displays the relationships of the six generic features of action to the whole of action. Action itself, the completed act or *fulfillment,* is the central focus, and thus is in the center of the wheel, surrounded by the six features.

Meaning legitimates and orients missions. It provides the

Figure 5.1. The Action Wheel.

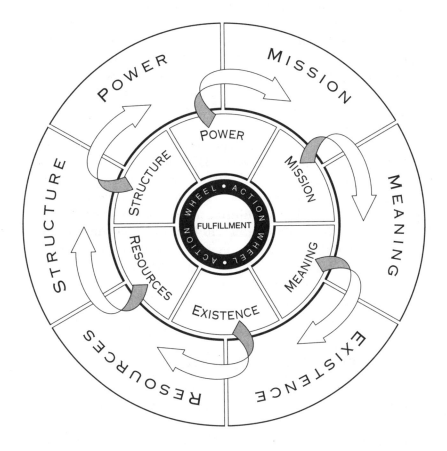

cultural justification of actions. *Missions,* be they small or large, direct and focus power. The value of a mission is judged by the significance of its related meaning. *Power,* quickened by mission, energizes and modifies structures. *Structures* sustain power, generate new ideas, and press missions forward. *Resources* equip structures and come from what is actually or potentially available in existence. *Existence* both limits resources and makes them possible.

Meaning and existence touch on the wheel. Each informs the other. As we enter any stream of ongoing human action, it is already infused with meaning from the past. These messages from our cultural past set boundaries for our action. As we mature and question

our cultural heritage, we are challenged to examine the past and reject, modify, or reaffirm meaning passed down to us. And the Action Wheel rolls on.

From the Holocaust to spiritual transformation, the range of human action reveals the most base and the most glorious actions of the human species. Leadership, to be true to the full range of action, must acknowledge and embrace all of human action as it seeks to engage it.

The following examples show how the relationships between the features of action play out in real-life decision making. Alice is considering whether to run for office. She discusses her options with friends and colleagues and goes through months of soul searching. Eventually, she decides to run, outlines her campaign strategies, secures staff and money, and embarks on the campaign trail. In this small vignette, all the features of action are present, as they must be. Alice's soul searching raises the question of meaning. Once she concludes that the struggle will be worthwhile and that the setting is open to real possibilities, her mission becomes clear: run for office. Her commitment, or power, energizes her structure and resources decisions, and she moves into action. It would not make sense for her to create solutions or seek resources if the meaning and mission questions were unresolved. Meaning clarifies mission, which in turn empowers appropriate decisions about structure and resources. None of this action would have occurred if existence had offered no opportunities. Yet existence also sets limits of place and circumstance.

The relationship between mission and power is often misunderstood in issue framing. For example, we typically describe a couple's fight as a power struggle. But what are they really fighting over? Mission. This is true even when the fight is over who will win. Then winning becomes the mission and directs the energy of the fight. Thus, what we often call power struggles are mission struggles.

Mission directs. Power energizes and modifies structures. We all know that on a highway with a fifty-five–mile-per-hour speed limit, cars blur past us, going sixty to eighty miles per hour. The formal structure of the law posts the limit, but the informal structure of the highway system permits the energy of the car coupled

with the decision of the driver to exceed the formal constraint. Thus, power energizes and modifies structure. When police enforce the law, legitimate power confronts illegitimate power, to align the formal and informal structures.

Similarly, some managers give minimal attention to elaborate personnel evaluation forms while others thoughtfully evaluate simple forms. It is power that gives life to these forms. If we dislike a structure, we will spend endless energy avoiding it or seeking ways to change it. If we want something to happen, we will use whatever structures are available, even if we have to circumvent their formal rules.

It is easy to confuse money and power or knowledge and power. However, it is not necessarily true that the rich are powerful. We become powerful only by using our resources to accomplish some mission. Likewise, the fact that information is a potential resource does not mean it will invariably empower. It can be ignored or misused, or it can overwhelm and flood the mind with irrelevant data.

Structure allocates and generates resources. If an organization is low on resources, it cannot simply will them into existence. Individuals must formulate a process to generate them. Conversely, resources limit and infuse structure. If I have $100,000, I have more options than if I have $1,000. However, even if I am rich, I may choose not to use my wealth to accomplish any particular purpose. Structure also channels and sustains power. Even though power energizes structure, structures such as laws, rules, and regulations restrict power when they are enforced. Owing to its public legitimacy, the Supreme Court was able to confront the presidency after the Watergate break-in and to enforce the relevant structures.

Resources only become resources after mission is clarified. If my mission is to build roads, I will need road construction equipment. It is mission that distinguishes between resources and stuff. The relationship between mission and resources also tells us why throwing money at a problem does not necessarily accomplish desired goals. Raising salaries, for example, is no guarantee of better results. The only sure thing we get from higher wages is better-paid employees, or employees attracted for the money. To produce better results from those employees, we have to address questions of mean-

ing, mission, power, structure, resources, and existence within the organization.

Meaning expresses significance and legitimacy. Mission highlights a narrow spectrum of concern; meaning then puts mission in context, conferring significance on the proposed direction. However, existence, as the setting from which action arises, limits possibility. A ringing phrase such as "Remember the Maine" cannot inspire anyone who does not understand its context—in this case, the events leading to the Spanish-American War.

History is replete with those who, to their great detriment, persisted in seeing the world through glasses framed with outmoded or false notions. At the famous Battle of Agincourt (1415), for example, French noblemen weighed down by medieval armor and an obsolete chivalrous code died by the thousands as English commoners and their longbows unleashed a rain of armor-piercing arrows that "blotted out the sun," in the words of one medieval chronicler. More recently, the English found their outdated colonial values bested by Mahatma Gandhi's ethic of nonviolent resistance.

The great difficulty for leadership, then, is to avoid being framed in by the way it frames issues. Like a CAT scan that reveals the inner workings of the body, the Action Wheel is a tool that enables us to diagnose the real problems leadership faces.

My hypothesis that all human action is structured the same, in every act and in every situation, sets the stage for the second and I think more critical hypothesis of the leadership theory: *The way we frame an issue invariably determines how well we focus the issue, judge what is really happening, and direct our attention and intervention for change.* This hypothesis is critical because we typically frame issues poorly, thereby misfocusing, misjudging, misdirecting, and failing in our leadership. Our ability to assess existing perspectives on leadership and to provide a new perspective that helps leaders to inform and direct engagement with the world hangs on a deep appreciation of the second hypothesis. Framing of issues is a skill that is crucial to effective leadership diagnosis and action because that is one major part of what leadership does. It frames issues.

Moreover, the ability to exercise the framing skill from multiple perspectives assumes fresh importance and urgency when leaders confront rapid, complex change. Schön (1983) highlights this importance, as do Bolman and Deal (1991), who observe that "multi-framed thinking is challenging and, at times, counter intuitive. To see the same organizations *simultaneously* [through four different frames] requires the capacity to think in different ways at the same time about the same thing. The power to reframe will be vital to the leader of the future. The ability to see new possibilities and create new opportunities will enable leaders to discover choice even when their options seem severely constrained and define hope even amid fear and despair. Choice is at the heart of freedom, and freedom is essential to achieving the twin goals of commitment and flexibility" (p. 450). In many ways, Bolman and Deal (1991) propose a similar approach to mine. Their four frames (machine, family, jungle, and theater) match closely with four of the generic features of action. What they lack, I believe, is a frame behind the frame. Their work implies a model of action but does not make it explicit. Nevertheless, their book is the best to date that illustrates the critical leadership role of multiple framing.

In framing an issue, two steps are required to answer the question, What is really going on? Step 1: *Locate the perceived issue or problem on the Diagnostic Wheel.* After careful listening, we should be able to group responses around one of the six generic features of action. The comments that typically indicate a problem with a particular feature are listed here.

Existence

When the responses that leaders hear or feel suggest helplessness, the agency of fate, chance, or an accident, the issue being indicated is existence. The following comments often emerge:

- The situation is terminal.
- There is nothing to draw on for help.
- I can't break my addictions.
- My habits have been established over many years.
- The forces battering us are beyond our control.
- History is against us.
- Life is one damn thing after another.

- The environment is overwhelming us.
- The situation can't change.
- The situation is not far enough along to do what we need.
- I was in an organization like this ten years ago and it failed.
- We have a terrible track record.
- The world doesn't respond.
- Nothing is coming to me.
- Sometimes I wonder if I really exist.

Resources

A resource issue is being indicated when the following are heard:

- We are not sure what we need to complete the task.
- Resources are available, but I can't get my hands on them.
- We need more, or less, of X for us to do our work.
- I don't have the skills or knowledge to do the job.
- It is just not there for us to use.
- The things we have don't work.
- We can't make do with what we have.
- X is in the wrong place.
- We can't create from nothing.
- I don't know what tools to use.
- I don't know what we need.

Structure

Structure is the issue being named when these remarks are heard:

- We tried that before. It didn't work then, and it won't work now.
- The job is not clearly defined. I don't know what I'm supposed to do.
- The company is poorly organized.
- The ways I used to get things done don't work any more.
- Our hands are so tied by red tape, we can't operate.
- The place is so loose, anything goes.
- There is no coordination among jobs.
- The organizational chart doesn't reflect the way things happen.

- There is no rhyme or reason to the way we are organized.
- The decision-making process is vague or undefined.

Power

Power issues are being indicated when leaders hear:

- People who have no right to be involved are in on the decision.
- Why doesn't someone just do something?
- People are abusing each other.
- The decision making is by fiat.
- All decisions are already made; it's a sham.
- We can't get things done.
- No one knows how to make things happen.
- I don't know what's happening. I just know that I was deeply upset and uneasy when I left work.
- It's like warfare.
- My energy level is really low.
- Morale is down.
- I'm scared, fearful, excited, or hopeful.

Mission

Mission issues are being discussed when leaders hear:

- I don't know if we're successful.
- We are never successful.
- We are not clear about our future direction.
- We've lost our way.
- There's nothing to hope or dream for anymore.
- People operate on selfish, narrow interests.
- Nobody cares about this place.
- We have conflicting policies.
- One policy undermines others.

Meaning

Meaning issues are the subject when the comments leaders hear are like these:

- I don't know why I come to work anymore.
- Things just aren't fair.
- They don't do things right anymore.
- This is a crazy world.
- I have never experienced this before.
- Things don't make sense.
- Why are we doing this anyway?

To practice this part of issue framing, leaders can draw the action diagram on paper, record people's responses according to the feature that is being discussed, and observe where the features cluster. It is advisable to press respondents for clarification and more thoughtful observations if their initial responses are not as helpful as we require for our diagnosis of what is really going on.

Once the information is gathered, we are ready for the second step of analysis. This is the most critical practical aspect of the model and is also especially relevant for a comprehensive theory of leadership.

Knowing What Is *Really* Going On

The diagnostic insight that the model generates is illustrated by the design of the Action Wheel (see Figure 5.1). The inner wheel represents the preliminary diagnosis of the presenting issue. The outer wheel represents strategic intervention of the issue. To find out what is really going on, begin Step 2: *Follow the arrows clockwise from the inner wheel to the outer wheel.* Whatever feature we think an issue represents, it really represents the next feature clockwise on the Action Wheel. A corollary insight is this: We typically, and mistakenly, try to frame an issue as representing the feature counterclockwise on the Action Wheel.

Thus, there are two steps in using the model. The first is analytic, the second strategic. The analytic stage locates the issue on the inner wheel. To act strategically, focus the action on the outer wheel. Follow the arrows. If the presenting issue is power, notice that the arrow goes through power to mission. Leadership focuses first on power, then addresses mission.

All aspects of the model are implicitly present in every act.

Therefore, all features of action must eventually be addressed in any proposed action. What is critical is the location of our attention and the direction of our engagement at the outset of the leadership task. Over the years, I have found that most issues center on meaning, mission, and power, but that our leadership slides too quickly to structure, resources, and existence. We reorganize (structure), throw money at the problem (resources), or pray for a miracle (existence)!

We focus our attention inappropriately for three reasons. It is easier, quicker, and safer to move counterclockwise rather than clockwise. When we address fundamentally authentic issues of meaning, mission, and power, we are dealing with the heart and soul of a culture or a person's life. It is easier, quicker, and safer to reorganize, count things, or hope for an environmental change. My evidence for this major division in how we regard parts of the model is in part intuitive, in part anecdotal, and in part garnered from working with hundreds of groups and speaking to thousands of people here and abroad. These people quickly agree when I claim that the critical issues today are meaning, mission, and power but that all of us rush to focus on structure, resources, and existence as our solutions.

Intuitively, the division seems right. The more mechanical and objective reality appears, the more easily, safely, and quickly it seems to be addressed. Exploring the realms of power, mission, and meaning goes to the complex heart of human life and, therefore, arouses more fear, anxiety, and uncertainty than investigating the other three realms. This intuitive view is confirmed by Bolman and Deal (1991) when they report that more attention has been given to resource and structure frames than political and symbolic frames (p. 178).

Anecdotal reports from people who have tested the model, time after time, confirm that the critical issues are meaning, mission, and power even though, time after time, these people see issues being framed as problems of structure, resources, and existence.

Finally, there is the confirmation that comes more systematically from evaluative feedback collected over the last ten years. Repeatedly, the message is the same. The model is useful as a diagnostic tool with mission, meaning, and power as the critical issues of action. Currently, a team of researchers from Midwest Extension Services is creating an instrument based on the model so that these ideas can be further tested and refined.

As I have mentioned, leadership must eventually attend to all dimensions of action for each leadership issue. Once we have dealt with the appropriate feature, it is then essential that we cover all the remaining aspects of action. If the real issue turns out to be mission, for example, we would clarify the real mission and then attend to power, structure, and resources.

What if the issue is meaning? Where do we go from there? Recall that serious meaning intersects with existence. A meaning issue calls us to revisit our history for fresh insight about our possibilities. It is from our history and setting that we create new meanings to make sense out of events. Social movements, for example, dig into history to find the deep roots upon which to build a future. In profound cases, revisiting existence becomes a spiritual quest as both our faith and our cynicism struggle to wrest meaning from bittersweet experiences.

Let me illustrate how this works with a story. A colleague had gone to speak to a group of white men about white racism, and had been attacked as a "male hater." His audience told him, "You don't understand us or yourself." "We have to learn to care deeply about each other and about ourselves." "We men have to rediscover our own roots." "It is not just that women are oppressed. We are all oppressed and caught in a vicious oppressive cycle."

As he told me about the intense hostility, we used the model to make a quick diagnosis. He had talked about white men's power and privilege, shared my parable of ups and downs (see Chapter Eight), and discussed how institutional racism worked to white advantage. That is, he had started with power and shifted counterclockwise to structure (institutional racism). These men, however, as part of the men's movement popularized by Robert Bly, were focused on meaning, seeking to revisit their existence. In the men's movement, such activities as writing and reading poetry, making masks, drumming, dancing, and mythological storytelling are ways for men to gain access to their roots, and to rediscover and reaffirm themselves as strong, caring persons. My colleague failed to read the focus of the group and failed to use an appropriate strategy to make his points with them.

My colleague talked color; they talked gender. Instead, he could have used a leadership strategy in which he, as a man, identified with their struggle and then introduced the issue of race as one that liberated, caring men had to address as part of their male responsibility. But because he had not diagnosed the group appropriately, a battle ensued. Ironically, under personal attack, the men in the group became inauthentic as well. Instead of pursuing spiritual insights of caring, they reverted to their old political behaviors as dominating, controlling white males.

Thus, when meaning is the issue, we revisit existence in a spiritual search for ground in a newly claimed but poorly comprehended reality.

Finally, because this model is a directive or *focus of attention model*, rather than a developmental model, there is no connection between an individual's personal development and his or her ability to use the model. This distinction should be borne in mind by those who wish to compare the Action Wheel with the work of Maslow and other developmental theorists.

The Theory in Practice

Two of the criteria by which I suggested a theory should be judged were utility and insight generation. I believe the best way for me to show how the Action Wheel meets these criteria is to provide some examples from my and my colleagues' consulting experience.

Situation 1

Some years ago, I was invited to be a consultant to educational media specialists in a Midwestern state. They had been together for over ten years, but their earlier camaraderie and team spirit had disappeared, and they wanted to rekindle it. I listened to their situation. In the previous decade, they had had limited resources but a clear mission of becoming the most valued media specialists in the state. Now, they had well-established state-supported funding, were recognized, and were quite rich. However, though on the surface they were friendly, underneath they were plagued by envy, suspicion, and lack of cooperation. They spent their meetings jockeying for power and prestige.

When I applied the framing tool, the perceived issue was power, which meant that the real problem was mission. However, the specialists' desired solution was to change structure, and they asked me to help them engage in team building. I shared my alternative point of view with them, and after serious discussion, they agreed with it. Therefore, on their own, they sweated over a mission statement they could agree on. Yet, right after they thought they had clarified their mission, they had one of the worst meetings in their history. Now, they wondered whether they had done something wrong or whether my approach had failed.

I asked to see the mission statement. It was entitled "The Role of Media Director." Instead of a mission statement, they had produced a job description. They had reverted to structure to solve a mission problem. A structure solution was easy, quick, and safe, but it missed the point. To jog their thinking, I suggested that the group disband. Immediately, one of them said, indignantly, "Then we wouldn't have political clout with the legislature." "Now," I said, "you're doing real mission work."

People frequently resort to structure solutions to cope with change without realizing that altered environments or resources require a reassessment of mission and meaning.

Situation 2

Owing to an enrollment decline, an elementary school was slated to be closed in two years. The principal reported that this had resulted in an apparent power problem, because of a lack of commitment and energy. The president of the local Parent-Teacher Association (PTA) had proposed a massive recruitment drive as a solution. Of course, the drive would not work because the real solution required a redefinition of the school's mission in the light of changing circumstances. The principal later reported that they had adopted a new mission: to help the children make as smooth a transition as possible during the school's closing. With this redefined mission in hand, the energy was available to recruit new PTA members and bolster and redirect those already on board.

Situation 3

A codirector of a gender-fair technical assistance center faced a problem with a male staff member. She and the other director, a man, were meeting with four women and the problem employee. After the codirectors left, the problem employee dominated the meeting, angering the women by interrupting them and making derogatory remarks. Afterward, the women suggested that at subsequent meetings the man be seated so he would be removed from the center of any discussion.

This problem can easily be analyzed as a power problem. The proposed solution, however, was structural, to rearrange the seating. To me, this was like rearranging deck chairs on the Titanic. Everyone is busy, but the whole operation is going under. The solution was for the codirector to ask the problem employee how his mission meshed with the organizational mission. Since the organizational mission was to provide technical assistance to schools to reduce sexism, his own sexist behavior had to change. The man refused to change his behavior and is no longer with the organization.

Situation 4

An issue that often surfaces when human resources are discussed is homosexuality. Asked my view of gay rights, I usually respond by asking, "What is your stand on birth control?" If the person says he or she favors birth control, then I retort (tongue in cheek), "If you use birth control, then you should have no problem with homosexuality in principle, and if you do, you are homophobic."

My answer is explained by the use of the Action Wheel as a framing tool. Questions about homosexuality are rarely about information. Rather, they conceal conflict and control issues between gays and straights. Society typically tries to solve the conflict by framing it as a structure issue. Laws are passed either to guarantee justice for gays and lesbians or to reaffirm a discriminatory practice if the society wants to institutionalize the discrimination. The unexamined issue here is mission: namely, what is the real purpose of sexuality? And beyond mission is the issue of meaning.

If the stated mission of sexuality is procreation, then only heterosexual sex is natural. If the stated mission of sexuality is lovemaking, then the gender of the lovers is irrelevant and anything goes (between consenting adults). To a person who practices birth control, the mission of sexuality is lovemaking, and thus, anyone can make love. If a person who practices birth control opposes the legitimizing of homosexual relationships, very likely an irrational fear, generated by mistrust of an unfamiliar reality, is driving his or her reaction.

At the preliminary level of analysis, leadership should focus on the question of mission to bring such contradictions to the surface. Is there alignment between a person's walk and his or her talk?

However, the model also suggests that perhaps the real issue is meaning. When any argument is taken to the level of meaning, then careful and thoughtful work is required, but reactions and personal disdain no longer count in the discussion. Moreover, internal consistency arguments do not address substantive theological or philosophical arguments. At this level, good people may differ and differ profoundly. In my view, much of the debate over gay and lesbian rights never gets to meaning, and simple focus on consistency exposes much of the prevailing inauthenticity. Consider the number of Protestant denominations that welcome gays and lesbians into the ministry as long as they remain celibate. Is that truly a theological issue, or a fear issue?

Situation 5

A new high school principal found that the school's academic and vocational teachers were in a state of virtual warfare. A young, aggressive man had taken charge of the vocational program, and the academics believed he was trying to dominate the school. He berated the academics as lazy and shiftless and tried to take their resources. The principal had tried to resolve this situation with a training program in which the two sides were brought together to "walk in each other's moccasins." The program was a disaster. People had left barely speaking to each other. The situation sounded like an unresolved mission problem, if not a meaning problem. The next question was how to intervene. When I present this case to others, most people suggest bringing the two groups together for a shared mission discussion. The difficulty with that approach was that the vocational people had no compelling interest that could force them into serious conversation with the academics. Therefore, my suggestion was to convene the heads of the academic departments—English, history, chemistry, and so on.

I listened for an hour to their amazing array of "ain't it awful" stories. The litany of the vocational director's sins was endless. They questioned his fundamentalist proselytizing and even mentioned rumors of sexual improprieties with female students. They wanted him fired, but they thought the principal was either taking sides with him or had been duped by him. After listening closely to them, I laid out the model and had them analyze their own situation. Very quickly, they identified power as their problem. Pushing further, I challenged them to examine their relationship with the vocational division, suggesting that they really had a mission problem. In their preoccupation with the vocational group, they were neglecting their own mission. I told them, "You can be for yourself without being against anyone else." I repeated it. There was a silence, and then one person said, "I'll be damned. I think that's true." Another person asked, "Do you mean I'll have to give up hating the vocational person? I'm not sure I want to do that. I've been doing that for years." The half-dozen people in the room began to get excited. After some discussion, they said, "We buy this, but we don't think it will fly with the total academic faculty." We arranged to repeat the process with a larger group of faculty.

The larger group went through the same process, relating the stories, learning the model, and hearing the maxim, "You can be for yourself without being against anyone else." And, like the department heads, the faculty said, "That's right. Let us take charge of our own lives. Let us get on with our own mission." There was a tremendous release of energy as they defined their values, set up an academic council, and took a hard look at what they needed to accomplish their own work.

About a year later, I learned from the principal that the council was working hard on tough issues. The vocational program had an afternoon work-study session that had forced the academic program to crowd chemistry, physics, and other courses together in the morning. The vocational director was also enticing some of the best students with good jobs. However, the council was having some success in restructuring the work-study program and in attracting and keeping college-bound students. In addition, the vocational director had become much more interested in cooperating with the academics. By taking charge of and asserting their own power and mission, the academics had gotten the attention of the person who thought he had nothing to gain from cooperation. The academics had exhibited leadership.

Situation 6

Imagine an intense family fight in which one of the combatants has the presence of mind to ask, What is the real mission of this fight? The fight could end in laughter and insight if the parties were able to step back and examine the issues that were arousing and directing their energy.

In the heat of battle, people will say, "Don't you ever do that again!" On the surface, this looks like a mission that is being given to the other person, and to some extent, it is. It is meant to direct that person's energy. However, if we ask the leadership question, What is the purpose of that rule, and why should it be accepted? it will become apparent that the purpose is power, which then drops down to structure. Or, let us suppose that a couple is battling over a concern about their children. As the struggle heats up, one partner shifts his or her mission from discussing the children to winning by any means necessary. This is a sure recipe for dirty fighting. Only if the real mission is identified is authentic action possible.

Situation 7

Sometimes, I forget to use the model and consequently fail to know what is really happening. Many years ago, I was about two weeks into teaching a course on leadership ethics, when I began hearing disgruntled remarks from participants. Then, two or three people dropped the course. Morale was low, commitment dropping. What was the problem? Power. What did I do? I listened, unthinkingly chose structure as the issue, and reordered the curriculum. Only after a colleague in the class reminded me of my own framing tool did I realize that my restructuring did not deal with the real issue. When I focused on mission, I discovered that some students wanted to examine case studies of ethical problems and some wanted to reflect on ethical theories. The course was designed for the latter, so those interested in the former were dropping out. Instead of going down the hierarchy, I should have been clear with myself about the seminar's real meaning and mission and have owned up to that mission and meaning. As it was, I did not exhibit leadership, even though I was the positional leader.

Situation 8

I learned a similar lesson when I assisted a mayor and her council to clarify the mission of their city, a bedroom suburb with a few small high-tech plants. For two days, I used every technique I could think of to focus the group on mission, but we could not produce a succinct statement that focused the desires of both the council and the mayor. Finally, one man said, "The problem with this city is that we don't know what we want to be when we grow up. The question for us is, Do we want to be a suburb, or do we want to be a self-contained city? Do we want to imitate a big city, or do we want to set our own agenda and create a city with our own boundaries?" As he was talking, the energy in the room increased, and when he finished, applause broke out.

        Using the model, I found I had been trying to force a mission solution, when the real issue was meaning. The more this fellow talked and the more the group's energy increased, the clearer it became that he was struggling to define the meaning of being a city. Once this meaning was clarified, the mayor decided her mission was to help the city become a self-contained unit. That mission would involve major changes in how roads were built, businesses developed, and cultural facilities established. Examining meaning opened the possibility of an entirely new mission and released new energy.

Situation 9

Suppose we wanted to apply the model as a leadership tool to figure out what was really happening with employees, in order to motivate them. The model can figure out not only what is going on but also what motivational approaches we might anticipate using.

First, what are the current ways in which workers are motivated? The most basic is reflected in the management attitude that says to workers, You should be thankful you have a job. This approach touches workers on the existence level, implying not only that they should be thankful that others in the organization let them show up but also that they could be let go if they don't act right. A second common motivational strategy is to increase pay and perks. By manipulating the availability and distribution of resources, managers believe they trigger sustained motivation. The third approach is to institute good personnel practices and policies so that the structure is fair. A personnel manual can be considered a justice document. It shows the way the organization *ought* to function. A popular approach today is shared decision making, committee work, quality circles, or self-directed teams. In each of these approaches, power is the primary issue. Individuals' motivation is understood to be tied to their having decision-making power over issues that affect their well-being. Finally, great attention has been given to excellence. The heart of Tom Peters and Nancy Austin's approach to motivation (1985) is that mission clarity energizes long-term worker satisfaction.

Although the motivators of worker participation and mission are relative newcomers to industry, they receive a major share of the attention in motivation studies today. The Action Wheel, however, anticipates an issue already sweeping organizational life—quality. Positional leaders and businesses will find it insufficient to articulate what they are good at doing. Instead, the question will be whether what they are doing is any good. This question will force the issue of social responsibility to the forefront, challenging organizations to provide products or services that meet a standard of quality that goes beyond excellence (Clancy, 1989). The wheel also anticipates the possible demise of the Quality Movement. Reduce it to a structure or a set of skills, and it will die. Quality is meaning, a philosophy of an organization. Today's anticipatory leadership will give serious attention to quality and will concentrate on the power and mission features of motivation as the clues to inspiring long-term commitment from all organizational participants.

Critical Questions About Framing Issues

When people study and apply the model, certain questions tend to recur. Here are my responses to five of those questions.

Are Resource and Structure Missions Possible?

People often ask if they can have a resource or structure mission. The answer is yes. A resource or structure issue, such as a goal to raise money or to be economically secure, meets the toward which criterion of a mission. However, once a mission of raising money or becoming economically secure is stated, the real issue may then become meaning. If we want to see an organization die, for example, all we need do is state that its mission is to survive. To keep it alive, we need to say why survival is necessary. Similarly, missions to raise money or be economically secure require us to ask, Why raise money? Or, Why be economically secure?

Also, when one of the other features of the model is posited as a mission, we must always test whether a hidden mission lies behind the stated mission. For example, the real mission behind raising money might be long-term effectiveness. If long-term effectiveness is the real mission, then raising money, even though it sounds like a mission, is actually a resource. When we use the model, we should be ready to have a "conversation with the situation" (Schön, 1983, p. 157), to be playful in our investigations. The model is not designed to be mechanically applied here and there until it achieves a tight fit with reality. It opens new inquiries. It helps us get unstuck.

Is the Model Useful, or True?

A second frequently raised question centers on the status of the Action Wheel. Is it to be judged by criteria of truth or of utility? I can answer this question most clearly with a story.

A group of administrators were trying to make the model work but were stuck. On the wall, they had taped sheets labeled mission, power, structure, and resources, with lists of key items under each heading. Frustration exuded from the group and motivation was low. After I listened to them struggle with the model, it became obvious that they were seeking to clarify an issue of culture, especially racial diversity. I suggested that they not use the model, and one administrator broke into a knowing grin. "You're messing with us, right?" she mused. "You just taught us something about the model that we forgot." They had forgotten something that the model itself predicted. Since the model is a "through which," its structure had gotten in the way of their mission.

Their mission was to solve a real-world political diversity issue. However, they had shifted from power to structure—in this case, the structure of the model—to frame their political problem. I took the issue to the real mission—diversity—and suggested that the model's structure was blocking effective framing and preventing them from addressing the real issue. Of course, and this was the cause of our shared smiles, I was using the model to suggest not using the model.

Is the model useful, or true? I like to think it is both. However, at this stage in the analysis, I'll settle for useful. Definitive discussions of the model's own authenticity await a later investigation.

Why Is the Model Creative?

Another question frequently raised focuses on the creative use of the model. My taking the model's insight and then simply moving clockwise seems mechanical and too simple. Life's richness mitigates against mechanical or simplistic structures. Therefore, where do creativity and divergent thinking come into play?

Since the tool is a focus of attention scheme, creativity in the tool's use is essential if the tool is to produce diagnostic wisdom. Again, let me illustrate with a story. Like others in the world, I have been bewildered and bedeviled by the issue of abortion. What is really going on? What are the possible solutions to a seemingly intractable conflict? For quite a while, I framed the issue as a debate between existence and resources—the right of the fetus to be born in order to be in existence was on one side and the right of the mother to choose resource options was on the other side. Thus, what appeared to be really going on was a structure issue requiring that the rights of the fetus and of the mother be balanced in some structural harmony.

Then Minnesota senator John Brandl proposed a legal framework as a political compromise. His structure solution seemingly offended everyone equally. The demise of Brandl's proposal triggered an insight in me. Maybe the issue is best framed as a conflict of missions: right to fetal life versus right to mother's choice—and is, therefore, really a question of meaning. The meaning question asks why such intense emotional and political commitment and conviction are attached to all sides of this issue in the United States when the debate in other countries seems much less emotional.

Reframing the issue opened a fresh line of inquiry for me. Perhaps the meaning crisis centers on the extent to which this culture values, or fails to value, life in general. However, because of the difficulty of debating an issue that is so emotional as to be unmanageable, we attach disproportionate energy to a more definable set of meanings. If this analysis is at all accurate, then diagnosing the issue at the meaning level opens up the possibility that we can reach joint strategies for affirming the gift of life in other areas. In time, perhaps, the sharp edges of the mission fight might blur to permit authentic dialogue, discovery, and possibly common ground.

My point here is not to offer definitive analysis of the abortion conflict, but to affirm the necessity of our being continually creative in our diagnoses. The model is not mechanical; we use it to create a virtual, or imagined, world, engage in a conversation with that world, and test our hypotheses. Schön (1983) observes that "a sculptor learns to infer from the feel of a maquette in his hand the qualities of a monumental figure that will be built from it. Engineers become adept at the uses of scale models, wind tunnels, and computer simulations. In an orchestra rehearsal, conductors experiment with tempo, phrasing, and instrumental balance. [Similarly], virtual worlds are contexts for experiment within which practitioners can suspend or control some of the everyday impediments through rigorous reflection-in-action. . . . Practice in the construction, maintenance and use of virtual worlds develops the capacity for reflection-in-action which we call artistry" (p. 162). The Action Wheel provides a guiding structure, or a through which, for practice and play. Without practice and play, the structure will become empty and the model will fail to produce the insight it is capable of.

Who Can Lead?

The model does not limit leadership to a few. In the example in which the city leaders' mission debate had failed to address the city's meaning, leadership came not from the mayor, a positional person, or the consultant, the expert, but from a discussion participant.

Figuring out what is happening and what ought to happen is not the property of position or particular knowledge. Leadership is widely distributed in our population. Slight alterations to two popular lyrics say it all: Where have all the leaders gone? They only appear to be gone because we look for them in all the wrong places.

Teaching the Model

For years, I have lectured on the action model, naively thinking that clarity of presentation could substitute for reflective practice. I now know better. The current method at the Reflective Leadership Center is to use multiple approaches. Knowing these approaches may help readers to hone their own issue-framing skills.

To create learning readiness, a group is given a case. Without benefit of the model, the group identifies the problem and proposes solutions. Inevitably, the solutions are framed away from the real problem. Then the model is presented to the group and the case is worked again. Watching the light dawn is a delight.

To study the boundaries of the generic features, the group counts off by six. Each subgroup, or team, is assigned a term: meaning, mission, power, structure, resources, or existence. (Fulfillment is not used for this exercise.) The groups are organized in a circle following the Action Wheel. After hearing brief definitions of the terms, each team defines its term further. Anytime one team steps on another's turf, that other team is to counter by illustrating where a boundary has been blurred. As the teams define and defend their terms, the features become clear and distinct. Sometimes the teams are asked to build a virtual house. Each team has to claim its term's part of the house building. This method stresses contrast and bumping up against differences as a mode of learning. Once action's generic features are isolated, the entire group relates the generic features to each other to establish the model's inner logic.

Finally, working in groups of five, participants each give a five-minute presentation of the model. Based on the theory that the best way to learn something is to have to teach it, this exercise requires internal sorting and clarity. After hearing each other struggle to be precise about the model, the group members make a remarkable improvement in understanding.

Summary

At the beginning of Chapter Four, I distinguished four criteria to judge the adequacy of the Action Wheel. The exercise at the end of Chapter Four provided an initial test of application criteria—the features had to be irreducible, distinguishable, inclusive, and easy to apply. In this chapter, I have indicated how the model meets the fifth and sixth criteria of establishing connections between the features and generating insight.

Issue framing is one of leadership's most critical tasks. Every action contains six generic features of action, each of which can be the central issue that must be addressed; therefore the Action Wheel can be used as a framing tool. However, the model is not mechanistic. Leadership must apply creativity and playfulness to locate the presenting issue and to identify the underlying real issue that will lie clockwise to the presenting issue on the Action Wheel. Leadership also requires a knowledge of the ways the features of action interact and shape each other. Moreover, in any intervention, all the features must eventually be addressed and aligned since a change in one feature affects all the features.

Action is one human universe that we must understand in order to lead. The other is authenticity—the link between thought and action, and action's ever-present partner.

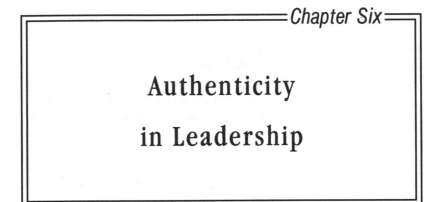

=Chapter Six=

Authenticity
in Leadership

Leadership is a subset of action. But not all action is leadership. Leadership is authentic action, a unique and honorific mode of engagement in life. In this chapter, I will define authenticity and explore its particular relevance for our times. Once I have linked action and authenticity, subsequent chapters will set the stage for a seventh view of leadership that will make this theory of leadership truly comprehensive.

Authenticity Defined

Authenticity, like any category of thought, carries with it historical baggage. The term's original meaning and multiple contemporary interpretations both limit and provide the foundation for my definition.

The word *authentic* derives originally from Greek sources meaning one who accomplishes. To be authentic is to act, to embody, to engage, and to participate in life. *Webster's New Interna-*

tional Unabridged Dictionary defines *authenticity* as "fidelity, actuality and fact, compatibility with a certain source or origin, accordance with usage or tradition, a complete sincerity without feigning or hypocrisy." However, this dictionary definition does not reveal all the word's philosophical complexity.

Mike Martin (1986) presents more of authenticity's connotations when he describes what he labels the Authenticity Tradition. In this tradition, authenticity "is defined in terms of avoiding self-deception. This emphasis leads to intensified criticism of virtually all self-deception—not just self-deception about wrongdoing—as cowardly and dishonest. . . . Existentialists, who represent the main current in the Authenticity Tradition, are preoccupied with the process of decision making. Their concern is not so much with *what* choices are made as with *how* they are made. Decisions, they insist, must be made in a fully honest way, based on a courageous willingness to acknowledge the significant features of the human condition, of one's immediate situation, and of one's personal responses" (p. 53).

One of these existentialists is Jean-Paul Sartre. Sartre clarified his understanding of authenticity by contrasting it with *sincerity*, a contrast that both Martin and I also find illuminating. In daily speech, sincerity and authenticity are often used interchangeably. Connotations of single-mindedness, moral purity, the avoidance of unjustified deceit, and openness (Martin, 1986, p. 70) can accompany either term. But a close look at both words reveals helpful distinctions in their connotations. Martin points out that sincerity "rules out unwarranted dissimulation, intentional deception, hypocrisy, duplicity, bad-faith commitments, and doublemindedness. Frequently it retains the positive connotation of purity derived from its Latin root *sincerus,* which means unadulterated. Talk about sincerity usually presupposes some positive standard for good motives, intentions, or attitudes against which insincerity is condemned" (p. 68). Promises are insincere if the person making them intends to renege. Hidden agendas also reflect insincerity of motive. In addition, Martin observes that "usually only desirable types of motives are called sincere or insincere." Both sincere love and insincere love sound possible, whereas sincere jealousy sounds redundant and insincere jealousy sounds contradictory.

In contrast, says Martin, authenticity "is captured by the idea of genuineness rather than purity. The authentic is the bona fide (insurance policy), real (Chinese tapestry), official (commemorative stamp), or authoritative (executive order), as opposed to the fake, imitative, unofficial, or unauthorized. . . . An authentic compliment is one that succeeds in praising someone, in contrast to a sincere compliment, which need only be intended to express feelings of admiration" (p. 69).

In addition to distinguishing genuineness and purity, Martin distinguishes the internal consistency, or congruence, that accompanies authenticity from that which accompanies sincerity. While consistency is a part of authenticity, it fails to comprehend the full experience of authenticity. Sincerity, however, can be viewed as an unmitigated consistency that limits a full exploration of self *and* world. Instead of asking what is really going on, it says, Be true to yourself, ignoring that the self may be unreflective, insensitive, or destructive. Martin provides an example from art history: "Rousseau and some other romantics viewed sincere artists as those who accurately revealed and expressed what they felt. In practice, this often inspired narcissism and exhibitionist displays of the sordid aspects of life neglected by conventional artists. . . . [The] ideal of sincerity with oneself [as] congruence . . . allows that the motives for the congruence may have little to do with striving for significant truths or an honest understanding of one's present attributes" (p. 71).

Thus sincerity treats the self as limitation. Authenticity, while rooted in the limit and possibility of existence, moves around on the Action Wheel and expands possibilities. "A free consciousness," says Martin, "assures that we are always more than our present attributes, for to be conscious of them is to transcend them . . . by freely giving them a meaning or by initiating actions to modify them" (p. 71).

Because we are self-conscious, we are never totally reducible to inherited traits, although a person who demands sincerity of others may wish to make it seem that the others are locked into a historical legacy. Martin's example of "outing" makes the same point: "To insist that the person who deceives himself about his homosexuality openly acknowledge it . . . may well be an attempt to degrade the person. The champion of sincerity views the homosexual as a thing whose homosexuality is a determined destiny rather than a free sexual response. The confession is demanded in order to [remove, as Sartre says], 'a disturbing freedom from a trait.' The freedom is disturbing, in part because it raises our anxiety about ourselves being free and in part because its recognition would reveal our kinship as free beings" (p. 72).

Thus, authenticity refers to certain fulfilled characteristics of an action; sincerity focuses on intent and motive. Authenticity is guided and judged by genuineness and trustworthiness; sincerity by purity of intent. A sincere compliment is meant; an authentic compliment fulfills the mission of complimenting. Finally, authenticity opens possibilities; sincerity limits them.

Authenticity and Social Self

Sartre's affirmation of radical individualism and its authenticity gives insufficient weight to our social interdependence. For social selves—that is, persons in communities—the tasks of authenticity are even greater than for individuals. Both self and community continually face issues of authenticity. For example, resources can be either authentic or inauthentic. Imitation Rolex watches, cooked numbers, and subliminal messages are real yet untrue. Structures can be public or hidden. Formal decision making versus secret pacts and nondiscrimination laws versus redlining illustrate this distinction. Power may be legitimately or pseudo-legitimately experienced and justified. Authentic power enforces law; inauthentic power abuses law, yet does so in the name of law. Authentic power resists oppression; inauthentic power terrorizes the innocent.

Likewise, missions can mislead. Missions that publicly propose one direction but have hidden agendas proposing another are usually inauthentic. Persons who intentionally distort someone else's mission to serve their own are inauthentic. Watch the debate about homosexuals in the military. The imputation of motives undermines real dialogue. The result is fear of difference, suspicion of the other.

However, some missions seem to require hidden agendas to ensure the desired action. Sting operations, placebos in controlled health research, and spying are examples. While serving important services to society, they also pinpoint dilemmas. Should there be public oversight of stings by judges? Should there be informed consent by patients? And should there be congressional review of the CIA? With the possibility of power abuse, the ethics of power and the core values of the society come to the fore in any thoughtful discussion of undisclosed missions.

Meaning gives reasons or rationalizations, the big truth or the big lie, the real or trumped-up justification. Nor does the vehicle that carries the meaning guarantee its truth. Metaphors can disclose or obscure what is real and true. Virtual reality can enrich or distort our understanding of the real world. Humor flourishes in the presumption of the inauthentic. Outrageous disconnections between appearance and reality delight audiences endlessly. But humor can also perpetuate untruths.

Identifying authenticity as one of the two human universes from which leadership flows raises serious questions. What justifies authenticity as a goal or means of action or both? Does authenticity entail a constraining and directing ethic? If so, what is that ethic? Is it personal or social? Is the ethic culturally bound or universal? What does leadership do if, in the name of authenticity, a person or group bludgeons another in a genuine conflict over principle, process, or fact? What is the relationship between a personal vision and a social vision? Are there authentic and inauthentic visions of reality? Does authenticity mean that leadership should embrace a particular vision?

There are yet more questions raised by authenticity's role in leadership. Is freedom, central especially to Sartre, an appropriate starting point for an argument about authenticity? What is freedom? Are there justifiable limits to freedom, and therefore to authenticity? Is there any time to be justifiably inauthentic or partially inauthentic? Can each of us be authentic alone, or are we caught in the web of others' inauthenticities? Is even authentic leadership historically situated, constrained by time and place, or is it able to transcend limits to new possibilities? What sustains authenticity? Does authenticity entail a spiritual underpinning? If it does, what then is the relationship between leadership and spirituality?

As each of these issues surfaces and is addressed here and in later chapters, one underlying notion of authenticity cuts across them all. Authenticity entails action that is both *true* and *real* in *ourselves* and in the *world*. We are authentic when we discern, seek, and live into truth, as persons in diverse communities and in the real world. What distinguishes leadership from other forms of action, including other forms of authentic action, is that leadership calls forth authentic action in the commons. The commons are those public places and spaces where leadership lives, moves, and expresses itself. To call forth authentic action requires courage and hope for the human community. Leadership is a response to a deep sense of disconnection in the human community, even if that sense is unarticulated. We doubt. Life is not what it appears to be or as it is described to be. When we do not know what is really going on, we fall into the chasm of confusion. If confusion and contradiction drive our action, we become robot-like, capricious, arbitrary, random, and exceedingly dangerous. Our life disconnects from the past, as we rewrite history without regard to what really happened. Our life disconnects from the present, as we frame current events to distort rather than disclose what is really going on. And our life disconnects from the future, as we fail to understand what will happen.

Thus, we need authenticity to ask for us, What are our anchors? To what can we hold? Is there any continuity in a time of radical discontinuity? We need authenticity in leadership to identify for us what is really going on.

The Age of Authenticity

From the echoes from the Garden of Eden to contemporary voices today, tales of distortion, denial, and avoidance abound. Listen to Christopher Columbus (1987), who, on Sunday, September 9, 1492, wrote in his journal, "This day we completely lost sight of land, and many men sighed and wept for fear they would not see it again for a long time. I comforted them with great promises of lands and riches. To sustain their hope and dispel their fears of a long voyage, I decided to reckon fewer leads than we actually made. I did this that they might not think themselves so great a distance from Spain as they really were. For myself, I will keep a confidential accurate reckoning" (p. 62).

We have not cornered the market on infidelity, broken promises, hidden agendas, political intrigue, and double messages. What, then, makes authenticity a more salient issue today than it was in past ages? The fact of inauthenticity is not new, but the depth and scope of it are well beyond past experience. Many of us sense a deep, pervasive, and profoundly disturbing disconnection between the world that we experience as we actually live in it and the world that we create and describe in our rhetoric and imagination.

Many of us grasp the disconnection intuitively. Others search for evidence. All of us are responding to an erosion of reality. Few doubt the current rapidity of change or underestimate the likelihood of its increased acceleration. What is uncertain and unsettling is the unknown direction of that change. Is it heading toward promise or peril?

One of the few social theorists to use authenticity explicitly in his conceptual work is Amitai Etzioni (1968), who believes that "authenticity exists where responsiveness exists and is experienced as such. The world responds to the actor's efforts, and its dynamics are comprehensible" (p. 620). In other words, reflective engagement matters. The world is at least partially malleable to a person's or group's bidding and that malleability is understandable. In contrast, inauthenticity exists if a relationship, institution, or society "provides the appearance of responsiveness while the underlying condition is alienating" (p. 619). Etzioni makes an important distinction between simple alienation and inauthenticity: "Subjectively, to be alienated is to experience a sense of not belonging and to feel that one's efforts are without meaning. To be involved inauthentically is to feel cheated and manipulated. The alienated feel that they have no power; the inauthentic feel they have pulled a disconnected lever without quite knowing where and how, so that shadows are confused with reality. The alienated are imprisoned, the inauthentic work at Sisyphean labor" (pp. 619–620).

According to Etzioni's distinction, black South Africans under white-controlled apartheid experience alienation; U.S. citizens experience inauthenticity. My only reservation about this distinction is that when power expresses itself as aggression, the alienating power wielders rationalize their action with inauthentic meaning. Rarely is brute force left undefended and unjustified. Even so, Etzioni opens the door to a better view of the pervasiveness of inauthenticity. But what is generating the abiding sense that we do not know what is really going on and what to do about it? What is creating this unique setting for leadership?

Using the Action Wheel as a guide, I identify six contributing factors to our emerging preoccupation with authenticity:

- A deep, yet undefined, sense of disconnection
- The introduction of a new resource
- A worry about the viability of institutional structures
- A willingness to create virtual reality
- A fragility of shared purposes
- A crisis of universality versus relativism

An experience of inauthenticity presupposes a knowledge of the authentic. In discussing these six factors, I will also cite examples of the authentic responses that we implicitly acknowledge when we call other responses inauthentic.

Deep Disconnection

Authenticity is speaking, however dimly, to more and more of us, calling us to recognize the pervasiveness of the new inauthenticity. Something is not right, and we sense that what is not right is expressing itself in many forms, from global issues to personal concerns. We have an intuitive sense of disconnection from the very institutions and people we believe we should be connected with. This abiding feeling cuts across ideological lines, as liberals, conservatives, and radicals alike acknowledge the immensity of contemporary events. The promise of a new world order conflicts with the peril of international and national conflicts running out of control. Which is the appearance and which is the reality? Is it a time for hope or for despair? A profound disturbance, a doubt, rooted in disconnection triggers our questions about authenticity.

A New Resource

In contemporary societies, the new resource of information is another trigger for the experience of disconnection. While it is common to say that technology-rich societies have shifted from production-based to information-based activity, what is not widely understood is the character of that shift.

Cleveland (1985) identifies five characteristics of the new resource with great precision. First, information is "expandable without any obvious limits, the facts are never all in—and facts are available in such profusion that uncertainty becomes the most important planning factor." We experience this characteristic as "information overload" (p. 30).

Second, and paradoxically, information is "compressible. . . . This infinitely expandable resource can be concentrated, integrated, summarized—miniaturized, if you will—for easier handling" (p. 31).

Third, information is increasingly being substituted for capital, labor, and land. For example, "people who use computers hooked up to telecommunications don't need much real estate to be efficient" (p. 31).

Fourth, "information is transportable—at the speed of light" (p. 31). Information is also "diffusive"; it has a natural propensity to leak! We expect natural resources to stay put until we "capture" them by mining, pumping, or other means. With information, the more it leaks, the more of it we have, and the more of us have it. Some of the sources of this leakage are "the Xerox machine . . . high-resolution photography, parabolic listening devices, remote sensing, electronic computation, satellite communication, and, closer to home, universal education combined with the human urge to pass a secret along" (p. 33).

And fifth, information is "shareable." Drawing on the work of communication theorist Colin Cherry, Cleveland asserts that "information by nature cannot give rise to exchange transactions, only to *sharing* transactions. Things are exchanged: if I give you a flower or sell you my automobile, you have it and I don't. But if I sell you an idea, we both have it" (p. 33).

The resource of information confounds old patterns of thought and behavior and directly contributes to the experience of disconnection. For Cleveland, who writes with great enthusiasm and optimism about information-rich societies, information is a great social leveler. When there is universal access to information, poor and rich can play on a level playing field; organizational hierarchies can be flattened. Cleveland, however, tends to play down possible ominous consequences of information technology, such as invasion of privacy, gene transformation, political control, data overload, and babble replacing wisdom.

Information richness is a mixed blessing, creating new possibilities for human achievement, but also raising the specter of abuse. What is true? What is real? What is likely to occur as information dominates high-technology societies?

Viability of Organizations

Are the structures we have designed to channel resources, including the new information resource, functioning well? Are we creating and managing flexible and adaptive processes to sustain our social and personal health? Again, a sense of disconnection is part of our mixed experience with functional and dysfunctional organizational and institutional structures. What were once touted as the best educational, health, and financial systems in the world are under siege. A pervading sense of personal and social sickness erodes our confidence in our basic social institutions. Categories of personal dysfunctions and social disorders fill the print and the electronic media. I often wonder what it would be like to meet a healthy person! Today, a person who claims to be healthy might be diagnosed as a victim of self-denial and delusion.

What was once taken for granted in education is no longer assumed. Schools formerly perceived as great are now having to justify their effectiveness. The burden of proof has shifted. Authenticity credits no longer cash out in available currency, and the credibility's bank account stands in arrears. The story is the same for health-care institutions. The savings and loan crisis illustrates the breakdown of structural controls. There is a constant worry about the breakdown of family structure. A trip through large metropolitan areas produces the sense that large cities may not be governable. Sprawling urban areas spin out of control, triggering worries that no processes are in place, or can be put in place, to channel the conflicting centers of energy. Are the mechanisms of governance functioning well? Our abiding sense is that they are not. Even information structures strain, as we have seen in the damage caused by computer viruses and the fear that just the threat of them arouses.

Proposals abound to reorganize, tighten controls, manage systems more closely. All kinds of alternatives to restructure institutions are being explored simultaneously. In Minnesota, for example, almost every conceivable option for school reform is being explored at once. Yet some are contradictory. The state is pioneering in "choice," standardized outcomes, effective schools, same race schools, voluntary statewide desegregation, multicultural education, institutional rule and procedural reform, and strategic planning, to name just a few of these school reform efforts.

Deep disquiet and disorientation lead to flailing about, trying this, trying that. Almost every idea is being tested somewhere. What is effective? It is difficult to discern. Appropriate reform is difficult to chart. Institutional skepticism erodes authentic action.

Some structures work well. Head Start, World Weather Watch, Red Cross disaster relief, civil aviation, and the treaties governing use of the Antarctic are just a few of the structures that seem to deliver what they promise. We all have personal examples also. My car dealership and mortgage lender both manage processes effectively.

The result of this crisis of authenticity is a new stirring of creativity. Old forms lose some of their grip as they lose credibility; new forms emerge as provocatively, if tentatively, promising. Nevertheless, we look out at the institutional landscape and wonder what is really going on and what is functional for the new society that is emerging. We ask ourselves what kinds of structures need to be in place as effective channels for action, channels neither too rigid nor too loose to carry our commitments forward.

The Creation of Reality

Building on the information resource and the concerns over institutional dysfunction is an exponential explosion of human power to create both reality and unreality. Scientists now believe they can map the entire human gene. As they progress in their work, I remember what a biologist once told me: "If we can understand it, we will mess with it!" When I have visited biotechnical organizations such as Pioneer Corn and the Garst Corporation, and heard about their work, the tension between working with natural processes and transforming them becomes abundantly clear. Much of this agricultural research focuses on mapping genes to speed plant breeding so that experiments that would take years using slower growing plants can be accelerated. Science in this instance is not changing natural patterns but speeding them up.

In other scientific work on genes, however, the goal is to transform natural patterns. The power of human intervention is unleashed onto the ecological system. These bold actions send shock waves through ecologists who deplore transformation of nature and advocate conformity and cooperation with it. Unleashed human power in other areas also threatens many people's sensibilities. Unleashed power challenges old boundaries, creating the prospect of an arbitrary and capricious future of unaccountable change. Just the fact that we can debate the permissible extent of human intervention in nature is disturbing. If natural law can be recast and rewritten, then it is problematic for us to use natural patterns as a test when building a global ethic. What can be counted on if we can change the fundamental order and predictability of the world? Our creativity coupled with our fear of abuse feeds our feelings of disconnection. What kind of a future awaits? Who is in charge?

However, there is another dimension to human power that contributes even more directly to our perception of increased inauthenticity. Etzioni (1968) first brought it to my attention that information-driven societies possess a geometrically expanding capacity to shape the appearance of events, thereby creating the illusion of reality in order to accomplish intentionally willed outcomes. A new vocabulary reflects the presence of this virtual reality—*spin control, plausible deniability, disinformation, doublespeak,* and *docudramas.* In each instance, we create unreality on purpose. An elected official makes an uninformed or just plain dumb remark. Out trots the *spin doctor* to "doctor" reality by putting the best "spin" on the embarrassing comment. Plausible deniability is a pervasive political criterion. What can I plausibly not know, yet get away with actually knowing? Disinformation is misleading information intentionally designed to change some perception of reality. Disinformation is so serious a problem that there is now a center to study it. Doublespeak pervades political life. William Lutz (1990) cites hundreds of examples of language used to disguise rather than disclose what is really going on.

Docudrama completes the litany of intentional distortions. Television docudramas merge fact and fiction to such an extent that only a viewer extremely well versed in the subject matter can untangle them. Yet calling these programs docudramas precludes criticism. If their truth is questioned, the retort by television executives is that the programs are drama. If the aesthetic quality is challenged, the documentary aspect of the programs is defended. A case in point is the docudrama based on the Walker family spy case. The program stated that the U.S. Navy knew of the spying. According to the investigator overseeing the trial, the Navy did not know. Who can benefit from this one-sided presentation?

As I mentioned earlier, Mitroff and Bennis (1989) characterize contemporary culture as an "unreality industry." They believe that the deliberate creation of unreality is "one of the most pivotal social forces shaping our time" (p. xi). Reality has lost out as individuals neither want to nor seem able to address the realities flooding into their experience. In Mitroff and Bennis's view, the fascination with unreality is psychopathic, generated by reality avoidance. They contrast the new global reality and the new unrealities in six areas:

Characteristics of the New Global Reality	*Characteristics of the New Unrealities*
1. Increased, if not overwhelming complexity through longer and longer trains of thought necessary to achieve a proper understanding of any event or phenomenon in modern society.	1. Greater and greater simplified, if not trivialized versions of everything through the presentation of vast amounts of uncorrelated data, quick-moving and un-related images, so that not only is there no need to connect them, but that it literally defies anyone to connect them in a coherent pattern.

2. More and more spheres of life that are thrown together into instant and strange conjunctions than ever before.

2. More and more 15- to 20-second snips or sound bites of limited and simplified contextless information which concentrate mainly on a single point of view through the use of one-liners, and countless disconnected images.

3. The quickened pace of all events through the ability to communicate rapidly through computers; increased general stress in our lives.

3. The focus on short-term goals such as money, notoriety, instant fame, the attempt to create stability by refusing to update our view of the world.

4. Socially, economically, and morally we are soon becoming if have not already become a second-rate nation.

4. We continue to believe that we are the biggest and the best.

5. More and more our destiny is controlled by other nations.

5. We continue to believe we can get along just fine without others.

6. More and more our values are severely in question.

6. We continue to believe we are God's chosen people, that our moral destiny is to shape the world [p. xiv].

Nevertheless, against this bleak backdrop are signs of hope. Elected officials in the United States are being held to the "appearance" standard. An action that appears to indicate a conflict of interest is tantamount to being one. Internationally, we have recently seen profound instances of previously unimaginable authenticity. Nations have admitted political abuses, apologizing and offering reparations. Nations have admitted failed economic policies. A political system that divided a country collapsed and was renounced. We have tasted global authenticity even in the midst of continued inauthenticity. Within the United States, television executives are saying that authenticity sells. Thus, a spate of purportedly true programs floods the airwaves—real rescues, behind-the-scenes exposés, a real "24 Hours." While we are busy creating unreality, we are also busy revealing reality.

The power of human energy and creativity is a mixed blessing. On the one hand, it opens new insights and makes progress possible. On the other, it abuses, dominates, exploits, and unleashes destructive forces. In part, unreality is checked by the authentic act of naming it. Mitroff and Bennis's implicit advocacy of authenticity qualifies their critique. Just as an analysis of dysfunctional structures presupposes an understanding of functional ones, so, too, does worry about unreality presuppose a deep and abiding confidence in reality.

The Status of Common Purpose

If the information resource, institutions, and power are problematic, on what can we base our trust? For many people, the foundation for trust is not the past but a vision of hope for the future. Thus, we can imagine the profound sense of unease that would result if those visions of hope themselves turned out to be suspect.

Clancy (1989) argues persuasively that the three broad purposes of business—production, wealth, and institutional maintenance—have lost their legitimacy. Because "a corporation is chartered by society, its legitimacy clearly must flow from society's agreement to an acceptable purpose for the business" (pp. 281–282), but the public is no longer quietly agreeable. When production creates floods of trivial products, wealth results in endless greed, and the maintenance of an economic system produces junk bonds, a crisis of purpose erupts.

Social ethicist Gibson Winter (1981) strikes an even more strident tone. Not only business purposes are suspect; our total societal vision wavers on the brink of illegitimacy. The West's overwhelming confidence in and commitment to technical mastery and technical solutions to all problems increasingly fall short of comprehending and addressing the fundamental problems of "social dwelling." Technical manipulation can neither understand nor fix the profound crisis of our ecological condition. Winter proposes that life be understood as art (see Chapter Eight). Responsible participation, in his view, must replace overconfidence in experts and societal manipulation.

Major systems of philosophical ethics are also under review. For years, two dominant principles have directed and legitimated ethical debate and theories: utilitarianism, which promotes the greatest good for the greatest number, and deontology, which advocates doing what is right (one's duty) regardless of the consequences. An alternative is emerging out of this review, which is led by ethicists, moral developers, and those who have assessed the debate over the good versus the right as a dead-end stalemate. Carol Gilligan (1982) reports that women use love and responsibility as central criteria for decision making, in contrast to men, who stress freedom and justice. Kohlberg explores whether there is a seventh stage of moral development beyond the duty to be just (Munsey, 1980). Philosopher Richard McKeon (1990) proposes that the ethic of responsibility was introduced to escape the stalemated debate over the good versus the right (p. 77). Helmut Richard Niebuhr (1963), another social ethicist, also proposes a responsibility for doing the "fitting" as an alternative to the good versus right debate (p. 56).

And so, in the deep recesses of the academy as well as in our daily walks of life, the profound wrestling with purposes continues. Ideas like these may be "invisible powers," as Clancy (1989) says, but their impact is broad and deep. When they are questioned and jerked into the foreground of our attention for review, we are unsettled and unnerved. Yet if the purposes that we once took for granted are now suspected to be inauthentic, there is no way to move ahead authentically until those purposes have been reviewed and alternatives proposed.

A personal story illustrates how it is possible to ignore but then have to face one of these changing purposes. I was invited to conduct a strategic planning session with the Midwest Conference of the United Methodist Church. Church attendance was dropping, financial giving was slowing, motivation was lagging. They needed to know what was wrong and what corrective action should be undertaken. For two days, fifty of us struggled to complete the strategic planning process. We analyzed the church's strengths and weaknesses and its opportunities and threats, clarified the mission, isolated strategic issues. Yet, on reflection, our team became convinced that we had failed to shape a strategic hypothesis, the fundamental idea that would direct all the other ideas.

At a second three-day session, we experienced great success and empowering results. Instead of focusing on techniques of strategic planning, we examined the central issue—the loss of direction. We asked ourselves what fundamental orienting metaphor was informing parishioner and clergy thinking about the church.

I took the participants through a metaphor exercise, asking them in which metaphor of the ones I offered they thought the church was currently living, and which metaphor offered the most promise as a depiction of the new realities of the church in society. To a person, they framed the current metaphor as body and the appropriate new metaphor as journey. The orienting metaphor of the church as a body, which at one time had contributed to church success, was now the church's undoing. The body metaphor directed clergy and lay positional leaders to look inward, to seek ways to nurture and grow the body. Membership drives, every-member canvasses, programs for all ages had been intensified, only to fail to deliver the desired results. Interestingly, Callahan (1990), a commentator on church leadership, had anticipated the need for this very shift on the part of churches, from looking inward toward their own functions and "conserving" resources to looking outward toward their relationships with the world and becoming "God's missionaries" (p. 34).

Universal Meaning Versus Relativism

In addition to the information resource, structural skepticism, ambivalence about power, and a sense that traditional social purposes are failing us, one further factor contributes to our concern over authenticity. Some radical skeptics argue that we can *never* know what is true or real or what is the good, the right, or the fitting. We are, they say, trapped in an ethnocentric envelope, peering only at ourselves and our own culture. Therefore, we face the specter of a profound relativism in which there is no sure foundation for any thought or action. It is becoming commonplace in leadership circles to observe that this is a time of paradigm change. However, I believe that some thinkers find it a time of paradigm shear, or even a time when any possibility of creating enduring or comprehensive paradigms has collapsed.

Few possess the courage to go to a philosophical precipice and step into the abyss. The great gift of these pioneering philosophers or artists is to return, through their essays and artworks, to report the terror and the promise. I have found Richard Bernstein's writings an excellent and reliable guide to the intellectual puzzle of relativism. Bernstein's *Beyond Objectivism and Relativism* (1985) is especially insightful. Bernstein (1985) observes an intellectual and cultural "uneasiness" that affects almost every discipline and aspect of our lives. This uneasinesss is experienced as the opposition between objectivism and relativism: rationality versus irrationality, objectivity versus subjectivity, and realism versus antirealism (p. 1).

Bernstein's reflective research for the sources and symptoms of this opposition takes him back to the philosophy of René Descartes, a pivotal figure in Western philosophy. Descartes's inquiry took him in two directions, one relying on reason and one on faith. His well-known conclusion, "I think, therefore I am," was an affirmation of reason. However, in his search for surety he also exhibited a tormented, troubled, faith-seeking side. Bernstein quotes Descartes's description of this torment, which was "reflected in the allusions to madness, darkness, the dread of waking from a self-deceptive dream world, the fear of having 'all of a sudden fallen into a very deep water' where 'I can neither make certain of setting my feet on the bottom, nor can I swim and so support on the surface, and the anxiety of imagining that I may be nothing more than the plaything of an all-powerful, evil demon'" (pp. 17–18).

Under Descartes's fear, as Bernstein acknowledges, lies a profound dichotomy with which many wrestle: "*Either* there's some support for our being, a fixed foundation of our knowledge, *or* we cannot escape the forces of darkness that envelop us with madness, with intellectual and moral chaos" (p. 18). Descartes's answer is to acknowledge his dependence on a "beneficient God" and "to set aside all the doubts of these past days as hyperbolical and ridiculous . . . for because God is in no way a deceiver, it follows that I am not deceived in this" (p. 18).

Either/or thinking is rampant in Western thought, beguiling constructive thought and creating false choices. I believe that the dispute between the relativists and the objectivists, or absolutists, is another of these either/or debates with deceptive choices. Relativists, who resist any claim to absolute truth, view their perspective as a safeguard against dogmatism, tyranny, and all other oppressions instituted by those who believe they have certain knowledge of the truth. Absolutists, in contrast, depict relativism as offering an intellectual haven for any abuse of power, because relativism lacks a universal ethical principle. Relativists, they argue, reduce truth to power, politics, and opinion.

What makes Descartes such a pivotal figure for Western culture is that he locked individuals into their own egos. From his time on, the outside world constituted a doubtful world. The only confidence in reality came through thinking and, finally, through a belief in God. Descartes could not believe that God's greatness would deceive him into believing that there was a real external world. But, as Barrett (1958) reminds us, "The ghost of subjectivism (and solipsism too) is there and haunts the whole of modern philosophy" (p. 193).

Descartes's solution turned out to be pernicious for our culture and our leadership. What he pulled asunder few thinkers have reconnected. Yet there is hope that we can rise above his either/or thinking. Bernstein (1985) observes that philosphers are reaching "a new understanding of rationality that has important ramifications for both theoretical and practical life." As they converse their dialogue "presupposes a background of inter-subjective agreements and a tacit sense of relevance," despite different emphases by different participants (p. 2). Bernstein confirms, I believe, the deepest suspicion that triggers and sustains our sense of inauthenticity. What we are told about either/or meaning disconnects from our deepest and most reflective experience. Yet the new inquiry he describes offers a glimmer of a way out.

I have argued that for six reasons authenticity deserves to be taken seriously at this time and this place in history. Our (1) intuitive sense of disconnection is buttressed by (2) the presence of the information resource, (3) a question about the functionality of our traditional structures, (4) our power to create virtual reality and transform nature, (5) a question about global and organizational direction, and (6) our ultimate question of what is really true, believable, and trustworthy. In each case of disconnection resides an implicit reconnection. Thus, a glimmer of authenticity also resides in our perceptions of inauthenticity. The interplay of authenticity and inauthenticity informs contemporary experience, grounding and creating the impetus for personal and societal change. As Cleveland (1988) reminds us, change requires two factors. There must be a perceived problem and a perceived hope to improve the situation. Problem identification without hope increases fear and a reluctance to change. Hope without problem identification ends in unembodied dreams. Authenticity faces the inauthentic, names it, and in hope, seeks to transform it into a new authenticity.

Authenticity and Leadership

A quest for authenticity informs our age and our thinking about leadership. However, the six reasons why authenticity occupies a central role in leadership differ from those that locate authenticity as a contemporary issue. Once again, the Action Wheel identifies the areas to investigate.

Personality Preference

Because subjectivity is a part of the way we think (but not, I believe, the only part), I must first admit to a subjective bias. Well before taking the Myers-Briggs Type Inventory, I had been intrigued with authenticity as a concept. I had written about it (1981) and thought I had explored new ground. After taking the Myers-Briggs instrument, I turned to Keirsey and Bates's *Please Understand Me* (1978) to review the portrait of my type. To my horror, surprise, and finally delight, I read the following: "ENFPs strive toward the authentic, even when acting spontaneously, and this intent is usually communicated nonverbally to others, who find this characteristic attractive. ENFPs, however, find their own efforts of authenticity and spontaneity always lacking, and tend to heap coals of fire on themselves, always berating themselves for being so conscious of self" (p. 173). I remember thinking, "My whole life is a footnote of my Myers-Briggs score!" So, perhaps, some of my interest in authenticity is genetic—it is my limit and my possibility. I can do no other.

However, the MBTI does not exhaust reality, and there are other critical reasons for focusing on authenticity as a source for leadership.

Inclusiveness

Just as the six features of action permit leadership to analyze all parts of every action, authenticity too is inclusive. It permits us to select different units of analysis—a person, an organization, a society—as centers of authenticity while also permitting us to explore the authentic relationships among these entities. For example, we can analyze the authenticity of a school district, a local school building, a class, a teacher, or a student. We can also explore the authenticity of teachers with each other, classes with each other, and students with each other. As a tool and a test, authenticity can transform apparent opposites into polarities and typologies, reaching out to embrace differences while holding to a recognizable center. Thus, the concept of authenticity serves a comprehensive function in model building. It is broad yet concrete, theoretical yet practical, unifying yet open to diversity. When I review the six perspectives on leadership (Chapter Nine) with which this book started, authenticity will play a major part in the shaping of my seventh and inclusive view.

Self-Correction

Authenticity self-corrects. It contains within itself an impetus to change as it reveals what is denied, discounted, hidden, and misleading. In other words, authenticity entices us to recognize the ever-present possibility that the inauthentic lies just beyond our full awareness. Authenticity holds together what we know and do in living tension with what we do not know, avoid doing, or have misled in doing. Therefore, while the test of the leadership ideas of action and authenticity is initially their utility, it is ultimately their own authenticity. Authenticity itself will test whether action and authenticity form a comprehensive and unique framework, one that both adds to our theoretical understanding of leadership and offers practical guidance for leaders.

Call to Engagement

Authenticity requires embodiment; it propels us to participate in life; it empowers. Authenticity resists idle speculation and encourages reflective engagement. Through its call to engagement, or accomplishment, authenticity requires action, forging a critical partnership for leadership and framework building.

Directional Orientation

Authenticity sets direction. It not only informs the means of action but defines a desirable future. It is visionary, picturing selves and the world as living an authentic life.

Ethical Foundation

Authenticity offers the possibility that we can construct a universal social ethic that preserves and enhances diversity. It provides the most fruitful approach I know of to transcend the relativism-absolutism debate. It is the presupposition of all human action, and a prerequisite to the creation of a viable future for all of us and for our ecology. It entails the acceptance of ethical categories such as love, justice, freedom as a part of leadership, giving each category its due yet uniting them in an inclusive ethical perspective.

When authenticity couples with action, when it is at the center of the Action Wheel, the wheel no longer spins in place. Rather, the grounding of action in what is most true and real propels the wheel forward toward a self-renewing future.

Summary

Authenticity is genuineness and a refusal to engage in self-deception. An authentic action is one that succeeds in accomplishing its mission. We live in an age in which attention to authenticity is becoming more essential as inauthenticity becomes more pervasive. We see real or potential inauthenticity in applications of the information resource, in the functioning of institutions, in our power to create virtual reality and usurp nature, in the fading of our common purposes, and in the crisis of thought over whether we are locked in our own egos, unable to communicate shared meanings.

At the same time, we see signs that out of these concerns can come beneficial uses of information and power, new purposes and structures, and a new view of meaning that does not require us to be either subjective or objective with no middle ground.

The concept of authenticity is as essential to leadership as the concept of action, helping us to frame issues and discover true answers. In the next four chapters, I use these two concepts to further unwrap the leadership enigma, especially regarding the current leadership issues deserving most critical attention: ethics, vision, and power.

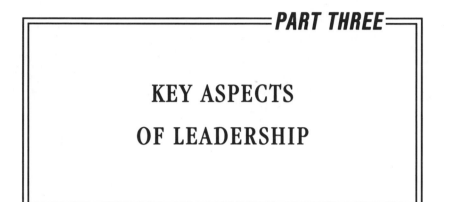

PART THREE

KEY ASPECTS
OF LEADERSHIP

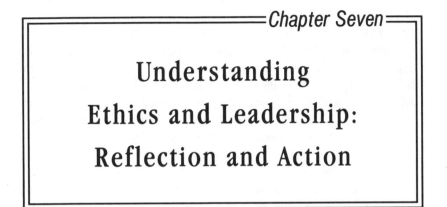

Chapter Seven

Understanding
Ethics and Leadership:
Reflection and Action

It violates common sense to argue that ethics is essential, even in-trinsic, to leadership. When Burns (1978) asserted just this case, he confounded the obvious. Yet, to this day, most leadership theorists, even those who acknowledge an intellectual debt to Burns, out-rightly reject or ignore Burns's most provocative contribution to leadership theory.

One question reveals whether a given theorist or practitioner holds the intrinsic or extrinsic ethical perspective: Can there be unethical leadership? If the person agrees that *ethical* and *unethical* can modify the term leadership, then he or she believes that ethical thought and action are external to leadership. We hope for ethical leadership, we can even teach and urge potential leaders to be eth-ical. But leadership itself is something other than ethical in its essential nature. Burns's claim about leadership is extraordinary because, for him, unethical leadership does not exist!

What is at stake in this discussion? Why is it not enough to assert the importance of ethics and leave it at that? Our definition of leadership sets the stage for whom we consider a leader. For Burns, Hitler was not a leader; he was a tyrant. However, most commentators on leadership would include Hitler in any leadership litany. It could be argued that this issue is merely a word game. Hitler's inclusion among the ranks of leaders does not mean he should be emulated. But it is not just a word game, because it does have real consequences for future leadership studies. Regardless of the outcome of the debate, the process itself will sharpen and refine our perspectives, press the outer boundaries of our thought, and bring clarity to such leadership concerns as leadership by whom, for what, and justified by what principles. We ought to be able to define leadership in a way that is "intellectually and morally defensible." There is an ethical imperative in the inquiry itself.

What is especially crucial is that, if ethics is not perceived as essential in leadership, it will continue to be ignored or included in leadership programs solely for idiosyncratic reasons—the instructors' interests, the culture's latest fad, or the participants' whims. Only what is perceived to be essential in leadership is *always* included. Even when ethical leadership is included in a leadership program, all too often key ethical principles are not identified, evaluated, or placed in a useful relation to each other. Urging ethical behavior is not the same as thoughtful wrestling with ethical principles or problems. More is required of us as teachers than a peripheral nod to ethical thinking.

A Time for Ethics

Authenticity precedes ethics. Or, to put it another way, an ethical view depends on a sense of the authentic. Therefore, it is not surprising that we see a deep worry over the apparent increase in unethical behavior at the same time as we see a deep concern with rising inauthenticity. And just as a concern with inauthenticity is an implicit recognition of our need for authenticity, a concern with unethical behavior is an implicit recognition of our need for ethics. Indeed, that implicit knowledge is rapidly becoming explicit.

We are bombarded by reports of public officials who exploit public power for private gain; banks that buckle under the, at best, questionable ethical practices of their directors, who benefit from these practices; and scandals and infighting in religious communities. Patterson and Kim (1991) report astonishing findings from a massive survey, concluding in part that "at this time, America has no moral leadership. . . . Americans are making up their own rules and laws. . . . There is absolutely no moral consensus in this country—as there was in the 1950s and 1960s. There is very little respect for the law" (p. 235). When Barbara Toffler (1986) asked managers for a definition of *ethical* she found that "although the common thread of these definitions is that 'ethical' has something to do with right and wrong, good and evil, virtue and vice, there is no agreement on the substance of right and wrong, its source or on the universality of applications" (p. 10). At the same time, people are becoming more assertive about their individual rights.

As a nation, we increasingly face profound ethical quandaries about issues in which there is no clear right and wrong: for example, Should doctors assist in suicides? Should law enforcement agencies be allowed to use computerized data banks to determine whether a person ought to be jailed or allowed out on bond? Good people differ; proposals for solutions differ. We are also witnessing clashes of opposing ethical principles deeply rooted to some sacred tradition. The premier example today, of course, is abortion, on which, at least in the near term, no consensus exists or is likely to emerge.

If we step back from the immediacy of U.S. society, another factor appears that contributes to our new interest in ethics and to the dilemma of connecting ethics to leadership. We face profound global diversity. What ethic will inspire a universal commitment to a global and diverse community that is also ecologically sane? The meaning of reason itself differs in various cultural traditions.

Amid this ethical erosion and malaise, communities and organizations are fighting back. The Corporation for Public Broadcasting presented the television series "Fixing America" in 1989. "Living an ethical life," wrote the proponents of the series, "is like playing an instrument: it takes practice'" (Public Broadcasting System, 1989, p. 2). Michael Josephson started the Josephson Institute of Ethics in Marina del Rey, California, hoping to create an "ethics core" to address teaching ethics in the 1990s. Conferences are held solely to address ethical issues. Harvard University received millions of dollars to incorporate an ethical focus into its business curriculum. Other business schools are following suit. Public and private organizations are developing codes of ethics for themselves in response to public concern over ethical failures. When staffs of elected officials at the Humphrey Institute attending seminars were asked if ethical mania is sweeping across the political landscape, their answer was an astounding yes. The land is astir with ethical debates and concern.

Despite the public ferment over ethics, there is no clear publicly acknowledged definition of ethical behavior. I believe that a publicly acceptable definition is possible. In the remainder of this chapter, I will discuss a definition of ethics; a clarification of the dimensions of ethical actions; an explicit linking of authenticity, action, and ethics; the construction of an ethical framing method for leaders; and practical examples that test the method.

Defining Ethics

Ethics, formally defined, is a branch of philosophy that considers questions of personal, organizational, and societal judgments. It is particularly interested in evaluative judgments, those that recommend certain classes of actions. (See William Frankena's *Ethics* for an excellent introduction to the field of philosophical ethics.)

Ethical judgments can be studied from a variety of perspectives. *Descriptive* ethics uses empirical inquiry to examine how people actually make ethical judgments. Kohlberg, the expert in moral development whose views were important to Burns's work, exemplifies this perspective. *Normative* ethics articulates and defends a particular set of criteria, standards, or principles that are intended to inform our judgments. I shall be proposing such a set of standards, rooted in the idea of authenticity. *Meta-ethics* asks, Why be ethical at all? It also investigates the meaning of key ethical categories. Meta-ethics steps back from the ethical enterprise itself in order to examine ethics from a comprehensive perspective. I shall use meta-ethical analysis, also.

We all make many more ethical judgments than we might think. These can be positioned along a scale ranging from nonreflective to profoundly reflective. *Instinctual* ethical utterances are usually reactive, nonreflective, and triggered by an external threat: "Don't hurt me!" "Don't harm my child!" Our personal or social survival is most likely at stake. Ethical statements can be expressed as *tastes* or *desires*. We use such phrases as "I like . . ." or "I want. . . ." These minimally reflective statements are often the product of childhood socialization and expose deeply held convictions. *Moral rules* or *codes of conduct* are ethical statements formed through collective deliberation in an organizational or institutional context. Federal employees, for example, promise to report "fraud, waste and abuse," as part of their professional responsibility. Ethical statements can also express *collective interests.* "Bring the hostages home" was a collective ethical demand of the president when U.S. citizens were hostages in Tehran and Beirut. Such statements are typically caused by a public event that evokes shared responses.

Ethical statements of *principle* exhibit a high level of reflection and abstraction and give direction to moral rules and collective interests. "Do what's right, regardless of the consequences"; "Do the greatest good for the greatest number"; "Love the Lord your God with all your heart" and "Love your neighbor as yourself"; and "Do unto others as you would have them do unto you" are four major principles often proposed in the philosophical or theological thought of many cultures. *Transcendental* ethical statements are the most reflective. They incorporate comprehensive beliefs about the meaning of life and the nature of the universe.

Ethical reflection and ethical statements are central to human experience, informing that experience and making sense of it. Therefore, it is surprising how little is known about the relationship between ethical thought and action. Even in the field of moral development relatively little is known about the connection between levels of moral development and particular behaviors. Nor do we know the best way to intervene in human development in order to improve ethical behavior.

Ethical Action

The Diagnostic Wheel suggests six areas that should be considered in a definition of reflective ethical action.

- *Ethical sensibility* (existence). Without the socialization that produces values, we could not recognize any situation as an ethical dilemma requiring reflective attention.
- *Ethical tools* (resources). Just as the science of economics uses such concepts as supply and demand, marginal utility, and cost-benefit to analyze economic issues, ethical reflection has its tools of analysis. These tools are such concepts as love, justice, and freedom, which must be built into any comprehensive ethical framework.
- *Ethical methods* (structure). Methods link tools to issues, reflection to action. Appeals to scripture, third-party scrutiny, or recognized social standards fit this category.
- *Ethical motivation* (power). Motivation, or commitment, is the energizer. It engages the methods and links methods to principles. Without commitment, there is no spur to engagement.
- *Ethical principles* (mission). Principles point the way to ethical action. Without ethical principles, particular actions get lost in detail or stray off the course.
- *Meta-ethics* (meaning). Doubt accompanies ethical reflection and action. Why be ethical? What supports ethical action and encourages it to endure? Not everyone asks meta-ethical questions. Yet in times of great distress, these questions demand attention.

Authenticity, Action, Ethics, and Leadership—The Connection

Burns, and others, believe ethics is at the heart of leadership. Not only are many skeptical of his perspective, but he, himself, while courageously opening the door to the inquiry, only partially enters the next room. It is authenticity that now invites us in.

Authenticity and Action

Authenticity informs and directs action; action grounds authenticity in life. The abstract and the concrete are joined in authentic action. Without authenticity, action drifts. Without action, authenticity remains idle conjecture and wishful thinking.

Given these assertions, what is the argument behind them? I begin with two postulates:

- Authenticity is conceptually and experientially presupposed in any reflections about action.
- Lived authenticity is a prerequisite to building an enduring, thriving, and hope-filled future.

Authenticity as Presupposition

Authenticity is ubiquitous, calling us to be true to ourselves and true to the world, real in ourselves and real in the world. When authenticity is denied, thought and experience cease to be sensible, action to be justifiable. When authenticity is acknowledged, we admit our foibles, mistakes, and protected secrets, the parts of ourselves and society that are fearful and hide in the shadows of existence.

Even when we lie, whether intentionally or unintentionally, authenticity is present, reminding us that more is expected of us, that more is actually happening than we admit or want to admit. Denial presupposes that someone knows what is being denied. Through our courage, what has been denied can be known. Authenticity can distinguish appearance and reality, and it can unite them. Furthermore, authenticity is presupposed in any argument mounted to reject it because that argument, if it is genuine, is itself a proof of authenticity's existence. The rejecter is authentic in his or her rejection. As Huston Smith (1988) says,

> Relativism sets out to reduce every kind of absoluteness to a relativity while making an illogical exception for its own case. In effect, it declares it to be true that there is no such thing as truth; that it is absolutely true that only the relatively true exists. . . .
>
> Relativism holds that one can never escape human subjectivity. If that were true, the statement itself would have no objective value; it would fall by its own verdict. It happens, however, that human beings are quite capable of breaking out of subjectivity; were we unable to do so we would not know what subjectivity is. A dog *is* enclosed in its subjectivity, the proof being that it is unaware of its condition, for, unlike a man

or a woman, it does not possess the gift of objectivity
[pp. 149–150].

Not to know everything does not entail knowing nothing.
Partial knowledge is still authentic knowledge. Authenticity requires us to do what is possible—to know and be known, to bump
against others' partial knowledge, to discern a more comprehensive
perspective.

Lying, keeping secrets, and self-deception all presuppose authenticity. Lying itself entails that someone knows the truth. For
what is the mission of lying, but to disconnect appearance and
reality?

Jody Powell, former press secretary for President Carter, vividly exposed the overwhelming presence of authenticity as action's
partner when he spoke at the 1987 Washington conference entitled
"Scandals, Scoundrels, and Saints—Ethics and Integrity in the Federal Government." Powell, you may recall, intentionally lied to the
American people when the U.S. government embarked on a rescue
mission of the U.S. hostages in Iran. When asked to report on truth-
telling and lying as a part of a justifiable form of government action, he affirmed authenticity through this comment: "The reason
we should tell the truth in government most of the time is so that
when we lie we are believed" (Powell, 1987).

The ground around Kant's grave shuddered at the utterance.
Powell reversed the ends and means of government. The purpose of
government is to lie, the means to perpetuate the lie is truth-telling!
I admit I am stretching Powell's point. But what his statement also
reveals is a backhanded recognition and affirmation of authenticity.
Without authenticity as the benchmark, lying is impossible. Successful fraud and sting operations, and even mystery novel plots,
require splitting perception from reality. Yet reality is always
known by someone in the deception process.

To hold a secret implies knowing the secret, to engage in self-
deception implies, at least conceptually, a touchstone of clarity. I
am not, of course, debating whether or not to lie and deceive. That
territory has been well traversed (Bok, 1978, 1983; Goleman, 1985).
My contention is simply that authenticity is presupposed even when
engaging in any of these activities.

Authenticity logically and experientially precedes any ethical requirement for us to act in a particular way. Therefore, if *ought* implies *can*, as I think it does, no one can be expected to do the conceptually or existentially impossible. I do not claim, at this juncture, that people will willingly admit and take responsibility for their self-deceptions. As Goleman (1985) states, "There is almost a gravitational pull toward putting out of mind unpleasant facts" (p. 244). Nor am I assessing the psychological and social mechanisms that disconnect us from ourselves, others, the globe, and even God. That territory has been well covered by others (Goleman, 1985; Martin, 1986). Mine is a simple point: to experience disconnection presupposes some referent point for prior connection, no matter how dimly known.

The presupposition of authenticity has provided two answers to the question, Why be authentic? The first answer is rational—it is self-contradictory not to be authentic. The negation of authenticity affirms its claims upon us. The second answer is experiential. Authenticity's presence is confirmed by the experience of disconnection.

There is one more sense in which authenticity is presupposed in all human action. As I mentioned earlier, authenticity is social; it transcends autonomous, self-reflective decision making. Authenticity enhances self *and* world.

Sartre, a prime exemplar of the Authenticity Tradition, and to a lesser extent, Kierkegaard, represent the individualistic side of authenticity. Sartre's central thesis is that "freedom is the unique foundation of values and that nothing, absolutely nothing, justifies me in adopting this or that particular value, this or that particular scale of values" (Martin, 1986, p. 60). Nevertheless, he finds that "as soon as there is a commitment, I am obliged to will the liberty of others at the same time as my own. I cannot make liberty my aim unless I make that of others equally my aim" (Martin, 1986, p. 65). Authenticity's press for categorical commitments drives Sartre to guarantee for others what he necessarily claims for himself. And as others claim their authenticity, he in turn is more assured of achieving his own possibilities.

For Kierkegaard, the route to recognizing human interdependence is somewhat different. His religious faith led him to assert that Christ is in all one's neighbors, especially one's enemies. Thus, a spiritual bond transcended reason's claims for categorical consistency.

Although arriving by different paths, both Sartre and Kierkegaard affirmed John Donne's famous metaphor, "No man is an island, entire to itself." Yet, perhaps, a more apt statement would be that we are all islands, unique and connected. Each of us possesses his or her unique shoreline, topography, and location, yet each is solidly linked in a common landmass, separated by water, united by rock. To be authentic is to be true and real in both self and world. Authenticity is socially interdependent. Human beings are social selves engaged in social action. Ethics, therefore, is fundamentally social ethics.

The problem confronting a concept of leadership that includes ethics is not subjectivity or the privatization of ethics, as opposed to objectivity. Ethical thought arises from and is shared in communities of persons; it is objective. The real challenge to ethics is relativism.

Authenticity as a Prerequisite

Authenticity justified is not necessarily authenticity engaged; hence, the second postulate is also required: *lived authenticity is a prerequisite required to build an enduring, thriving, and hope-filled future.* Radical diversity does exist, and it continually challenges authenticity to reach across cultural divides. Are we forever stuck in our own cultural and conceptual envelope, or can we build a universal global ethic that both affirms our human oneness while simultaneously affirming and guaranteeing our differences? Lakoff (1987), himself a conceptual relativist, frames the issue by comparing "diverse ways of comprehending experience" to a diverse "gene pool." Both are necessary if our "species is to survive under a wide variety of conditions." Lakoff believes that "conceptual relativism of the sort that appears to exist does not rule out universal ethical standards of some sort. . . . Nor does it seem to tell us very much about what such standards should be. However, a *refusal* to recognize conceptual relativism where it exists does have ethical consequences. It leads directly to conceptual elitism and imperialism—

to the assumption that our behavior is rational and that of other people is not, and to attempt to impose our ways of thinking on others" (p. 337).

Since diversity exists everywhere, what ethic is applicable to families, organizations, communities, nations, and the globe? What is the starting point for a comprehensive leadership ethic that heeds Lakoff's warning about domination but avoids the absurd relativism pointed out by Smith? An ethics that begins with any one faith or philosophical tradition alienates other traditions; therefore, a relatively neutral starting point is needed.

I think there are two minimum requirements for entities that adhere to a social ethic that both is universal and protects and enhances diversity. This ethic holds in appropriate tension the one and the many. The requirements are these:

- Show up
- Be willing to engage and to claim your own authenticity

An entity that shows up establishes its presence as a fact of existence; an entity that lays claim to its own authenticity must engage with others to make that claim.

The entity that shows up and engages can be a particular person, an organization, a country, a nation, or a cluster of all of these. Showing up does require a physical presence, although that presence may stand in for something else. Representative persons and/or artifacts such as flags, styles of talking, and other symbols can represent a group's or nation's presence. When we say that General Motors and the United Auto Workers show up at the bargaining table, obviously, we do not mean that the entire organizations surround the table. Instead, representatives with defined powers and responsibilities appear, observing carefully choreographed seating arrangements and other structural procedures. Shared meanings make it possible to understand who is and who is not showing up appropriately and what actions are appropriate when a representative appears.

Each entity, or center of claimed authenticity, lives within a symbolic boundary and, as such, becomes a locus of action. Each center can be analyzed, using the Action Wheel. Thus, each center embodies meaning, mission, power, structure, resources, and existence in its engagement with other centers, which are similarly structured.

Now, the stage is set to construct the ethic. Given the two starting points, what is required to ensure that the authentic action centers can endure together in a hope-filled future? On what must they agree if they are to maintain themselves as centers?

I identify six ethical requirements, or principles. Each is an aspect of a generic feature of action. These requirements are responsibility (meaning), love (mission), participation (power), justice (structure), freedom (resources), and dwelling (existence). The following parable describes how these ethical requirements are called forth and applied in our lives. In this parable, two centers of authenticity show up. I call one center Us, the other Them.

The Story of Strangers

The community of Us rejoiced as its renewal celebration concluded, marking the beginning of a new year. Hope stirred in Us. It had been a prosperous year; the community looked ahead to the next year with justifiable optimism.

Looking across the broad stretch of land toward the horizon, a few of Us noticed a barely visible cloud of dust. As it settled, large numbers of Them could be seen, moving relentlessly toward Us. Our hope quickly gave way to fear. A few of Us asked, What is going on? but, nevertheless, rumors spread with the speed and intensity of a raging fire. Invasion, enemies, destruction! Still, some of Us remained curious. "Wait and watch," they counseled. "See what happens."

And a curious thing did happen. Instead of moving closer, as was expected, the group of Them stopped. It became apparent to Us that many of Them were settling in and taking up what looked like permanent residence adjacent to Us. A few of Us wept. Life would never be the same. Yet others of Us were intrigued. What would life for Us be like, living next to Them?

Some of Us convened a council to determine what to do. Slowly, after serious, intensive, and often fear-filled debate, a strategy emerged. A few of Us, selected for insight and strength, would attempt to meet Them. Many warnings went with the investigative party—"Be always on guard," "Return immediately if you are in danger." A skeptical few were not even sure a meeting with Them would be possible.

When the team returned, the whole community of Us could hardly wait to hear the news. Was the community of Them warlike, friendly, or like Us at all? Two facts from the visit hit Us hard. The most troubling was the apparent permanence of the new settlement. The second was how different the community of Them was from Us. Language, customs, appearance, manners—all were different, and that scared many of Us.

As time passed, and periodic meetings between Us and Them occurred, a small, intense group of Us argued forcefully that the only strategy to address the ever-present danger of Them was to attack, to eliminate Them before it was too late. A majority of Us, while deeply concerned about the permanent presence of Them, did not agree, even though small parties of Them had been sighted venturing closer to Us. The danger was not sufficient for Us to mount a preemptive attack on Them. Moreover, one of Us pointed out that a victory by Us was not assured. It was an unsettling debate for all of Us.

Amid the doubts and suspicions that Us had of Them and, presumably, Them had of Us, members of Us went about life's daily routines, securing the necessities of life, caring for the children, exchanging goods, producing, buying, and selling, and generally flourishing. Yet there was a difference. A watchful, suspicious eye was continuously trained on Them. Although the community of Us still experienced its own freedom relatively unchecked, and showed a great potential and possibility to thrive in spite of Them, fear still surged among the community.

One day, at a council meeting, a new strategy to deal with Them emerged from the community dialogue. We could make agreements with Them to recognize each other's existence, not to invade each other, and to structure regular exchanges between Us and Them. The council rejoiced. A breakthrough! But would the community of Them agree and would they keep their promises? There was no doubt that promises made by Us would be honored, for lurking behind our concern about Them was an arrogance about Us. Almost all of Us knew, in our heart of hearts, that the community of Us was culturally and morally more advanced than Them.

The members of the team that would engage in the dialogue were selected on six criteria: Who were most representative of Us? Who best understood and could articulate the team's mission? Who were suspicious of Them? Who best understood Them? Who possessed the best dialogical and negotiating skills? And who carried the collective historical memory of Us?

The team's visit to Them lasted several days, and team members were both astonished and pleased with the overall results. In the discussions with Them, it had become abundantly clear that the community of Them believed they were morally and culturally superior to Us! In order to find a basis for an initial agreement, the parties finally had to agree that the communities of Us and Them had equal claims to moral and cultural supremacy. From there, it was politically difficult, yet intellectually easy, for each community to recognize and affirm the other's existence, meaning, and resources by promising not to invade and agreeing to create opportunities for exchange.

Another unanticipated result of the meeting, beyond the agreement about mutual supremacy, was the agreement made in response to questions raised by Them about our commitment to equality. What if some of Them or Us got into trouble, perhaps owing to a natural disaster or a market failure? What would be just? Through more probing dialogue, a promise was made. Minimum fairness meant equal access and treatment to available and created resources. In addition, both parties agreed to the principles of equity and adequacy. If conditions warranted, Us and Them would assist each other proportionately, not just equally, to make up for inequities caused by new situations. The communities also reached a clear recognition that any need for new rules and arrangements would be tested by adequacy, because what is appropriate at one time may be inappropriate at another, owing to new knowledge, technology, or other shifting factors.

The suspicion that prevailed during the dialogue also surprised Us since the community of Us believed itself to be totally trustworthy. Given the mutuality of suspicion, however, Us and Them agreed to reciprocal monitoring of each other's commitments.

Afterward, a sense of calm and relative well-being pervaded Us. We had *freedom* because we had potential and possibility. We were not threatened by arbitrary discrimination or exclusion or by lack of information. We had *dwelling*, our necessary space, place, and time, and we were free from the threat of genocide and murder. And we had *justice*, or fairness, which mitigated against the breaking of promises and opposed underdevelopment and rigidity. Yet, as many of Us soon realized, no system functions smoothly. As the community of Us matured in wisdom, it also experienced new worries. Rules were diversely interpreted by Us and Them, and at times, each claimed the other had violated the rules and broken promises. Disturbingly, many of Us began to take for granted that the promises made to Them functioned independently of human action. The community of Us became passive. Waning energy and commitment opened the door to abuses of power by those seeking to exploit the vulnerabilities of Them. Aggression by those perceived to have the upper hand triggered deviousness in those who felt less powerful. Commitments to justice were ignored and new oppressive behaviors rationalized. Only lip service was given to prior promises. The new behaviors sent shock waves of fear through many of Us. Was all that had been accomplished to be lost to the actions of an adventuresome few? Calls for a preemptive strike reemerged. If the threat presented by Them could not be removed through agreement, then it should be resolved by aggression.

Two strategies for a peaceful solution were developed; each aimed to build lasting relationships between Us and Them. At a council meeting, it was decided to share power with Them in regional governance, thereby encouraging *participation* by both groups. Further, a serious effort was to be made to care for the well-being of Them, as well as Us. Instead of relying upon the constant threat of overthrow to maintain the participation of both communities, the communities would rely on sharing power. Moreover, by attending to the well-being of Them by understanding Them, the community of Us would know the genuine interests of Them and would discern the common ground that could be acted upon. The community of Us could not afford to be indifferent or apathetic toward Them; nor could it rely on pseudo-insight about Them. The community of Us decided it had to *love* Them.

As in the past, some arrogance accompanied these actions. Thus, love sometimes veered toward self-righteousness, and caring deviated into caretaking. Nevertheless, in spite of these aberrations, serious attention to the new actions produced amazing results. Listening to each other encouraged storytelling. As both communities swapped history, myths, and experiences and as trust and credibility expanded, exchanges that started on the safe ground of swapping yarns were transformed into serious dialogues. Differences, while still real, gave way to the discovery of commonalities. Stories pinpointed similar struggles and similar heroic efforts to overcome adversity. The communities of Us and Them began to refer to the members of both communities as We. Fears about each other were named, anxieties disclosed, and claimed superiority was replaced with mutual acceptance, regard, and respect. The communities of Us and Them both admitted to breaking promises and seeking to exploit the other's vulnerabilities. Mutual remorse opened the possibility of forgiveness, not in the sense of forgiving and forgetting, but in the sense of breaking a spiral of escalating revenge, blame, shame, and humiliation.

A danger still haunted both communities. Love needed an anchor to limit its sentimentality. Alongside the newly discovered and appreciated oneness, there was also difference. The one and the many were equally real. The communities realized that attention had to be given to both Us *and* Them. *Responsibility* had to be taken for the history of each community as well as for the communities' connections. To show up as Us, not just initially but continually, required Us to take responsibility for both our laudatory and destructive aspects. To be responsible is to embrace the width and depth of existence, the bad news and the good news, the fears and the hopes, the peril and the promise. Embracing reality required both communities to face reality. Facing reality required courage, and to endure, it required faith in the ultimate worthwhileness of the endeavor.

What the Parable Reveals

The six ethical principles, their relation to each other, and their link to the Action Wheel are displayed in a grid in Table 7.1. The principles possess both personal and communal aspects, which operate in tandem. In addition, as the story and the contents of the table illustrate, authenticity entails more than simple consistency. Neither Us nor Them could endure and thrive in a hope-filled world if the ethical principles were ignored or denied. Any guarantee that authentic dialogue will persist and deepen over time requires that the parties to the dialogue increasingly understand and accept their own heritage, sense deep freedom, be just, participate, love, and be responsible. The alternatives are genocide, discrimination, deception, oppression, apathy, and abdication of responsibility. In other words, authenticity entails being committed to keeping authenticity alive in oneself and in others.

Can any group claiming authenticity assert its rights and expect to prevail? The answer is no. What authenticity proposes is that both goals *and* procedures be reviewed for their authenticity. We cannot achieve authentic ends by inauthentic means. Thus, even though an entity claiming authenticity shows up and engages, it can be critiqued by the authenticity's criteria.

Earlier, I remarked on the apparent stalemate between the absolutists and the relativists. Each claims the other opens the door to abuses of power. The absolutists fear that the relativists see all perspectives as justifiable, and the relativists fear that the absolutists are ethical imperialists.

My proposal of lived authenticity seeks to confound both groups. Only in unity, by agreeing to the six universal principles, can diversity flourish, and only in diversity can unity be discussed and valued. Without the many, there is no need for the one; without the one, the many will be extinguished. Pluralism, the one and the many, surmounts false either/or choices of absolutism or relativism. An entity's willingness to show up and engage both presupposes authenticity and is a prerequisite for its fulfillment. When we feel overwhelmed with diversity, it is instructive to remember how many nations signed the United Nations Declaration of Human Rights.

Table 7.1. Authenticity and Ethical Principles Framed by the Action Wheel.

Generic Features of Action	Lived Authenticity: Prerequisite for Self	Lived Authenticity: Prerequisite for Community	Ethical Principles (Affirmations and Denials in Showing Up and Engaging)
Meaning	Possess wise judgment	Build an enduring and thriving future	Responsibility Affirms accountability to and for authentic action Denies abdication
Mission	Understand self and others	Discover and support knowledge, mutuality, regard, and respect	Love Affirms attention, caring, and forgiveness Denies indifference, apathy, and self-righteousness
Power	Possess empowerment and consent	Share power in dialogue over collective interests	Participation Affirms actual engagement Denies aggression and deviousness
Structure	Exhibit personal growth and development	Possess equitable and adequate distribution systems	Justice Affirms fairness Denies promise breaking, underdevelopment, and rigidity
Resources	Possess necessities of living	Produce and distribute adequate resources	Freedom Affirms potential and possibility Denies arbitrary discrimination, exclusion, and lack of information
Existence	Possess life—physical development	Promote ecological diversity and survival	Dwelling Affirms dwelling as necessary place, space, and time Denies murder and genocide

That does not mean everyone practices all its principles, but the very fact that over a hundred nations could participate in that discussion means that cultural diversity is not an overwhelming obstacle to discerning a commonwealth in the midst of a diverse commons.

Authenticity, Action, and Leadership

Leadership is essentially ethical, although it is not reducible to ethics. It is crucial to include the central findings of the visionary, political, functional/positional, team, and personal schools for a comprehensive perspective on leadership. As I will show, leadership must also embrace courage and spirituality. Nevertheless ethics is an essential component in leadership. To demonstrate why this is so, I must recall certain stages of my argument.

- Action and authenticity are the twin human universes within which leadership inheres.
- Every action can be analytically separated into seven generic features.
- Six of these features form the Action Wheel. The Action Wheel is an issue-framing tool.
- Authenticity is both at risk and in demand today.
- Authenticity requires us to be true and real in ourselves and in the world. Ethics is also at risk and in demand.
- Authenticity entails an ethic that is both personal and social.
- Violations of the universal ethical principles erode diversity's potential to exist and endure.

Leadership as an idea and as an experience cannot be divorced from either logic or life. If we are expected as human beings to be true and real in ourselves and in the world, how can leadership be anything less? Leadership's primary mission is to enhance our authenticity as persons in communities. If leadership is to enhance authenticity, it must embody what authenticity requires.

Burns was right to reject Hitler as a leader, but not solely because Hitler was a tyrant. Hitler violated leadership because he perpetuated and lived the lie of supremacy. Even if he believed his own rhetoric, the consequences to the oppressed were calamitous. His social inauthenticity masked the ethical requirements of authenticity, undermining human possibility, decency, and diversity.

Nevertheless, there is a serious danger in this kind of pronouncement. As the story of strangers illustrates, self-righteousness is an ever-present threat to authenticity. Authenticity, inappropriately understood, having no love for others and no responsibility for its actions, can abuse and too quickly condemn others. Authenticity ripped from the ethic it entails is inauthenticity.

Martin (1986) illuminates this point when he discusses Sartre's critique of anti-Semitism. "Anti-Semites adopt fear as their basic attitude toward truth about themselves and others . . . and passionately cling to simplistic explanations of the world. Yet the main objection to anti-Semites is not their threat to authenticity *per se* but, instead, the ways in which their self-deception renders them insensitive to humane values. [Sartre says], 'a man who finds it entirely natural to denounce other men cannot have our conception of humanity.' The self-deception of the anti-Semite is immoral because it spawns cruelty, suppression of liberty, and irrationality" (pp. 66–67).

Leadership calls forth authentic action in the commons. However, it should be a gentle, reflective authenticity. For, very likely, the criticism directed at others applies to oneself as well. To strike unempathetically at others is to condemn oneself harshly. Lest we become what we fear and imitate what we despise, we are better off as "committed seekers after truth rather than discoverers of any particular truths" (p. 78). Self-righteousness is often painfully real; however, it does not go hand in hand with serious ethical reflection. Self-righteousness flows from insecurities, which cause us to demand at least the appearance of certainty. Ethical people do not have to be, nor are they, self-righteous.

Leadership thrives on a boundary. It acts at the intersection of the inauthentic and authentic, acknowledging and owning the inauthentic in ourselves and the world and seeking ways to tilt the world and ourselves toward the authentic. Ethically hard cases do not yield easy answers; however, reflective dialogue over time presses for consensus and often yields it. For example, reflective practitioners found themselves simultaneously confronted with new life-sustaining technology for terminal patients and with a need for donated organs for transplants. Together, the practitioners decided on a definition of death. As the result, most states have adopted a formal agreement that death is defined by the absence of brain waves. Although not perfect, the definition generally works well.

No doubt many persons would like to be excused from making judgments. Yet, renaming and disguising ethical criteria with psychological or sociological terminology only makes it more difficult to address what is really going on. Naming and addressing the authentic opens clear and straightforward possibilities for community building. Making judgments is not a task to be feared; it is a task to be relished. Since it is already going on, as I have demonstrated, why not own what is really happening?

Ethical discussions often conceal vested interests. Yet the ethical judgment may not discard these interests. We must first ask whether they are worth pursuing. Niebuhr suggests that organizations and nations can only be interested, not ethical (1960). Current leadership mostly agrees, in the short term. In the larger view, however, interests are expressions of profound and pervasive ethical commitments that can and do manifest themselves in direct public policy. Leadership must reject Niebuhr's cynical view.

Leadership That Practices Ethics

It requires courage to be ethical. Often what is ethical and what furthers a particular interest overlap. However, that is not always the case. Ethics is not reducible to self-interest and expediency. Practicing ethics does not guarantee professional or personal success, especially if that success is measured in traditional terms of position, power, and wealth. Yet authentic action entailing ethical action is a prerequisite to building a hope-filled future. What is it then to practice ethics?

One aspect of ethics is knowing what to do, the other is doing it. Some problems embody serious ambiguity that demand commensurate serious thought. In others the problem is not the ambiguity of the issue, it is instead willingness to act on what is already known to be good, right, or fitting.

The leadership objective has not changed. It is to frame issues. Therefore, among its other questions, leadership must ask what is really going on ethically. Once the ethical question is raised, the Action Wheel, depicted again as a grid in Table 7.1, comes into play. Like the use of the Action Wheel, the use of the ethical grid requires the equivalent of clockwise movement: that leadership frame ethical issues a level or more above the presenting issue.

The cases that follow are opportunities for leaders to practice framing ethical issues.

Case 1

A proposal that is being floated in Washington, D.C., recommends that a portion of our national park reserves be set aside as rescue-free zones. People who voluntarily entered these zones would not be rescued if they became endangered. The ethical question is, Should federal policy encourage rescue-free zones on federal land?

Case 2

You are a member of a hospital board of ethical advisors. The hospital research team has just discovered a cure for AIDS. You have doses for one hundred people; one thousand people need it immediately. What is the ethical issue?

Case 3

You are a teacher. One of your students is a bully. The other class members are angry at the student's behavior. What is the issue you face?

In case 1, the presenting ethical issue is freedom. (It is similar to the issue of whether people should be required to wear seat belts.) However, the ethical issue that must be addressed is justice—What is our duty to one another? We will get into ethical difficulty if we do what we might be inclined to do—namely, address the issues as a matter of existence and let nature take its course. The justice question is the one that raises the ethical quandary.

In case 2, the presenting ethical issue is distributive justice. Most people reading this case propose some form of lottery. Leadership would take the issue to the dimension of power. It would ask about those who will get around any fair lottery process and about those who should be included in the decision making. When the issue is framed this way, it suggests that the stakeholders be involved in determining the mechanism of a lottery or in deciding that some other device for choosing is appropriate.

In the third case, the presenting issue is participation; thus, the real issue, according to the model, is love. If we try a structure solution, the power abuser will only find another way around it. Caring for the non-caring bully challenges him to face his own mission. Caring for the bully quickens love.

Case 4

The first three were relatively easy cases. The following one is more difficult. For five years, a community has successfully administered an Adopt-the-Road Program. Each community group that partic-ipates, and by implication its civic virtue, is acknowledged by a sign at the appropriate point on the highway. Now, the Ku Klux Klan wants to participate in the program. What should the responsible city administrator do? Should the Klan be allowed a section of the road?

Ethical framing can also inform tough cases such as the abor-tion issue. Earlier, I shared my dilemma in framing the abortion case. For a long time, I thought justice was the issue, rather than the right to choose (freedom) and the right to life (dwelling). Now, I believe, the problem is more accurately stated as a love issue, reaching for shared responsibility for enhancing all of life. (Dionne, 1991, also sees the issue as one that requires an ethical rather than a political debate.)

Conclusions

Earlier, I identified six aspects of ethical action. In conclusion, I review them in Table 7.2 to complete the discussion of rethinking leadership and ethics.

Leadership is logically, experientially, and practically ex-pected to be ethical. However, leadership is more than ethics. It is also expected to be visionary, but it does not condone all visions.

**Table 7.2. Ethical Action and Authentic Action
Framed by the Diagnostic Wheel.**

Generic Features of Action	Dimensions of Ethical Action	Authentic Action Results
Meaning	Meta-ethics	Consequences in thought; alignment in experience
Mission	Ethical principles	Concern with authenticity
Power	Ethical motivation	Concern with reason and courage
Structure	Ethical methods	Focus on moving clockwise
Resources	Ethical tools	Focus on dwelling, freedom, justice, love, participation, responsibility
Existence	Ethical sensibility	Deep sense of disconnection

When Barker (1985b) confronts business executives with the phrase, "If you think it is impossible, get out of the way of those who are doing it," the ethical ire of reflective leaders rises up. Are we to get out of the way of anything that is doable? Just because something is doable does not mean it should be done. Leadership as ethics says be wary of the visionary who refuses to address ethical questions.

Ethics is intrinsic to leadership. Because ethical behavior is currently a "hot" topic, it is easy to link ethics discussion to leadership. However, the current popularity of ethical interest is not the reason that ethics is intrinsic in leadership. Leadership is ethical because of the relationship of ethics to authentic action. Authenticity is presupposed as a partner in all human action. Authenticity also entails the ethical principles of responsibility, love, participation, justice, freedom, and dwelling. If we as humans must be authentic, and thereby ethical, then so must our leadership.

Ethics and vision are reciprocal. Ethical reflection offers us the rationale by which to select a vision and a metaphor for life. Visions and metaphors cradle, expand, and orient the ethical principles. The visions that should direct leadership in order to create an enduring, thriving, and hope-filled future are the subject of the next chapter.

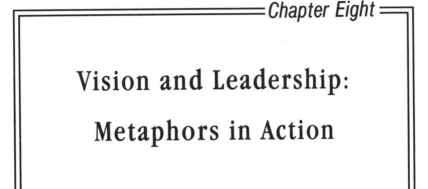

Chapter Eight

Vision and Leadership:
Metaphors in Action

The lights dim, the energy level subsides as old friends and new acquaintances come to order. Another futuring conference begins. Three hours and numerous scenarios later one wonders. The visions of these futures differ radically. What is true and real? What future is likely? Can we ever know?

In another city, an executive leadership program nears completion. An artist's work awaits unveiling. For five days, the executives have been engaged in guided imagery, body movement exercises, dance, and role-playing. Some even dared to walk on hot coals. Now the artist reveals his airbrush painting of the group's organizational vision, the result of a day and a half of dreaming, reflecting, and hoping.

These stories describe what is occurring with increased frequency across the United States. Visioning and intuiting have captured the imagination and dollars of the corporate community as executives seek clues about the future and ways to anticipate it. As

157

I illustrated in Chapter Three, vision is an aspect of leadership that many theorists find essential to leadership.

It is my belief that effective vision is shared vision, because, as Senge (1990) says: "a shared vision is the answer to the question, 'What do we want to create?' Just as personal visions are pictures or images people carry in their heads and hearts, so too are shared visions pictures that people throughout an organization carry. They create a sense of commonality that permeates the organization and gives coherence to diverse activities. . . . Shared visions derive their power from a common caring. In fact, we have to come to believe that one of the reasons people seek to build shared visions is their desire to be connected in an important undertaking" (p. 206).

Vision and Metaphor

But what directs vision and what allows it to be shared? I suggest that the directing agency is metaphor. In some leadership literature, metaphors are emphasized as technical tools that enrich language, rather than as frames to better understand reality. This technical view trivializes the function of metaphor and ignores the centrality of metaphor in our perceptions of reality.

The most important aspect of metaphor for leadership development is the way metaphor functions to orient our views. Orienting metaphors, or, as they are sometimes called, root metaphors, are the fundamental frameworks that direct our attention to a wide array of human experience by uniting that array under one notion.

Not only do orienting metaphors allow us to understand a large number of seemingly disparate items by discovering their profound similarities but they also direct our attention toward the future by providing models and maps that both describe and prescribe societal actions. In other words, metaphors describe a way in which the world works and, when the world does not act as the metaphoric model suggests, the same metaphors imply the broad sets of action that should be taken to realign the world with the original vision. Thus, metaphors are linked to the generic feature of mission in the Action Wheel. Yet metaphors also cradle specific meanings. Therefore, leadership must ask the validity of metaphors. From what perspectives should metaphors be judged adequate and thus advocated as appropriate for visionary leadership? And which orienting metaphors should receive close attention?

My answer resides in the relationship between action, ethics, metaphors, and authenticity. Action contains generic features. Ethics frames the deep meaning and justification of the features of action. Metaphors contextualize ethics, carrying ethical principles into the world of action. And authenticity cuts across the whole discussion, calling for worldly engagement that challenges vision directed by metaphor to be true to itself, while at the same time inviting a leadership inquiry clockwise on the Action Wheel for a more complete understanding of what is really going on.

Let me illustrate why action, ethics, and authenticity are essential to a discussion of metaphor. As I mentioned before, Clancy (1989) argues that the popular purposes of business have lost their ethical legitimacy. He proposes that businesses adopt a voyage metaphor to define their purposes and give them new legitimacy (p. 287). Likewise, Kouzes and Posner (1987) use a journey metaphor to communicate "the active pioneering nature of leadership" (p. 119). Journey is also an explicit organizing principle in the thinking of Reich (1987), Bolman and Deal (1991), Peters and Waterman (1982), Senge (1990), and Adams (1984, 1986). However, none of these authors explicitly articulates the deep meaning or ethical principles that guided the choice of the journey metaphor. Nor do these authors state why the metaphor is adequate for leadership theory development. Nor do they explore a number of other metaphors that might offer complementary insights. In addition, it is one thing to urge metaphorical thinking in general, quite another to articulate what is entailed in a particular metaphorical view of the world. Thus, I particularly appreciate Clancy's work (1989) and his willingness to be publicly accountable for his world view. All too often, leadership theorists act as if their perspective is value neutral. In my judgment, leadership perspectives are not and cannot be value neutral. Our orienting metaphors and our perspective on leadership itself causes us to frame policy issues differently. To be authentic in leadership theory, it seems to me, is to make explicit the policy implications of our own perspective and take ownership of these implications.

The remainder of this chapter will explore leadership and

metaphors in more detail, identify six metaphors that are commonly used as frames for understanding life, and relate the metaphors to action theory and ethics. I will also share my methods for teaching metaphorical vision.

Metaphors Defined

Metaphors open windows onto reality. They identify the unknown from the known, the novel from the familiar. They link the well established with the less well understood. Paul Ricoeur, phenomenologist and linguist, suggests that metaphor is a "calculated error that brings together that which heretofore did not go together" (Bolan, 1985, p. 353). Richard Bolan states that a metaphor simultaneously asserts that "A is B" and "A is not B." This entails a deep contradiction. In Ricoeur's words: "Such a process creates a tension between the two words employed. Resemblance plays a role but nonetheless the tension, the contradiction, between the words demands a dual interpretation of the words, one literal and the other figurative. . . . A metaphor, in short, tells us something new about reality" (Bolan, pp. 353–354). "A tractor is a machine" is a literal statement about a direct perception. "Life is a machine" is a metaphor. The metaphor anchors a direct experience to something that goes well beyond it.

Lakoff and Johnson (1980) illustrate the ways metaphors shape perception by contrasting the metaphors argument is war and argument is dance. The idea that argument is war is common even though we may never have articulated it. Its currency is shown by the frequency with which it colors our everyday speech. We say:

> Your claims are *indefensible.*
> He *attacked every weak point* in my argument.
> His criticisms were *right on target.*
> I *demolished* his argument.
> I've never *won* an argument with him.
> You disagree; okay, *shoot!*
> If you use that *strategy,* he'll *wipe you out.*
> He *shot down* all of my arguments [p. 4].

Many of the things we *do* when we argue are also structured by the concept of argument as war. "We see the person we are arguing with as an opponent. . . . We attack his positions and we defend our own. We gain and lose ground. We plan and use strategies. If we find a position indefensible, we can abandon it and take a new line of attack" (p. 4).

Lakoff and Johnson suggest that their readers imagine a culture that views argument as dance. Using this frame, "participants are seen as performers and the goal is to perform in a balanced and aesthetically pleasing way." Using this perspective, "people would view arguments differently, experience them differently, carry them out differently, and talk about them differently" (p. 5).

Thus, metaphors not only are filters on reality, they also unite what *is* happening with implied suggestions about what *ought* to happen. They unite the true and the real in one vision of reality. In other words, metaphors mediate what is perceived to be authentic. Different metaphors yield different realities, resulting in different perceptions of what is really going on. Is a business's orienting metaphor journey or is it something else, say, a belief that a business is an organic system? Very different ideas and actions will arise from the different metaphors.

Deep disputes are conflicts over fundamental orienting metaphors. Everyone has facts to support his or her perception. Yet what is at stake in the debate is the unacknowledged partner, the orienting metaphor. It is the metaphor that determines how the facts are ordered and evaluated. It is for this reason that "fact flooding" frequently fails to dislodge someone else's view. For what is a serious fact according to one metaphor can be an insignificant fact to another. The sometimes violent confrontations that emerge from conflicting visions present leadership with a vexing set of problems. What should leaders do when faced with different visions? What vision or visions should hold sway? Understanding the metaphors behind the visions helps us see the actions that are being prescribed by the vision and, eventually, may help us to join visions together to expand our options for authentic action.

As Reich (1987) reminds us, metaphors and morality tales form the maps out of which leaders frame problems and advance proposals for policy. As an issue is framed, however, so it is solved.

Misframing a problem confounds the solution and compounds the problem rather than leading to authentic action. Or, as Schön (1983) puts it, "When practitioners are unaware of their frames for roles or problems, they do not experience the need to choose among them. They do not attend to the ways in which they *construct* the reality in which they function; for them, it is simply the given reality" (p. 310). Unreflective use of metaphors locks us into existence; reflective use of metaphors opens the possibility of choice and assessment. Frames then become resources for action.

Of late, leadership theorists have been giving a good deal of attention to particular metaphors. However, they often do not identify enough of our major social metaphors, and they offer very little theory to assess each metaphor's adequacy and truth. Fritz Capra (1982) cites only two metaphors: mechanical and organic. Gibson Winter (1981) introduces a third: art. Lee Bolman and Terence Deal (1984) propose four: structural, resource, political, and symbolic, which parallel the mission, power, structure, and resource features of the Action Wheel. Steven Pepper (1970) also offers four: formism, mechanism, contextualism, and organicism. And Garreth Morgan (1986) identifies nine—machine, organism, brain, culture, political, psychic, prison, flux and transformation, and instruments of domination. In addition, the authors do not tell us which metaphor to use when. To a large extent, multiple metaphorical analysis undergirds Ralph Stacey's provocative book, *Managing the Unknowable: Strategic Boundaries Between Order and Chaos in Organizations* (Stacey, 1992). "As soon as we recognize that the dynamic of a successful company is chaotic," he writes, "and the long-term future is unknowable, it becomes clear that long-term plans, mission statements, and visions are also bypass games (p. 116). Thus, expecting tight agreement on many values in a time of radical diversity exposes a false assumption about reality. "The absence of strongly shared cultural norms encourages the multiple perspectives required for innovative activity" (p. 144). What then is the fundamental challenge for leadership? Engage in metaphorical analyses from many points of view. Test boundaries. Become a complex learner in a complex learning organization in a complex learning society.

Six Metaphors for Leadership

Our creativity is proportional to our metaphorical diversity. The more metaphors we use, the more we enrich our view of life and the more unexamined aspects of life reveal themselves to us. Thus, I initially hesitated to advocate the use of a limited number of orienting metaphors in leadership studies. However, as I read the literature in the field and spoke, and reflected on the story of strangers and the Action Wheel, a pattern emerged. All metaphors are not equally salutary. Some are better than others.

The six metaphors I have selected are the ones that I believe *are* shaping current leadership and public policy debates and that I believe *ought* to shape those debates. Ethical principles and metaphors live in a reciprocal relationship. Principles legitimate actions; metaphors direct and interpret actions. When our ethical principles are known, we can make preliminary judgments about appropriate metaphors. However, metaphors themselves enrich the ethical principles, bring them to life, and trace out their significance for action. The metaphors I have selected also relate to and inform the generic features of action. The six metaphors are these:

- Life is a gift (existence).
- Life is a market (resources).
- Life is an organic body (structure).
- Life is ups versus downs (power).
- Life is a journey (mission).
- Life is art (meaning).

Since this is not a volume on policy and metaphors, a full treatment of each metaphor must await another time. Here I want simply to sketch the thrust of each metaphor and show how it directs leadership. I also show how each metaphor prescribes actions, using public policies, and especially educational policies, as examples. And I show how metaphors can function inauthentically, using racism as my example.

Life Is a Gift

Isabel Briggs Myers, as I mentioned earlier, called her book on personality types *Gifts Differing*. A number of us, however, build our world view on the idea that not only are our traits gifts but that life itself is a gift. Just what is a *gift?* Louis Hyde (1983) describes it as "a thing we do not get by our efforts. We cannot buy it; we cannot acquire it through an act of will. It is bestowed upon us. Thus, we rightly speak of 'talent' as a 'gift,' for although a talent can be perfected through an effort of the will, no effort in the world can cause its initial appearance. Mozart, composing on the harpsichord at the age of four, had a gift" (pp. xi–xii).

The gift metaphor is pervasive in religious traditions. Black Elk, a holy man of the Oglala Sioux, reflects on his gift of healing, "of course it was not I who cured. It was the power from the outer world, and the visions and ceremonies had only made me like a hole through which the power could come to the two-legged. If I thought that I was doing it myself, the hole would close up and no power would come through. Then everything would be foolish" (Neihardt, 1961, p. 209). Contemporary theologian Matthew Fox (1983) seeks to recover the gift metaphor as a shaper of religious vision. The Christian faith, in particular, he believes, has distorted the joy of the gift of creativity by its preoccupation with the fall-redemption metaphor.

When we use the gift metaphor, we link life to existence and make existence a gift, also. Existence is that from which human action moves. Existence is stubborn; it is pre-resource. By viewing existence as a gift, the "thatness" of existence is transformed. What is taken in, received, appropriated, enjoyed, and relished becomes internal rather than external to our lives. That which has been alien is now friendly; that which is strange, now familiar. Thus, the gift metaphor causes us to look at the givenness of life from a mode of cherished affirmation.

Policy Choices. Any metaphor that shapes our view and understanding of life also directs our policy choices. The policy implications of the gift metaphor are many. Life as a gift affirms diversity by directing us to rejoice in the richness of life's great givens. As a gift, diversity should not be homogenized, assimilated, or rejected. And yet the gift metaphor faces the brutal challenge of evil. If life is a gift, what about the Holocaust, Russian gulags, the nightmare visited on Kampuchea by Pol Pot, and other examples of human destructiveness? Is death a gift? Or sickness, or disease, or poverty? These are also givens of life. What of natural disasters—floods, earthquakes, hurricanes? History, at best, is bittersweet. Yet, says the gift metaphor, evil must be acknowledged and embraced.

If life is a gift, policy predilections follow: abortion is problematic, as are the selling of blood for transfusions and paid surrogate parenting. The purpose of education is viewed as the complete development of all the diverse talents belonging to each individual. Education is expected both to identify and to enhance those talents.

Life Is a Gift and Racism. Racism is a scourge on the earth. What we think it is and think that we should do about it depends on the metaphor used to analyze the situation. However, racism distorts each metaphor, recasting it in counterfeit ways. An examination of each metaphor from this viewpoint will suggest why racism persists, why particular advocates of one metaphor are threatened by another, and, perhaps most importantly, why proposed solutions from a single metaphor can be inauthentic, either intentionally or unintentionally.

Racism distorts the gift metaphor while appearing to affirm it. Racism says all people have gifts; however, some gifts are superior and some inferior, and this distinction is rooted in biology or theology.

We can call those who support this view *supremacists*. They argue that, while it is true that everyone has a right to exist, "natural" supremacy justifies control of the inferiors by the superiors. They neither hate nor eliminate inferiors, they claim, because there are no grounds to hate. It is not their fault that one group is superior to another. It is genetic or it is God's will. There is no need to eliminate inferior persons who understand their place and stay in it. However, if supremacists believe their survival is at stake, then all means, including genocide, may be used to ensure the superior group's continued existence.

Thus, a plurality of gifts is transformed into better and

poorer gifts even though the affirmation that all people deserve a place maintains the minimum requirement of the gift metaphor. In this way, racism distorts the metaphor but does not eliminate it.

Life Is a Market

The market metaphor thrives today. Margaret Thatcher in the United Kingdom and Ronald Reagan in the United States advocated it. It is the metaphor directing much of both the breakup of the Soviet Union and the development of the commonwealth that is replacing it.

The roots of the market metaphor lie in the Newtonian and Copernican revolutions, which depicted the universe as a perpetual motion machine (Capra, 1982). We have only to consider the mechanistic concepts of supply and demand, marginal utility, and cost-benefit analysis to realize the impact of the Newtonian and Copernican world views on economic theory. Etzioni (1968) states that the atomistic and aggregate approach to interpreting life experience, used by many economists, "explains the state of a society, economy or policy in terms of properties, relations, or actions of micro-units, rather than in terms of their super-unit macroscopic relations" (p. 62).

In other words, the market view focuses on a particular interrelation of parts. Persons or resources relate to other resources through a variety of voluntary contracts or exchanges. Anything that challenges this free exchange is a threat to the workings of the market. The sum of the parts, working freely, equals the good of the whole. From this atomistic perspective, a term like *the common good* is the sum of all the exchanges of all the private actors producing private goods. *Common goods* is a better description of the desired result than is *common good.*

The libertarian strain of this market perspective is illustrated by Milton Friedman and Rose Friedman (1980) when they say, "No external force, no coercion, no violation of freedom is necessary to produce cooperation among individuals, all of whom can benefit. That is why, as Adam Smith put it, an individual who 'intends only his own gain' is 'led by an invisible hand' to promote an end which was no part of his intention." As free-market advocates, the Friedmans believe that "the combination of economic and political power in the same hands is a sure recipe for tyranny." They worry that "the view that government's role is to serve as an umpire to prevent individuals from coercing each other was replaced by the view that government's role was to serve as a parent charged with the duty of coercing some to aid others." As a result, they say, "sooner or later . . . an even bigger government will destroy both the prosperity that we owe to the free market and the human freedom proclaimed so eloquently in the Declaration of Independence" (pp. 5–6).

On the face of it there would seem to be an inherent contradiction in the Friedmans' belief that a Newtonian deterministic model sustains individual freedom. However, Friedman and other free-market advocates see no contradiction. By preserving his or her own desires, each person is being true to his or her own nature. Supply and demand as lawful relationships among the parts in an economic exchange always hold as individuals pursue their own desires. The laws do not account for the desires, only for the character of the exchange.

Policy Choices. We see the policy implications of this metaphor daily in the United States. The belief that life is a market calls for deregulation, limited government, parental and student choice of schools, and privatization of the public sphere.

The purpose of education, in this view, is to develop individuals' skills so they can compete in the marketplace. These skills include reading, writing, computing, and so forth. The specific levels of these major skills and the specific subordinate skills that are called for depend upon the market's reading of the competitive situation.

Life Is a Market and Racism. In the market metaphor, racism is manifested as personal prejudice and institutional discrimination that restrict the entry of certain groups of people into a "free" market and deny the right of individual competition to a whole group. Racism is thus anti–free market and inauthentic.

In an authentic free market, everyone must be free to be secure *and* to develop his or her inherited abilities, or gifts, to the maximum. At their most authentic, free-market advocates are great civil libertarians because anything that threatens the freedom of the market is anathema.

Free-market advocates become racists when they attempt to restrict the freedom of the market to a particular group, such as whites. The Southern Christian Leadership Conference and the American Indian Movement are examples of organized groups that became threatening to some free-market advocates because admitting these groups into the so-called free market appeared to restrict its efficient allocation of freedom and resources, which had de facto been reserved for whites. From the perspective of the free-market racists, these new would-be traders in the market had to be challenged, resisted, and brought under appropriate legal constraint.

Thus come the inauthenticities: all people are supposed to be free and have equal access to the marketplace, but whites end up defending their own access. Ultimately, these self-alleged defenders of liberty openly restrict the freedom of people who are different. While racial supremacists are worrying about their own survival, racist free-market advocates worry that unrestricted allocation of human and material resources will restrict their own access. But it is racism itself that introduces inefficiency into an efficient market. Again, racism distorts the metaphor's essential vision.

Life Is a Body

One of the most dominant contemporary metaphors views life as an organic system. Life is a body. This metaphor undergirds a wide range of seemingly disparate activities, including the ecology movement, personal growth therapies, cooperative classrooms, and affirmative action. Capra (1982) summarizes the view of living systems that the organic metaphor conveys: "Living systems are organized in such a way that they form multi-leveled structures, each level consisting of sub-systems which are wholes in regard to their parts, and parts with respect to the larger wholes. . . . All these entities— from molecules to human beings, and on to social systems—can be regarded as wholes in the sense of being integrated structures, and also as parts of larger wholes at higher levels of complexity" (p. 43).

The organic metaphor informs "body politic," "body of knowledge," and similar phrases. During the Watergate hearings, presidential counsel John Dean drew upon this metaphor when he spoke of a cancer growing in the presidency.

Organicism is the viewpoint of most public television nature programs. Vivid images of balance and survival, adaptation and flexibility indicate nature's ordering principles. Life is portrayed as a complex web of interdependencies and all nature as a complex organism. Tampering with one part of the system has direct consequences for other parts. Inherent in this notion is the message that nature's survival is our own survival. Images of domination and exploitation are replaced with those of cooperation.

In some ways, the body metaphor parallels the gift metaphor; however, they differ in the role assigned to action. The gift is given to be accepted and treasured as it is. The organic system is susceptible to change at the hands of humans, who can invent new structures to make it more effective. Human agency is more pivotal in the systems model than in the gift model.

Policy Choices. The policy and change implications of this metaphor are enormous. First, how do we change a system? In this view, we must work with the system, rather than against it. Peter Senge, in one of his Innovation Associates seminars, offered this example of system change. Suppose we want to turn a large ship. An obvious approach would be to have a tugboat push the ship at right angles to the bow and in the desired direction. However, that is not effective. Pushing at the bow pushes against a tremendous weight of water on the other side. The harder the pushing, the more the resistance of the water's inertia. An easier way is to turn the captain's wheel, which turns the rudder. An even easier way is to use a trim tab on the rudder. This device uses very small amounts of energy to change the direction of a large ship. Thus, a small energy input can yield a large system output. The basic message of the body metaphor is, Work with, not against, the system. Figure out how the system works and look for those levers that bring the greatest amount of output with the least amount of energy input.

Organicists believe interventions must be careful, selective, and able to work within the body. They often criticize public policy decisions in which major changes are forced on a system without an understanding of how the system works. Thus, governments build low-income housing in the form of high-rise buildings, only to find that they become stifling ghettos for their residents.

Educators who employ this metaphor worry about community and push for self-worth courses, cooperative classrooms, and personal growth. They worry that parental school choice will undermine a neighborhood's sense of community and increase destructive rampant individualism. The purpose of education is self-understanding, global understanding, and the building of a global community of mutual respect and dignity. This can only occur as individuals affirm the larger organically related world.

Life Is a Body and Racism. In the authentic organic metaphor, racism is a social disease. What do we do with a disease? We find a cure. Since the body is an integrated whole, all parts of the system have to be healthy for any part to be healthy. Justice, understood as fairness (Rawls, 1971), is one of the ways health is maintained in the system. Therefore, justice that benefits only the few produces social sickness.

Those who are authentic in using this metaphor to understand life worry about personal deviance and nonadaptive structural processes. The antiracist task, as they see it, is to make up for past wrongs. Equal opportunity is insufficient. What is required is affirmative action that brings relief from past discrimination. Their antidote to racism is consensus building, teamwork, and cooperation. In order to maintain consensus and cooperation, advocates of this metaphor press toward assimilation of everyone into the common culture through educational, religious, and family socialization processes.

Just as advocates of other metaphors can become inauthentic when threatened by others, so too can systems advocates. Who needs surgery to be a healthy part of the body? "Them." The "victims" of racism are viewed as deprived and disadvantaged. The cure is "mainstreaming." The health of the society into which minorities are mainstreamed is not questioned. By naming victims and their institutions as the problems, systems racists assume their own systems are the standard of success.

When acting as racists, systems advocates become indistinguishable from authentic market advocates, who seek to guarantee minorities equal access in the market. An authentic rendering of the organic metaphor, however, directs individuals to reform the whole system for the benefit of all, not to focus on "them" and try to cure "their" problem.

Systems advocates were among the leaders in the Civil Rights movement. Yet some of them, instead of being true to themselves, unknowingly affirmed the market metaphor by focusing solely on assimilation of minorities into the larger culture. They were convinced that they were curing a disease and creating a healthy body, but instead of bringing about a new, just community for all, this assimilationist group affirmed and supported a sick society for everyone.

Pluralists represent another school of thought that uses the body metaphor. The pluralist view on racism argues that ethnic identity can be maintained while ethnic groups enjoy full participation in the United States. All minorities should follow the lead of the Jews, Irish, Italians, and other groups who came to the United States as poor and outcast minorities and achieved success by accepting a certain level of adaptation, while also enriching the culture to which they adapted.

We can see this orientation operationalized in many school cultural awareness programs, which focus primarily on blacks, Hispanics, Native Americans, and other victims of racism. The goal is to heighten the whites' awareness about minorities' contributions to society. In this process, however, the meaning of being white or the dynamics of oppression are rarely examined. Therefore, the inauthenticity within this orientation is essentially the same as that of the assimilationists, except that the pluralists acknowledge the significance of cultural identity.

Life Is Ups Versus Downs

Our everyday speech contains many up-down metaphors, each reflecting the belief that up is better than down. Friends have sent me a number of choice examples:

> The *heights* of ecstasy, the *depths* of despair.
> *Lower* than a snake's belly.

Morale is *up;* morale is *down.*
Elevated to bishop.
I'm not *up* to doing that.
I'm *under* the weather.
I'm *down* at the mouth.
The computer is being *upgraded.*
I am *down*hearted.
They are *beneath* contempt.

Those who order their lives in terms of up and down believe that the body metaphor disguises fundamental conflicts in a society that is a battleground of irreconcilable vested interests. Only through resistance and constant organizing will the oppressed *downs* eventually overthrow the powerful *ups.*

Although body metaphor advocates do not ignore conflict—disease infects the body, which tries to reject foreign substances—they see conflict as an abnormal process that threatens the larger harmony. For up-down disciples, conflict is a given. Typically, they frame reality in terms of two hierarchical groups in perpetual opposition: master-slave, rich-poor, white-black, male-female, straight-gay, ruler-ruled, colonizer-colonized. The essential mission is "the struggle"—the battle to ensure that resources are fairly distributed and that the oppressed achieve liberation and self-determination.

For example, most social movements are informed and directed by the up-down metaphor. Early labor history abounds with up-down language, as does much early Marxist thought. In this perspective, groups are powerful agents who dominate and exploit others, as each group attempts to maintain or secure an advantage. Just as there can be no master without a servant, there can be no ups without downs. They are dialectically related.

Much liberation theology also draws on insight derived from this metaphor. Karen Lebacqz (1986) quotes liberation theologian Gustavo Gutiérrez's observation that "Latin American theology starts with 'praxis,' with passionate and committed involvement in the struggle for liberation" (p. 101). This theology is committed to the political downs: "laborers, peasants, the elderly, the young, the unemployed, women, those from oppressed ethnic and racial groups"—people who have become nonpersons, "suffering misery and exploitation, deprived of the most elemental human rights, scarcely aware that they are human beings at all" (p. 101).

Policy Choices. Those who view the world through the up-down lens advocate political education. In contrast, current schooling, with its authoritarian control, often parallels imprisonment. Schools should be centers of learning about political self-determination. Education should be a commitment to the fundamental task of liberation, not an enforcement of conformity to a preordained hierarchical system.

Life Is Ups Versus Downs and Racism. Racism under the guise of the up-down metaphor is the unilateral use of power by ups to exploit, dominate, and tyrannize downs. In the United States, the exploitation of cheap black, Hispanic, or Chinese labor to maximize profits is a clear example of this kind of racism.

There are two schools of thought that use the up-down metaphor to analyze life: worker or class advocates and anti-neocolonialists. The former stress class only; the latter combine race and class in their diagnosis.

U.S. worker or class advocates become racist when whites control the organizing of labor or when the assumption is made that minority interests are identical to white working-class interests. That ethnocentrism leads ups to discount Hispanic concerns for bilingual, bicultural education or Native American concerns for tribal identity. Thus, white class advocates who say they fight for the freedom and shared power of all oppressed people paternalistically tie the fate of others to that of their own race. Their failure to distinguish color from class downplays the importance of culture. They can look and act like body advocates, and are sometimes criticized for acting "like liberals."

The anti-neocolonial advocates argue that the experience of oppressed people of color in the United States can best be understood if it is compared to the experience of colonization. U.S. minorities are concentrated in ghettos, in barrios, and on reservations, where they are exploited by U.S. whites just as the Europeans exploited their colonies. Race, in this view, is an interdependent variable; it is not reduced to class, but it accompanies class struggle

(Blauner, 1971). Anti-neocolonial advocates believe that whites cannot be trusted to lead U.S. society because they have lost the power to see the racist evil in their midst. They need constant monitoring by Third World leaders. In capable hands, the anti-neocolonial model is a powerful analytical tool for understanding the impact and functioning of white racism. However, a suspicion of all whites creates a contradiction. The liberators who seek to overthrow the oppressive system have created a language and analysis to perpetuate a new oppression. Now, the oppressed group becomes superior; its sensitivities become the justification for dominating its former oppressors. The oppressed will imitate the oppressor unless there is a cultural transformation of the oppressed mind-set and the oppressive culture (Freire, 1974).

The up-down metaphor has difficulty envisioning people standing side by side. Ups become downs and downs become ups and rarely do they figure out what it means to be in partnership.

Life Is a Journey

Patricia Hampl (1987) captures the essence and the paradox of the journey metaphor in the context of a comment about composer Antonin Dvořák's summer vacation in Spillville, Iowa: "There can be no pilgrimage without a destination, but the destination is also not the real point of the endeavor. Not the destination, but the willingness to wander in pursuit characterizes pilgrimage. Willingness: to hear the tales along the way, to make the casual choices of travel, to acquiesce even to boredom. That's pilgrimage—a mind full of journey" (p. 21).

Many writers explicitly use journey language as an ordering principle in their writings—for example, Robert Fritz, *The Path of Least Resistance* (1984); Nelle Morton, *Journey Is Home* (1986); and M. Scott Peck, *The Road Less Traveled* (1988). Often, it is the implicit backdrop, as in Ferguson's *The Aquarian Conspiracy* (1980) and Anthony, Ecker, and Wilber's *Spiritual Choices: The Problems of Recognizing Authentic Paths to Inner Transformation* (1987). They go so far as to argue that journey is *the* central theme throughout the romantic tradition.

Journey directs our attention inward and outward, highlighting the connection of self to community, nature, and God, while stressing our creative capacity to chart our own courses.

How each of us attends to and describes the experience of journey, of course, varies greatly. Keith Morton (1987), describing an Arctic journey, calls the Arctic a "place to be conquered. It is meant only to enlarge puny humans to mythic and heroic proportions" (p. 1). In contrast, Barry Lopez (1986) sees the adventures of the explorers who searched for a Northwest Passage as "the record of human longing to be free of some grim weight of life. That weight was ignorance, the poverty of spirit, indolence, and the threat of anonymity and destitution. [The] harsh landscape became the focus of a desire to separate oneself from those things and to overcome them. In these arctic narratives, then, are the threads of dreams that serve us all" (p. 310).

Many journey advocates propose a spiritual dimension. We seek to connect and touch at every level, redefining ourselves as we get to know others. The journey metaphor also embraces diversity. From this perspective, the up-down metaphor is too narrow, the market metaphor too mechanistic, the organic metaphor too structure-bound. Journeys are not recorded in analytic systems, mathematical models, or dialectical frameworks but in journals, diaries, tales, stories, and shared experiences.

In the diaries of Etty Hillesum we experience what Hillesum's editor, J. G. Gaarlandt, describes as "a journey" through Hillesum's "inner world" (Hillesum, 1985, p. xiv). Like Anne Frank, Etty was a Jew who lived in Holland during the Nazi reign of terror. Hers is the painful and glorious story of one person's struggle to address her own deepest fears and hopes as she loved in one of the most radical ways one can love. As Gaarlandt observes, "She did not want to escape the fate of the Jewish people. She believed she could do justice to life only if she did not abandon those in danger, and if she used her strength to bring light into the life of others. Survivors from the camp have confirmed that Etty was a 'luminous' personality to the last" (p. xv). She died in Auschwitz on November 30, 1943.

As Etty confronts her fears for the future, she moves through the language of up and down to another metaphor:

Life is difficult, it is true, a struggle from minute to minute (don't overdo it now, Etty!), but the struggle itself is thrilling. In the past I would live chaotically in the future, because I refused to live in the here and now. I wanted to be handed everything on a platter, like a badly spoiled child. Sometimes I had a certain rather undefined feeling that I would "make it" one day, that I had the capacity to do something "extraordinary," and at other times the wild fear that I would "go to the dogs" after all. I now realize why. I simply refused to do what needed to be done, what lay right under my nose. I refused to climb into the future one step at a time. And now, now that every minute is so full, so chock full of life and experience and struggle and victory and defeat, and more struggle and sometimes peace, now I no longer think of the future, that is, I no longer care whether or not I shall "make it," because I now have the inner certainty everything will be taken care of [pp. 17–18].

Policy Choices. The purpose of education in this view is to invite students on a journey of mutual discovery. Multiple criteria are better than one, offering many roads to travel. Exploring, bumping, challenging, and learning about others as we learn about ourselves become the central guiding mission.

Life Is a Journey and Racism. Since the journey metaphor is often manifested through storytelling, perhaps my personal odyssey can best illustrate how racism exploits this metaphor. My first job was an associate directorship at the Detroit Industrial Mission (DIM), an ecumenical agency working in industry on human value issues. Our DIM staff was all white males. In 1968, we decided to hire a black male, and Reverend Douglas Fitch came in for an interview. At that time, I was smugly content with my view of the world and, wanting him to know I was a "good" white, I asked him to read an essay I had written titled "Black Power: The White Hope." He did. What happened next transformed my life. He said, "Bob, this is a good piece on black power. The only problem is it's moving in the wrong direction with the wrong solution, and it won't get you anywhere. Why don't you figure out what it means to be white and let us worry about what it means to be black?" For reasons far beyond my comprehension, his question penetrated to the core of my being. The new direction it gave me still propels me today.

I called some white friends together. We began thinking and writing and slowly developed a novel idea—a new white consciousness. I wrote my thoughts down and they became my book, *For Whites Only* (1970). My book and Joe Barndt's *Liberating Our White Ghetto* (1972) were, at that time, the only books that proposed a self-conscious examination of whiteness. *For Whites Only* catapulted me into a new arena. I was considered a leader in the fight against racism, especially as I advocated this new white perspective. Then another important event occurred, one that threatened me to my core.

I was attending a racism conference at which the black participants had taken over, using Third World leadership as their rallying cry. I remember standing up when this happened and proposing that the whites should caucus to decide what we should do. All hell broke loose. I was called every name imaginable. As I entered my house that evening, my back went out. I spent two weeks in bed, and during those weeks, I spent a lot of time pondering what I was doing and why. I still remember the strength that came when I realized that I was dealing with racism because I had to. Racism violated my core being. I had to deal with it, whether I was supported or not, criticized or not. Amazingly then, I stood up for the first time in two weeks. My heart and head were aligned. I felt a deep peace and a kind of power that was not oppressive. I tasted authenticity.

What emerged for me was an analysis of *whiteness*. Not only did I look at myself in a new way, I asked a whole new set of questions about the world in which I was living. By confronting blackness, I was challenged to explore myself as part of white society. Many of us whites joined together to attend to our own racism. Sometimes we bashed each other, mostly we loved. As we tested the outer limits of our racism and searched for self-affirming new ways to treat our color as a gift in the liberation struggle of people of color and ourselves, we began to put together methods of engaging other whites in the journey. White-on-white seminars emerged, producing a set of structured learning activities (see Katz and Taylor, 1988).

We also joined and shared antiracist activities with people of color, forming the organization People Acting for Change Together (PACT), which became a vehicle for our sustained growth and development and lifelong learning and friendships. As I look back on those events I continue to be amazed. By being with blacks in common struggle, I learned about whites and my color in ways not possible without the contrast. I also learned that I would never completely understand the black experience. However, with the help of black friends, I could grasp my own experience of being a white participant in a white racist society. What a journey from naïveté to understanding.

The journey taught me many lessons. The two most basic were that what it meant to be white was "not to have to think about it," and that, as a white, I could understand and embrace whiteness as a destructive cultural force without guilt and commit my energies toward the mission—the elimination of racism and affirmation of pluralism. There is no way around the pervasiveness of the white culture in this country. By accepting the reality of being a racist, I could transcend it.

So we cared, we repented, we asked for forgiveness and we mobilized antiracist actions. Yet as our journey unfolded, we often lost vision and became less than we had promised. We failed to develop a new self-concept as "new whites," and thus had no foundation to resist manipulation and control by people of color. Instead of being a harbinger of a new, shared reality, new whiteness sometimes collapsed into a vitriolic ethnocentrism that came from those who had most thought they had escaped from its prison. New color consciousness looked very similar in behavior to old color consciousness. Cultural ethnocentrism runs deep and is persistent. The journey must continue, to find fresh ways for whites to address this issue of color directly.

Life Is Art

"When good jazz musicians improvise together, they also manifest 'feel for' their material and they make on-the-spot adjustments to the sounds they hear. Listening to one another and themselves, they feel the way the music is going and adjust their playing accordingly. . . . They are reflecting an action on the music they are collectively making and on their individual contribution to it. Thinking what they are doing, and in the process evolving their way of doing it" (Schön, 1983, pp. 55–56). Donald Schön's description of improvisational jazz provides a bridge from the journey to the art metaphor. In a journey, we attend to others, learn about ourselves, build relationships of caring and empathy, and grasp deep forgiveness as the act that breaks a revenge cycle. But there are many journeys, some unusual, some inward, some outward, some spiritual, some natural, some destructive, some constructive. In other words, the journey metaphor avoids the dilemma of evaluation. Yet conflict is perennially present, to be acknowledged, embraced, engaged, or transcended. A Quaker facing a Nazi still must decide, in love, whether to resist the Nazi. There comes a point of accountability for action, for war or for peace.

The concept that life is art offers a fragile hope for resolving this dilemma. It is not a new metaphor, but it fills modern everyday language. We "imagine scenarios," "sculpt visions," "act out roles," and "write the future" on the "stage of life." Improvisation, context, setting, and history are important to this metaphor. Art focuses on journey as a historical trip but highlights the receiving and creating aspect of human dwelling, the flow of past and future into each other that clarifies sense and significance for the journey itself. Art is that process which reveals our being to us, gives shape and substance to the journey, calls us not only to attend to ourselves and others, to care for ourselves and others, but also to stand, to present ourselves, to articulate values, and to be centers of authenticity.

The most comprehensive treatment of the art metaphor I have found was developed by Winter (1981), who believes we are in a time of transition between orienting metaphors. Our condition calls for a new vision, one that can embrace the past and explicate a future that affirms creative symbolic dwelling on the earth. For Winter, the very survival of the Western technological era is at stake. Its self-destructive process and goals are undermining a sustainable global future. The desire to dominate others and nature is realizing an unintended consequence of its own success. Human dwelling has been reduced to technological manipulation and management. When the hydrogen bomb can be considered technologically sweet, a cultural crisis of the most profound order demands attention. "Unless the question of the *meaning* of the human project is confronted, there can be no escape from the domination and injustice that follows upon the drive for mastery" (p. xi, emphasis added).

The art metaphor is best positioned to reveal and embody a new synthesis. Winter directs our attention to existence as the setting for meaning. Human beings dwell "symbolically on the earth," amid the "artistic event of receptivity and creativity" (p. xiii). Existence, as I have already argued, is infused with publicly shared meanings. Even though it has a givenness, a stubbornness, that refuses to disappear, it also invites inquiry and interpretation. If we are to clarify the meaning of existence, to explicate the sense and significance of its givenness, we must be open to the past and willing to reconstruct our vision of the future. The core of the human enterprise can thus be articulated by viewing symbolic dwelling as the basis for our full engagement in life.

Winter is radically historical. Like Karl Marx, he critiques journeys of philosophical idealism. Like Marx, he is dialectical, framing the artistic process in terms of thesis, antithesis, and synthesis. However, for Marx, symbols and metaphors block the way to reality. Culture is a product of political and economic forces, not the cause of them. For Winter, ideology and culture, including religion as fundamental meaning, constitute and direct human history. Thus, we must understand the real mission of technological society if we are to challenge it and propose an alternative. For Winter, ideas are not "above" human dwelling, as Plato has it, or "under," as Tillich has it when he posits God as the ground of being (1954).

The art metaphor opposes any process that reduces people to things, and it opens worlds "that have not been glimpsed or experienced" (p. 23). For example, when life is art, language is no mere tool with which to manipulate the world around us. Language is what allows us to be in the world while transcending it toward new possibilities. Language is our way of experiencing being in the world as working, loving, fearing, enjoying, or hoping (Winter, 1981, p. 55).

One way we learn about life as art is through the formal artistry of others. As poet Joseph Brodsky (1988) pointed out, in his Nobel Prize acceptance speech, "Every new aesthetic reality makes man's ethical reality more precise. For aesthetics is the mother of ethics" (p. 17). The artistic event challenges us to attend to what constitutes human life itself and from that perspective offers an evaluative frame for retrospective assessment and prospective anticipation. Art is the metaphor of responsibility. It decides the process of receiving and creating within the ebb and flow of human life, the core of full participation in one's dwelling on earth.

Not all art has this quality. Art can be misused as propaganda or money-making commodity just as a journey can be misused. Yet Brodsky suggests that "for a human being there is no other future save that outlined by art" (p. 20). B. F. Skinner (1976) and many Marxist writers also share the idea that art is fulfillment for the human species: Art is the telos of the journey; it is utopia.

Policy Choices. For Winter, the human species is fundamentally responsible for discernment of the quality of life. People and processes that sustain the capacity to review and redirect the human situation are to be encouraged. Aspects of life that destroy life are to be thwarted. Given this, who should be recognized as the carrier of a humane future? Is it the poor, as in liberation theology; the proletariat, as in Marx; people of color, as in racial liberation? It is every person's responsibility.

From this perspective, education is defined as a commitment to critical thinking. It invites us into paradox and the use of metaphorical language itself as an opening on life. Education relishes divergent as well as convergent thinking, challenging students to establish their own ethical foundations and take ownership of their own thinking.

Life Is Art and Racism. Viewed through the metaphor of art, racism is the denial of our personal and cultural shadow, as defined by Carl Jung. That denial is repressed and/or projected onto others. According to Hopcke (1989), Jung's *shadows* are "those unpleasant and immoral aspects of ourselves which we would like to pretend do not exist or have no effect on our lives—our inferiorities, our unacceptable impulses, our shameful actions and wishes—this shadowy side of our personality is difficult and painful to admit. It contradicts who we would like to see ourselves as, who we would like to seem to be in the eyes of others" (pp. 81–82). Jung believed deeply that we may project our shadow onto others, attributing to them negative qualities that we deny in ourselves. Our task is to create and then confront our full selves, to bring the shadow into consciousness and thereby deprive it of control. Cultures, as well as individuals, engage in this form of denial. Racism and ethnic hatred are problems that are seriously compounded by this human failing.

Formal art often examines how well or poorly we do at creating examined lives. Athol Fugard's play *"Master Harold"—and the Boys* (1982) is a penetrating expression of the price of refusing to confront our full selves. Set in South Africa, the play powerfully, poignantly, and painfully explores the consequences of white refusal to face the truth of whiteness, to admit that the roles of white "master" and black "boys" are roles chosen by whites. They are created and maintained by an inauthentic art orientation, which pretends these roles are given (gift) not created (art).

In this play, the direct confrontation between blacks and whites begins when one of the "boys" simply says that Harold can choose not to sit on a bench restricted to whites. If Harold were able to accept this idea, that single small action of choosing where to sit would have an enormous implication for him. It would force him to admit that he could review and redirect his own life, that he could start to undo a great inauthenticity through just one small authenticity, as we all can. But first we must see life as art; we must accept responsibility for ourselves and our ability to review and create our own situations, over and over again.

Metaphors, Action Theory, and Ethics

When Clancy (1989) critiques the three purposes of business (production of goods and services, creation of wealth, and economic institutional maintenance) he marries ethics to purpose. He states that "we must find a way to reorient business from the market fair, from '*le voyage sans but*' [the journey without an aim] and get it back to its proper role—assuring a better life for everyone, spiritually and materially. We need a new paradigm, and we need new metaphors for business. . . . We need a modern version of 'cathedral building,' . . . to inspire people to the challenging, rewarding, and socially responsible calling that business should be" (pp. 298–299). Clancy chooses not to detail a new vision that would be grounded in the very authenticity out of which his critique arises. Yet that is what authenticity demands of us, that we build our visions on an ethical base.

Ethical thinking is mediated through orienting metaphors. Lodged within each metaphor is a central ethical principle, directing our attention, telling us what is workable and what we *should* do. However, if a single metaphor totally shaped our perception, we would sink into the morass of cultural relativism. We would have no fulcrum for intellectual critique, no place from which to make ethical judgments about the ethical principle embodied in the metaphor. Authenticity critiques from both within and without, providing a conceptual and experiential touchstone for evaluation and recommendation.. Therefore, I will examine both the internal alignment and the external reach of the six metaphors as they are enriched and informed by the ethical principles outlined in Chapter Seven. (Table 8.1 outlines the relationships.)

When we define life as a gift, we transform the givenness of

**Table 8.1. Metaphors and Ethical Principles
Framed by the Action Wheel.**

Generic Features of Action	Metaphors	Ethical Principles
Meaning	Art	Responsibility
Mission	Journey	Love
Power	Ups versus downs	Participation
Structure	Body	Justice
Resources	Market	Freedom
Existence	Gift	Dwelling

existence into deep appreciation and affirmation of all of life, including death. Current leadership's preoccupation with fixing the world takes our attention away from the glory of creation. The gift metaphor redirects us to be with that which is, not to fix that which is. Although the gift metaphor in isolation can induce resignation, helplessness and quietism, and preservation of the status quo at all costs, it is also essential in our orientation if we are to understand the sacredness of our past and appreciate existence as a trigger for insight. Authentic action's home, its fundamental dwelling, is rooted in life is a gift.

A view of life as a market implies a freedom that complements the givenness of existence. At its best, the market opens our options for exploring our gifts. At its worst, it turns all gifts into utility objects, to be measured, controlled, and bargained over. Without freedom, gifts lie idle; with freedom, gifts are potentialities, to be chosen and tendered into the marketplace of ideas and material production in order to become essential resources.

The concept of life as an organic body corrects excesses that arise from an untempered market. Justice is framed as a regulative concept, insuring adequacy of production and fairness of distribution and redistribution of resources. Justice expresses itself in three sub-principles: equality, equity, and adequacy. Equality requires that we treat equals equally. Equity requires that we make up for past inequities by taking corrective action. And adequacy requires that particular distribution and redistribution criteria change as conditions change. Freedom without justice results in caprice and unfair externalities that the market cannot address on its own. As a friend of mine said, "Sometimes the invisible hand gives you the finger!" A market orientation maximizes efficiency; a body orientation concentrates on effectiveness. Market highlights exchange; body worries about sustainability and integrity of the total system.

The up-down metaphor brings energy to the social body. The body orientation seeks consensus; its natural tendency is to move toward equilibrium. The up-down orientation inspirits, testing whether the claims of justice are real. An open door takes us into another room only if we can choose to use that doorway, only if what is formally present in the system has been claimed by us through struggle and change. Equal opportunities are energized only by decision and commitment. At its worst, the up-down metaphor fails to transcend itself. Downs become ups and repeat the very patterns of oppression that once held them down. The struggle envisioned by this metaphor is an endless one that does not admit the possibility of side-by-side partnerships. At its best, up-down thinking marries dynamic to form, inspiriting both toward a shared journey. It undergirds full participation in life's sustaining opportunities.

A view of life as a journey justifies and energizes side-by-side partnerships. It transforms an up-down struggle into a shared voyage on which the sojourners attend to, care about, and learn from each other, regardless of status and political power. A journey orientation redirects power. Instead of facing in on itself or trying to fix others, it attends to being with the other. Love, identified as empathy, not sympathy, stands with others on their journeys, not to change these others but to be with them in their duress and joy. Justice cures; love cares. Henri Nouwen's comments on caring (1983) are instructive:

> The word "care" finds its roots in the Gothic "Kara" which means lament. The basic meaning of care is: to grieve, to experience sorrow, to cry out. I am very much struck by this background of the word care because we tend to look at caring as an attitude of the strong toward the weak, of the powerful toward the powerless, of the have's toward the have not's. And, in fact, we feel quite uncomfortable with an invitation to enter into someone's pain before doing something about it. . . . The friend who cares makes it clear that whatever happens in the external world, being present to each other is what really matters. In fact, it matters more than pain, illness, or even death. . . . Therefore, to care means first of all to be present to each other [pp. 34–36].

As I said in the story of strangers, love also forgives. Senge (1990) takes this forgiveness into the business environment as a part of management, in what I think is an inappropriate way: remarking

that "to encourage risk taking is to practice forgiveness. Real forgiveness includes 'forgive' and 'forget.' Sometimes, organizations
will 'forgive' in the sense of not firing someone if he makes a mistake, but the screw-up will always be hanging over the offender's
head. Real forgiveness includes 'reconciliation,' mending the relationships that may have been hurt by the mistake" (p. 300). In my
view, the popular adage "forgive and forget" misses the mark of
authentic engagement. Unless we have had frontal lobotomies, we
do not forget, nor can we. Far from meaning forgetting, reconciliation means admitting what is really going on. As Hannah Arendt
(1959) says, forgiveness breaks the revenge cycle of human interaction, opening new possibilities for continuing the journey that is
life (p. 221ff). Forgiveness remembers but declares a willingness to
continue the relationship without blame, shame, or humiliation.
Amnesty and pardon are political acts of societal forgiveness,
which, for humanitarian or political reasons, do not require repen-
tance. Ford pardoned Nixon; Carter offered amnesty to the Vietnam
War objectors. At its best, a journey orientation levels the experiential terrain, offering virtual equality amid actual disparities. At its
worst, this metaphor perpetuates ethnocentrism and advocates a
responsibility to judge the journeys of some cultures as better than
those of others.

    When we view life as art, we take responsibility for creation
and for our own creativity. This orientation adds accountability to
the life journey. Humans cannot escape the fact of responsibility.
Just as meaning intersects with existence in the Action Wheel, so
too does the art metaphor link up with the gift metaphor. As we
reflect on ourselves and others in action—as we create meaning—
is (gift) and ought (art), fact (gift) and value (art) unite. Life as art
says we ought to be responsible. Life as a gift declares that we are
responsible. The act of showing up and engaging in life implies
that we are accountable to ourselves and for others. One of Dostoyevsky's characters in *The Brothers Karamazov* reveals the unity
of fact and value when he says, "believe me, everyone is really responsible to all men for all men and for everything. I don't know
how to explain it to you, but I feel it is so, painfully even. And how
is it we went on then living, getting angry and not knowing?"
(quoted in Morris, 1961, p. 1).

Responsibility, as a word and a concept, is so deeply en-meshed in our everyday speech, we fail to realize that it may be the only really new and provocative idea that has entered the stream of ethical reflection in recent history. Its rapid acceptance is a clue to its importance, not only in our ethical tool kit, but more critically, to a comprehensive model of action and leadership. McKeon (1990) traces the concept of responsibility in English and French thinking back to 1787, roughly the same time *leadership* emerged as a word and concept. His review of all the layers of meaning that respon-sibility has accumulated over two centuries reveals why this idea is so essential for us today.

As originally applied to the operation of political institu-tions, responsibility had four criteria. Under these criteria, McKeon (1990) states, a government or republic is responsible "(1) if it op-erates within the framework of law in which official action and control are reasonably predictable and (2) if its government reflects the attitudes of its people through institutions that provide for the regular election of personnel and regular review of policy" (p. 80). These initial criteria concentrate on two conceptual precursors to a full-blown theory of responsibility: namely, accountability and immutability. Accountability entails punishability, not just the fact of it, but that it should be deserved. Immutability entails the exis-tence of free beings, deliberating and shaping their own destiny. Immutability will not become totally operational in the West, or elsewhere, until suffrage restrictions are totally removed. However, it is the concept of responsibility itself, not just political pressure, that has made it possible for governments to extend suffrage.

Accountability and immutability are negative criteria and are external to the person within the state. Accountability is demanded by the law; immutability is a product of the government's openness to constituents' influence. However, says McKeon, these criteria are supplemented by two positive and internal criteria: freedom and rationality. Freedom means that in "matters of the common good, the people are better judges than the uncontrolled ruler-elite. This idea challenged the idea that representative government or democ-racy will work only if the people are ready for it" (p. 81). Respon-sibility reverses that idea's order: people "acquire responsibility only by exercising it" (p. 81). Rationality means that "justice and the moral sense of community is better advanced by free choice of moral criteria rather than by imposition and pre-supposition, precisely because the decision is more likely to be rational and truth is more likely to be advanced by frequent competition among ideas than by authoritative prior decision concerning the true" (p. 81).

The idea of political responsibility led to cultural responsibility because citizens belong to many cultural communities and participate in many different commons. These commons are determined by "religion, education, taste, ethical diversity, economic situation, [and] occupation" (pp. 81–82). Political responsibilities of nations both reflect and protect citizens' treasured traditions, making each community "responsible to other countries as well as to its members" (p. 23). Overall, responsibility "reflects and depends on a common rationality and on common values revealed in discussion and sought in action. . . . Responsibility is a reflexive relation: the responsibility of the individual and the responsibility of the community of which he is a member are interdependent, and independent communities assume responsibilities with respect to each other which constitutes a kind of inclusive community" (p. 82).

McKeon's remarks demonstrate how responsibility discovers and makes public the We amid the Us and the Them. Responsibility is a driving force in leadership because it is coupled with dwelling, freedom, justice, participation, and love, and it presses toward convergence. The person and the community are interdependent, responsible to and for each other.

Furthermore, McKeon states that, over time, the external controls of accountability and immutability tend to become internalized. Persons in communities admit their actions and their actions' consequences. They do not blame the law for setting standards that are not their standards. Their preoccupation with their own interests changes to a recognition that their context includes self and others. Empathy opens the possibility of understanding the "problems, needs, and aspirations of others." In the process, "the understanding of interest may be transformed into an understanding of the common good and of common values" (p. 83).

At its best, the art metaphor intimately connects responsibility with creativity, innovation, invention, and meaning. Life is the stage, canvas, or commons for meaning to be discerned, explored, and created. At its worst, the art metaphor fosters counterfeit interpretations of life, denying the complex reality of existence. Escapist art is art; however, it disguises rather than reveals life in its fullest.

Leadership, Metaphors, and Authenticity

Leadership calls us to be authentic: to be true to ourselves and be true to the world. In order to be true to ourselves, we must look at any misalignment that exists between our professed metaphor and the behavior that is entailed by that metaphor. Thus, if the issue to be addressed is racism, the preliminary challenge to leadership is to invite supremacists to guarantee a place for all, discriminators to open access for all, social healers to sustain health for all, liberators to empower participation for all, journeyers to care for all, creators to take responsibility for all.

This call need not be harsh. Too often an attack on others only disguises gross incongruities in the very ones mounting the attack. Gentle authenticity offers ourselves and others more journey options. Better to ensure our own authenticity is in order than to flail about at others.

Paradoxically, the more secure we are in our own view, the more open we are to that of others and the easier it is to go clockwise on the Action Wheel. Thus, as we develop our visionary leadership and become comfortable with our personal metaphor, we can more readily perceive and receive the second step, which is to be expansive and inclusive of others' perspectives, to walk in the shoes of others and be true to the world.

Barker's insight challenged leadership to go into places that it would not ordinarily go. Metaphorical analysis may take us a level up to another metaphor. However, when we deal with public policy issues, a move to another metaphor is difficult. All too often, our own metaphor is invisible to us, even though it interprets and directs our actions. Only by sustained reflection and bumping against others can we begin to contemplate an alternative as a realm for understanding our actions.

Let me illustrate with two examples. The first shows the hidden interplay of ethics and metaphors. A young man who was a member of a leadership seminar group that had talked with Mitch

Snyder, the nationally known advocate for the poor and the homeless, just a few weeks prior to his death was deeply disturbed by Snyder. The true problem, the young man said, was empowerment and participation. Snyder should teach the poor to love and to take responsibility for their lives. The problem lay with the poor and with Snyder, who was not providing adequate ethical education to the homeless.

By using the Action Wheel, I saw that this young man was taking his ethical argument clockwise—which was totally appropriate. He moved the issue from power to mission and, therefore, had moved his ethical focus from participation to love. However, when he blamed the poor for their own plight, it was clear that the market metaphor was silently directing his view. I suggested to him that love was indeed the ethical issue, but that he had focused on the wrong group. The ups needed to love and take responsibility for their part of the social scene. Then Snyder would have something to discuss with him and them! There could be no real journey of mutual respect if the ups maintained indifference and apathy.

The second example illustrates how metaphorical discussions can open insight into situations in which "something is not right" but we don't know what it is. Vivian Nelsen, a consultant on racism, and I were asked to work with the troubled and perplexed staff of a nonprofit community organization. They had been told they were a team, yet they did not feel like or function as a team. After six hours of exploration with them, it became apparent that one problem was a collision of three metaphors. They didn't need each other to do their jobs, except for coordination (market); they talked as if they were family (body); and their social philosophy of service to the poor and excluded directed their organizational programming (up-down). Moreover, the director was challenging them to take on a new adventure (journey). Just surfacing the metaphorical complexity alleviated their disorientation and opened the possibility of improved understanding and informed decision making.

What is at stake in understanding our metaphors? Why are they so central to leadership?

Earlier, I used racism, one of our most persistently bedeviling issues, to illustrate the enormous consequences of orienting metaphors for leadership. As that example illustrated, our solutions, directed by our metaphors, bear on people's lives. Distorting a metaphor destroys its promise, limiting and misdirecting action. Each orienting metaphor, in a very real sense, comes from the people. It is not imposed by leadership but proposed, because each metaphor informs both leader and follower as, together, they seek a vision that answers the question, What is really going on? Out of the millions of possible metaphors, only a few are broad and deep enough to reveal highly significant connections among all the experiences of life, sustain attention over time, and inspire fruitful investigation into reality.

No one metaphor, however, exhausts reality. Metaphors reveal as well as conceal, bringing certain aspects of life and policies for action to the forefront of our attention and disguising others. Hence, multiple orienting perspectives are essential in leadership thinking. If we were concerned only with logical consistency, the advice to be true to self would be the entire truth here. However, talking, even shouting, across metaphorical camps only exacerbates any issue. Not only do we need to think with more than one metaphor, we need to marry metaphorical analysis to an independently justifiable ethical framework. A commitment to a metaphor does not justify the use of that metaphor. The justification comes from ethical argument. And it is ethical justification that spurs leadership to select particular metaphors and expand its metaphorical repertoire.

Teaching Metaphorical Thinking

When I teach metaphorical thinking, I divide the seminar participants into six equal groups and give each group one of the six metaphors. I ask each group to brainstorm all the ways life is really a gift, a market, and so forth. After ten minutes of brainstorming, I ask the groups to report their findings. Beginning with the gift metaphor and working toward art, I throw out policy issues to each group, asking the group to frame the problem from its metaphorical perspective: What is your view of abortion, surrogate parenting, rationing of scarce goods, and so on? After some practice and coaching to jumpstart the process, the groups find metaphorical analysis exciting and are surprised at how quickly they can frame issues from their metaphorical perspective.

After hearing three of the six groups (gift, market, and body), I point out how amazing they have been—framing problems with no data! Then the process continues; however, it also gets more difficult. We are all familiar with the market and body metaphors, but the up-down, journey, and art metaphors force the participants to reach for new thoughts. The art metaphor always proves to be the most difficult perspective to articulate.

Then I invite the participants to vote with their feet. Each person is asked to join the group that represents his or her strongest personal metaphor. Usually, all six metaphors are covered, although journey continually gets the most votes. Then I ask the participants two questions—what is the strength of your metaphor? And what does your metaphor conceal about life?

Next, the groups are invited to bump up against others' metaphors, each group listening to the strengths and weaknesses of the others, each trying to impress on the others the insight from its preferred position. The entire process takes two-and-a-half to three hours. I always ask each group to use its metaphor to define racism and propose a solution. I also ask the groups the purpose of education. I do this for two reasons. First, the answers differ so dramatically that the participants can easily see the informing power of each metaphor. And second, the issues are so much in debate today that the participants can easily recall current examples of solutions and can quickly connect those examples with the metaphorical perspectives that inform them.

As a final comment on this teaching method, I suggest that metaphorical analysis is also important in the case-study method of teaching, which is dominant in most U.S. business schools. I have little doubt that complicated real-life cases challenge participants to think creatively. However, unless students are taught to analyze cases with metaphors in mind, they will not realize what is actually guiding their conclusions. Too many business cases play against the market metaphor without anyone's attending to what that metaphor reveals and conceals about life. Using the process of moving around the Action Wheel, a full metaphorical inquiry can challenge participants to see more in a case than their single prevailing metaphor reveals.

Summary

Vision is controversial and difficult to define yet eagerly sought in current leadership theory and practice. In this chapter, I have critiqued current interpretations of vision and supplied the missing ethical and metaphorical foundation upon which leadership vision must be built. Vision is not imposed; it is proposed. It is even discovered in our midst. Wherever visionary leadership is found, it will possess orienting metaphors, ways of understanding life that direct both thinking and acting. Metaphors come and go, gain public currency, and then lose it. Six metaphors deserve our serious attention as central interpretive schemes in a comprehensive view of leadership: life as gift, market, body, ups versus downs, journey, and art. Each metaphor embodies a critical ethical principle, and both the principles and the metaphors are linked to the features of the Action Wheel. The degree to which leadership reflects the coherence and interdependence of these ethical principles, metaphors, and features of action determines that leadership's authenticity.

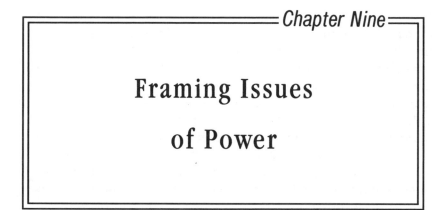

Chapter Nine

Framing Issues
of Power

When leadership addresses what is really going on, it must inevitably address power, either because power is the presenting issue or because eventually, each generic feature of action must be examined as it appears in relation to the presenting issue. Power is often unequally shared; ups can impose their will on downs more easily than downs can on ups. Leadership's first task when power is unevenly shared is to frame the power issue more specifically. Even though one group may hold more power than another, this imbalance does not mean that one group is authentic and the other inauthentic. Let a parable and three examples set the stage for this discussion:

The Parable of Ups and Downs

What makes an up an up and a down a down? An up can do more to a down than a down can do to an up. That's what keeps an up up and a down down. Ups tend to talk to each other and study the downs, asking the downs what's up, or what's coming down, for that matter.

The downs spend a lot of time taking the ups out to lunch and dinner to explain their downness. The ups listen attentively, often amazed about the lives of downs. They contrast one down's experience with another down's experience. At times they don't worry too much about what the downs are up to because the ups know that the downs never seem to get it together. If they did, the ups would have to shape up.

After a while, the downs weary of talking to the ups. They think, "If I have to explain my downness one more time to an up, I'll throw up." So downs form networks and form support groups. This makes some ups nervous, for ups know three ups standing together is a board meeting; three downs, pre-revolutionary activity.

In order to cope with this rising up of downness, some ups hire downs, dress them up, and send them down to see what the downs are up to. These downs are often called personnel or affirmative action officers. This creates a serious problem for the down who is dressed up. That down doesn't know whether he or she is up or down and that's why downs in the middle often burn up.

Sometimes ups, to smarten up, ask downs to come into a program created by ups to explain and justify their downness. The ups call this "human relations training." Of course, ups never have to explain their upness; that's why they're ups.

There's good news and bad news in this parable. The good news is that there is no such thing as a perfect up or a perfect down. If people were perfect ups, they wouldn't be able to stand up, they would be so heavily burdened with downness.

The bad news is that when ups are up, it often makes them stupid. I call this *dumb-upness*. Dumb-upness occurs because ups do not have to pay attention to downs the way downs have to pay attention to ups. The only time ups worry about downs is when downs get uppity, at which time they are put down by the ups. The ups' perception is that downs are overly sensitive; they have an attitude problem. It is never understood that the ups are "underly sensitive" and have an attitude problem.

I used to think that when downs became ups they would carry over their insight from their downness to their upness. Not so.

Smart down, dumb up! One can be smart one minute, dumb the next.

Three Examples Illustrating the Parable

The first example involves work that I did with a group of black and white men at a power company in the East. During the morning the blacks played a game they called "watch the honkey run" in which downs take cultural advantage of the ups. Because the ups did not really know what was going on, the downs could embarrass, cajole, and belittle the ups. It was a power game that was not particularly noble yet very dramatic. A white man would respond to black cajoling with stereotyped responses: "I live in a mixed racial neighborhood, some of my best friends are. . . ."

In the afternoon, a white female lawyer came to speak to this group of men about sexual harassment. In an amazing transformation, these men locked arms and went dumb up in unison! They said this woman had an attitude problem, that she was out to get them, that she didn't understand them. Color was not mentioned again all afternoon. The issue was now gender—men versus women. In her presentation on sexual harassment, the lawyer said that 95 percent of sexual crimes were perpetrated by men and only 5 percent by women. "That's what we want to deal with," exclaimed the men in unison. The woman shook her head. "These men are incorrigible," she muttered on the way out.

A second example is more personal. A colleague and I had formed a partnership, resulting in a solid collaborative relationship, and she had landed us consulting work in a large urban school district. Knowing she was only going to be in that city for another year because she had decided to pursue a theological education, I was called into a meeting with the superintendent of schools to plot a strategy and develop a comprehensive year-long plan. Here we were, two white males figuring what would be best to do in the district, never considering the participation of my new partner. At three o'clock the next morning, I got a call from my partner, who was absolutely irate that I had not represented her interests along with mine at the meeting. After all, she said, she was not leaving for a whole year.

Of course, she was right. I had fallen into dumb-upness and had inappropriately excluded a cherished colleague from authentic participation in shared work. There was no point in denying the truth. I admitted my own stupidity and luckily, she believed in forgiveness. I corrected the error and our partnership continued to deepen and grow.

Finally, here's a military example focusing on the debate about women in combat. General Colin Powell, chairman of the United States Joint Chiefs of Staff, the highest ranking U.S. military officer who is also black, was asked whether there are too many minorities in the military. "No, not at all," he replied on an NBC television interview with David Brinkley on January 14, 1990. "All people who are qualified should be able to serve." Later, in the same interview, he was asked to comment on the role of women in combat. "The restrictions of women in combat dictated by U.S. policy are fine," he said. With the controversy swirling around the issue, his answer seemed too facile. He was either simply stating U.S. policy or not recognizing the dumb-upness of his male response. More recently, Powell's comments on gays and lesbians in the military have continued his headlong slide into dumb-upness.

These three examples illustrate how downs know a lot more about ups than ups know about themselves. This view is supported by the thought of both Reinhold Niebuhr and contemporary liberation theologians, all of whom orient their thought within an up-down metaphor. They all affirm the "epistemological privilege" of the downs (see Lebacqz, 1986). The reasons downs know more about ups than ups know about downs is that downs experience the oppression, whereas ups rationalize it.

Ironically, it is ups who are frequently and popularly labeled as leaders. If we focus on dumb-upness, such a traditional view of leadership falls into serious disrepair—one does not want to follow a dumb-up leader. Both ups and downs can be authentically powerful and inauthentically powerful. Neither has a stranglehold on leadership or on the denial of leadership. Ups shift from authentic to inauthentic power by aggression; downs resort to deviousness. Ups go overt; downs covert. Fear of the other, perceived or real, acknowledged or unacknowledged, pushes and entices ups and downs into inauthentic behavior.

Table 9.1, which displays the Action Wheel in a power grid, outlines the actions leadership will investigate when framing issues of power. Each use of power by ups and downs is linked first to one of the generic features of action. (Even though power itself is a generic feature of action, when we examine it, we ask the questions posed by power's own subset of these actions.) Second, each use of power is linked to a generic expression of power—a broad category of power, or energy expenditure—that also helps us to understand the kind of power we are really facing.

However, let me stress that this discussion of power is in no way meant to justify the perpetuation of inauthentic up-down relationships. The ultimate goal is for individuals and groups to stand side by side in a caring journey. My discussion is intended to help leadership deal with the actual situations we face today, which must be addressed by leadership if we are to build new partnerships.

Power as Exploding Physical Force

At the existence level of action, power explodes as raw energy. Experienced as overwhelming force and might, it divides people into controller and controlled. Ups are entitled to command compliance and appropriately punish those who are disobedient if the purpose is publicly known, noble in intent, and legitimated by public consent. Forcefully clearing traffic to make way for fire trucks, trying alleged criminals, and defending against personal attacks are typical legitimate coercive activities. Lively debates, of course, occur over exact definitions of legitimate uses of coercive power.

When ups subvert or compromise shared public purposes, the ups' power is experienced by downs as arbitrary and capricious violence. Downs often retaliate with unorganized sporadic violence, such as stealing, shoplifting, or leaking damaging information.

Power as Personal Volition

On the resource dimension of action, power is the expenditure of energy by multiple exchanges, trade-offs, and bargains. The market metaphor is active, and power appears in the form of personal

Table 9.1. How Leadership Frames Issues of Power.

Generic Features of Action	Generic Expressions of Power	Inauthentic Power by Ups (Aggression)	Authentic Power by Ups	Authentic Power by Downs	Inauthentic Power by Downs (Deviousness)
Meaning (for which)	Creating and interpreting	Denying	Discovering and revealing	Acknowledging and admitting	Minimizing
Mission (toward which)	Aligning	Propagandizing	Persuading	Educating and offering	Disguising
Power (by which)	Collective volition	State-sponsored terrorizing	Pursuing legitimate interests	Claiming interests	Insurgent terrorizing
Structure (through which)	Growing and developing systems	Assimilating	Active including	Networking and supporting	Pretending
Resources (with which)	Personal volition	Exploiting	Selling and exchanging	Buying and exchanging	Sabotaging
Existence (from which)	Exploding physical force	Arbitrarily coercing	Commanding compliance	Voluntary and non-voluntary complying	Random resisting

volition as people choose how they will compete in the market. Because individuals make their own decisions, power and freedom are equated. In this view, power tends to be quantified. It is assumed there is only so much to go around.

In millions of these exchanges there is parity. People who are equals under the conditions of exchange come together, and both parties are satisfied. Up-down expressions of power occur when one actor accrues disproportionate decision-making power, leaving others unorganized and dispersed. Producers, for example, organized into large firms, exert more power than diffusely unorganized consumers. Witness the difficulty in organizing a product boycott. A highly organized government can exert its unified will on citizens' everyday affairs more easily than can unorganized individuals. Nevertheless, in the longer term, consumers can directly impact producers, and citizens can throw out elected rascals.

However, if the trade-offs are believed satisfactory to all parties, the exchange relationships go unchallenged. Abuse of power occurs when ups become aggressive, form monopolies, and exploit downs. Downs frustrated by exploitation resort to numerous forms of sabotage inside the work place. Politically, their deviance expresses itself as refusal to vote, or even withdrawal of any public participation. Deviousness is not viewed as morally reprehensible but rationalized as an appropriate response to blatant exploitation.

Power as Growing and Developing the System

The power that develops systems and is manifested in growth must be cumulative. Thus, government intervention to ensure active inclusion of all citizens is necessary. Cooperation between government and citizens, based on mutual obligations, provides the essential conditions for social growth. On this structural level, large corporations are not necessarily a problem if they are also good community citizens.

Downs take full advantage of opportunities to enter the mainstream using support structures like networking for their own and community benefit. Ups actively include downs in socially beneficial programs. Downs use these programs and the whole system benefits. Freedom expresses itself as socialized conformity. People have real choices; however, those real choices are constrained by cultural, political, and social structures.

However, ups can be inauthentic, saying one thing and practicing another. For example, the legal defense program of the War on Poverty was dismantled when power was claimed by downs who threatened the status quo of ups. When ups are inauthentic, downs may then revert to acting one way in public and another way in private, in order to accomplish their own silently stated goals, and the ups are often fooled into believing real cooperation is present.

Power as Collective Volition

When people see power's own power (rather than its meaning, mission, structure, resources, or existence) as its most important aspect, collective self-determination is active, and freedom is again equated with power. Organized social and political movements are important. Revolutionary politics are adopted by downs, establishment politics by ups. Ups and downs are locked in a struggle, seeking a transfer of power from one to the other. Ups, be they political or corporate, who pursue their own legitimate interests often believe their own actions benefit downs as well as ups. In contrast, downs perceive ups' interests as inimical to their own and perpetually claim their own interests. Conflict is inherent at this level. At its most intense, the conflict results in revolution. Prior to revolutionary action, negotiation of differences is always possible.

Ups resort to aggression and downs to deviousness when each group ceases to pursue its legitimate interests and turns to oppressing or overthrowing contrary interests.

Power as Aligning

Vision quickens power; conviction focuses it. People are preoccupied with movement toward the common good. Ups share their vision by persuading downs that the vision is viable and trustworthy. Downs, knowing that ups can deliver on the vision, educate ups to make the vision more responsive to diverse concerns.

Parents advise children on what is best for them. Children teach their parents about what they need and want. Top management articulates a corporate vision; middle management and workers recommend changes that better serve all parties. First World countries propose international policy for economic development; Third World countries suggest individualized alternatives.

When they believe they are threatened, ups resort to propaganda, downs resort to disguising their real interests. Ups brandish self-serving studies about welfare fraud and cheaters; downs lie to welfare worker ups about what is really happening for fear of retaliation. Men exaggerate women's weakness; women exaggerate their own strengths. Real interests lose out to defensive posturing because neither ups nor downs can align on a shared vision.

Power as Creating and Interpreting

When meaning is the issue and art is the metaphor for life, power is expressed as the creating and interpreting of reality, and freedom is understood as transcending power. Play is at the heart of this experience of power, since it is through play that energy is released from the constraints of old visions and enabled to test the authenticity of new visions. It is no wonder that artists are often seen to create a political threat. They constantly challenge traditional authority through their choices of what to create.

On this level, power discerns what is hidden in all personal and societal visions. It inspires authentic inquiry of both the delightful and the despicable in life. It brings to consciousness the fearful, the humorous, the ignoble, the paradoxical, and the ambiguous.

Ups' authentic power uncovers abuse, addiction, and denial. It creates alternative perspectives so that people can take responsibility for and transcend those denials. Downs' authentic power admits secret fears of victimization, abdication, inauthenticity, and denial. And it creates alternative prospects in order that people can take responsibility for and transcend those abuses. There is a clear mutual understanding that ups' and downs' experiences of power disparities are true and real.

When threatened, ups deny the severity of their aggression, in order to cushion and protect their own identity. In response, downs likewise minimize the impact of the ups' action, thereby cushioning and protecting their own identity. The courage to face what is really going on is lost. Inauthenticity and counterfeit identities emerge. In each expression of power, whether it be control or creativity, inauthenticity only creates more inauthenticity.

Applying the Action Wheel to Power

Leadership diagnoses and acts one dimension or more clockwise from where a presenting issue is initially discerned on the Action Wheel. This rule also applies to reframing power. If a previously healthy system resorts to expressing power through assimilation, the Action Wheel guides leadership toward collective volition as a solution. By pressing each group to claim its own collective self-determination, assimilation is challenged, and systems growth is reclaimed as an authentic possibility. Many positional white leaders missed this signal during the early days of the civil rights movement. Downs experienced assimilation; ups touted inclusion. The result was the uprising of black power, brown power, and red power, groups led by people of color. Furthermore, as movements take hold, the power issues shift. Leadership anticipates this shift by framing upward on the power grid.

Leadership resists aggression and deviousness. Neither is legitimate. When either exists, leadership's long-term credibility and viability are eroded. Therefore, leadership's calling is clear—reestablish authentic action. Name abuses of power by both ups and downs; admit abuses and act courageously.

What sounds ethically upright is, of course, not simple. Serious wrestling with power for many of us is difficult. However, I can suggest two bases for hope. Since we have all been both ups and downs, at different times, we have all been both the doers and the receivers of the abuse of power. We know both aggression and deviousness firsthand. As we understand them in ourselves, we can understand them in others. Thus, we have the possibility of transcending the abuse of power, based on our own experience and how we allow that experience to play itself out in our lives.

The second basis for hope is the action of the downs under duress. When ups become aggressive and downs resist, the downs often remain authentic far beyond what might reasonably be expected under the circumstances. Deviousness is a last resort. For example, what have people of color done to deserve the scorn of whites? People of color have authentic reasons for their anger at white-dominated societies, yet by and large, they remain faithful to authenticity, committed to creating an enduring future.

Not all inauthenticity is of equal magnitude and deserving of equal scorn and condemnation. In the matter of racism, at least, aggression is more heinous than deviousness. This interpretation rests on a moral judgment: Who's more noble, those with superior power aggressively overreacting to a nonexistent threat, or the ones fighting back with whatever means are available?

Summary

The parable of ups and downs illustrated how downs know a lot more about ups than ups know about themselves or about downs. Both ups and downs can be authentic or inauthentic in their expression of power.

Leadership frames issues of power two ways. First, it links power to one of the generic features of action; second, it links power to a generic expression of power. Depending on which generic feature of action is applied, power can be seen as exploding physical force, as personal volition, as cooperation within the system, as collective volition, as vision, or as creation.

The underlying fact in these reflections is that no one person or group is totally powerful or powerless. No one can act, therefore, with total impunity. There are always options and consequences. Downs do not exist totally at the mercy of ups. And ups can and do fight abuse in their own ranks. Without leadership on all sides, the spiral of revenge will destroy whatever blocks its path. Authenticity is always at work resisting that destruction and seeking to build a viable human future.

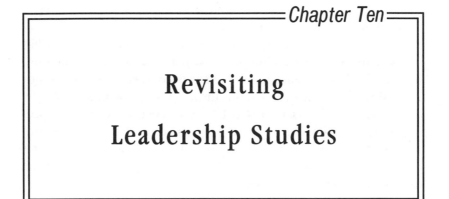

Chapter Ten

Revisiting

Leadership Studies

At the outset of this inquiry, I framed leadership as an enigma that both invited and resisted inquiry. Now, I revisit the enigma to sift and sort, in the light of the authentic action theory, some of the leadership dilemmas and perplexities that I described in the beginning. It turns out that the ferment and disarray in current leadership studies is not a sign of defeat; rather, it is the occasion for a new synthesis of leadership thinking. The comprehensive frame of authentic action for practical leadership can also become a comprehensive frame for leadership studies.

Thus, in this chapter, I will revisit the six schools of leadership thought and propose a way to understand, order, and appreciate all six schools, before I suggest a seventh perspective that embraces all the others. I will also demonstrate how leadership programs can be constructed around this ordering of perspectives. The remainder of the chapter will focus on three questions that continually arise in leadership studies: What is the difference between leadership, management, and technical expertise? What is the relationship between leadership and followership? Can leadership be taught, or is it only learned, and what is at stake in this question?

Bringing Leadership Perspectives Together

Each school of leadership studies claims to be an authentic perspective; it argues for its own truth and assumes it is grounded in what is real. Until now, each school has competed for our allegiance and support. One of my objectives here has been to cause the six major leadership perspectives to communicate among themselves. In the course of this conversation that I have created, issues were raised, boundaries clarified, core ideas sharpened, and weaknesses and strengths revealed. In Chapters Two and Three, the discussion was ordered so that one school's set of issues raised questions that the next school's perspective sought to address.

These six theories have persisted over time because each carries forward an essential theme in leadership. Initially, to help determine the generic features of all our actions I embraced the diverse leadership focuses suggested by each of the six leadership schools and incorporated these focuses into the Action Wheel. Then, I used the action features to identify, question, and interrelate areas of authentic action, ethical concerns, visionary metaphors, and authentic and inauthentic power. Now, I will turn back and use the same features, drawn from all the schools, to examine each school individually, since each view standing alone begs important questions. Therefore, I have opened up each perspective into its constitutive dimensions.

The meaning, mission, power, structure, resources, and existence aspects of leadership, as each school of thought perceives them, are presented in Table 10.1. Reading each vertical row gives a composite picture of a single school. Reading each horizontal row gives a composite picture of all the obligations of leadership that accompany each leadership action. The orienting focus of each school is indicated by bold type. As before, though the Diagnostic Wheel and the Action Wheel have been depicted in grid form, the Action Wheel principle still applies. On the flat display, the movement is up and to the left.

Table 10.1. Schools of Leadership Framed by the Action Wheel.

Generic Features of Action	Schools of Leadership					
	Ethical Leadership	Visionary Leadership	Political Leadership	Positional/ Functional Leadership	Team Leadership	Personal Leadership
Meaning	**Acts for a humane world**	Acts for social and personal transformation	Acts for confidence in self-determination	Acts for effective organizational and societal functioning	Acts for maximized productivity	Acts for recognition and appreciation of differing gifts
Mission	Aims to increase civic virtue	**Aims to increase public responsibility**	Aims to maximize shared interests	Aims to master relevant role responsibility	Aims to enhance personal and group functioning	Aims to improve results from followers
Power	Energizes through debates and dialogues	Energizes through reflection	**Energizes through identifying shared and conflicting interests**	Energizes through adapting to organizational and societal requirements	Energizes through matching skills and events	Energizes through seeing differences as strengths
Structure	Works through transforming	Works through intuiting	Works through organizing	**Works through developing**	Works through training	Works through nurturing
Resources	Supplies aspirations and needs	Supplies ideas and trends	Supplies diverse interests	Supplies roles and expectations	**Supplies specific skills**	Supplies identified personal traits
Existence	Understands values	Understands symbols	Understands forces	Understands systems	Understands history	**Understands birth or socialization**

Note: Bold type indicates orienting focus of each school.

Earlier, I said the personal, team, and positional/functional views were "traditional," while the political, visionary, and ethical views were "provocative." I also suggested that the critical demarcation in framing issues appears to be located between structure and power. Most problems in families, organizations, communities, and societies present themselves as power, mission, and meaning issues; however, we tend to tackle them by reorganizing structures, supplying more resources, or hoping for a miracle!

New thought in leadership studies also seems to recognize an essential difference between these two sets of perspectives. Each time I teach the six views, I ask the participants which school of thought they know the most about and which school is the one in which they think they live. I also ask them which school intrigues them the most, which they know least about, and which they would like to explore in more depth. Typically, the answers to the first set of questions are my traditional schools, and the answers to the second set are my provocative schools.

Rough and imprecise as these data are, I take them as a sign of restlessness in consumers of leadership education. Traditional programs are being implicitly, if not explicitly, challenged as inadequate. The inauthenticity of the partial approaches represented by these schools is beginning to be recognized by leadership program participants. More is being expected of leadership educators than most theories can deliver.

Designing Specific Leadership Programs

The Reflective Leadership Center employs the Action Wheel to design leadership programs that fit organizations' specific needs. The following two examples illustrate the program design procedure.

A Program for a School District

A delegation of teachers from a school district asked the Reflective Leadership Center to design and run a leadership program for them on strategic planning. Their superintendent of schools had been advocating strategic planning for two years and the district needed assistance to get started. In the center's judgment, the presenting problem was structure. The school district wanted to master the *process* of strategic planning. Yet the more the delegation members talked, the more apparent it became that the real issue was power (one level clockwise on the Action Wheel). Thus, the center proposed a seminar to help them take control of their own school.

The people who made up the delegation and participated in the program were not helpless, existence-laden teachers and principals. They had energy and were willing to work. They were, however, suspicious that strategic planning was a subterfuge for administrative hidden agendas. They perceived the real power to be hidden and abusive, and wondered if they could really shape their own agenda and set their own mission. Therefore, in the program design, empowerment was the organizing principle, with strategic planning as a secondary theme.

When my colleagues and I convened the first seminar, suspicion filled the room. The prevailing view of the participants was that the superintendent could not be trusted, the laws of the state were barriers, and the act of educating themselves in strategic planning would probably turn out to be a charade. After ten sessions, the participants concluded, "We can do what we need to do. The superintendent may not be authentic, but we will test him. We will assume he genuinely means what he says. We can do what we do through the law. We can even provide our own in-services. We possess the knowledge among ourselves to shape the future for our own schools. We are in charge of our own destiny." The contrast between the first and last sessions was dramatic. I believe this was due to the center's framing the leadership issue correctly.

A Program for Agricultural Extension Agents

Agricultural extension at the University of Minnesota invited the Reflective Leadership Center to be their partner in designing a leadership program for agricultural extension agents. It was to be a long-term, comprehensive, experiential, cognitive, expansive effort and, as a result, expensive. Assistant Director of Agricultural Extension Jerry Miller and his colleagues proposed four missions for the participants in the Leadership and Extension for Agricultural Development (LEAD) program:

- Understand and assess the future of agriculture locally, nationally, and internationally
- Enhance one's own political analysis skills
- Understand and participate in reforming the institution of extension
- Understand oneself as a leader and develop personal leadership capacities

At the outset, there was a match between Miller's vision and parts of the Action Wheel. Together, Miller and the center designed and implemented a comprehensive leadership curriculum. It took place over a period of four years. Four- to five-day sessions were conducted in various locations in Minnesota. The program also included a week in Washington, D.C. and an eighteen-day tour of France, the Netherlands, and Germany. The first session worked to build a learning community and introduced the six leadership perspectives. Each subsequent session explored one of the four missions and one of the schools of leadership. For example, reviewing the history of agriculture (existence) was matched with work on the Myers-Briggs Type Indicator (existence). Analysis of policy formulation and implementation was linked to political skills, such as dealing with conflict. Discussions on the future of agriculture were coupled with visioning skills. The European trip was included to counter the natural tendency to ethnocentrism. Only by bumping up against differences could participants surface their own biases and fundamentally open themselves to diverse perspectives.

The underlying principle of seminar design was authenticity. My colleagues and I wanted the program to be reflexive—that is, true to itself. We tried to ensure that theory and practice were aligned, both in the seminar content and in the instruction methods. Agricultural agents cocreated the program with the staff. As the seminar moved from region to region within the state, regional agents had the responsibility to design components of the seminar, secure and introduce speakers from the area, lead discussions of evaluations, and generally be in charge of the event. Whatever was taught at one seminar was reinforced, and expected to be used, at subsequent seminars. Participants were given ample time to reflect on speakers' presentations and on-site tours. We soon learned that we tended to overprogram and underreflect. Given this feedback, the staff continually made midcourse corrections.

Since leadership is action, not just thinking about action, each agent had to complete a project. Projects could be done alone or in teams (most were team projects). For example, three agents from three contiguous counties designed and constructed a co-leadership project modeled after ours. (Projects were not eagerly embraced. However, after much explanation and prodding, participants' resistance was transformed into productive action.)

One serious design flaw was the lack of spouse involvement. Long, intense programs are life transforming. Exclusion of spouses eroded the participants' long-term support at home and created some tensions that we had to address. In LEAD Two, the second four-year program, spouses came to a number of sessions, especially those that discussed generic ideas used throughout the seminar. For example, discussions of the Myers-Briggs instrument, the Action Wheel, and ethics were open to spouses.

Leadership, Management, and Technical Expertise

In order to introduce leadership program participants to the enigma of leadership, I ask them the tough leadership questions raised by current leadership studies. One question is this: Are the categories of leadership, management, and expertise clearly distinguishable, do they overlap, or are they useless and not worth maintaining? After a discussion, the participants are asked to vote. Typically, about one-third of them think the categories are distinguishable, two-thirds think the categories overlap, and no one votes for the last option. I think the appeal of the second option is that the intellectual task of defending it seems less onerous.

John Kotter (1990a) is one theorist who argues clearly and persuasively for the first position. Leadership and management are distinct and the differences crucial for understanding change. Management, Kotter argues, copes with complexity. In contrast, leadership copes with change. In coping with complexity, "good management brings a degree of order and consistency to key dimensions like the quality of profitability of products" (p. 4). Leadership, in contrast, focuses on the larger context for action and attends to the changes that are shaping the bureaucracy itself. Within this change context, managers plan and budget, organize and staff, and control and solve problems. In contrast, leaders establish direction, align people, and motivate and inspire (pp. 4–5).

In terms of the authentic action framework, both management and leadership expend energy (power). Leadership, however, tends toward mission and meaning, management toward structure and resources. Kotter's distinctions are crisp and useful and merit serious attention by theorists and practitioners alike.

Authentic action theory enriches Kotter's analyses by pinpointing a potential trap for both positional leaders and managers. If change and complexity threaten positional leaders' coping capacity, they tend to preoccupy themselves with power. Managers threatened by change give undue attention to structure. Value and direction lose currency as leaders seek political advantage. Likewise, managers tend to take their attention away from the energy necessary to inspirit organizational action and to preoccupy themselves with organizational maintenance and monitoring. But do managers need to be concerned with energizing?

The picture becomes more complicated when technical expertise is added to the litany of role options. Technical experts match resources to structural problems, offering advice, counsel, and hands-on informed practice. When threatened, instead of attending to their expert contribution to the organization, they may preoccupy themselves with their own importance. They focus counterclockwise from structure to resources, afraid that change will render their skills unnecessary.

Heifetz and Sinder's distinction (1988) between problems that are fixable and require technical expertise, problems that are partially correctable and require management, and problems that open unknown arenas of life and require leadership appears to match with the distinctions I am making here. Yet I know from personal conversations with Heifetz that he does not take the leadership/management/expertise distinction with great seriousness, and on reflection, I agree with his restiveness. If leadership is providing resources for people to do *real* work, as Sinder and Heifetz contend, or leadership is the courage to call forth authentic action in the commons, as I contend, then leadership is a more fundamental notion than that embodied in any distinction between leaders, managers, and experts. Leadership cuts across all three roles. Authentic action challenges leaders, managers, and technical experts to remain authentic, face their fears of changing complexity, and courageously take on the essential tasks of their roles.

As much as Kotter asserts that, in times of change, leadership must be widespread rather than at the top, the underlying assumption in distinguishing between leaders and managers is that leadership equates with position and authority. The power he sees in leadership is legitimized by institutional structure. But is not leadership more profound and widespread than position? Does it not transcend roles and call all people to engage in real work and authentic action? A leading expert, a leading manager, and a leading leader all have one thing in common. Each practices authentic engagement, framing issues for himself or herself and others clockwise. That engagement is positional leaders', managers', and experts' deepest and most salutary action. Thus, authentic action both affirms the distinction between leadership, management, and technical expertise and pushes beyond it, to a deeper unity of purpose and value.

Leadership and Followership

Conversations on leadership are frequently well sprinkled with comments about followers: "We get the leaders we deserve." "Don't follow like sheep." "Those people could be talked into anything." "Beware of the charismatic leader manipulating an unsuspecting crowd." None of the typical comments is very flattering to followers. Yet followership may be as critical to our understanding of leadership as leadership itself. For a few leadership theorists, followership is essential to the definition of leadership. For example, business consultant James Georges points out that "the guy in the street who has a sandwich board that says, 'The world is coming to an end' has a vision and is communicating it." But, "Is he a leader? Only if he has followers." Georges believes that the presence of followers is the "only sensible, verifiable measurement of leadership" (Lee, 1989, p. 20).

The longer I struggle with leadership the more I debate whether we need programs on followership akin to programs on leadership. I have even thought of setting up a followership institute that would focus on the process of creating better leaders through more creative followers. In part, this idea was sparked by an intriguing question someone asked me: What would you include in a course on followership that you would not put in a course on leadership? I was hard pressed for an answer.

Followership is little understood. Some people do not like the term because they find it suggests passive, almost robot-like adherents who exhibit nonreflective obedience. Leadership consultant Frank Pace suggests replacing *followers* with a term such as *constituency* or *partners*.

A story about the Thunderbirds, the precision Air Force flying team, reflects the ambivalence that the followership concept arouses. Thunderbird pilots key off the lead pilot in the formation. They say, "It makes no difference where the ground is because [our] eyes are on the leader." On the day the leader's stick did not work, the other three pilots continued to follow him, just as they had been trained to do, right into the ground. "They hit in formation, everybody doing his job. They didn't malfunction, there were four distinct crashes at Indian Springs but only one explosion anyone could hear" (Deford, 1987, pp. 70–71).

Total obedience is not the American way, yet paradoxically, the cooperativeness of the flight team symbolizes much of what is great about the United States. However, unreflective obedience must be replaced with reflective followership. As I stated earlier, Cleveland (1985) even suggests that followers identify the vision first. It is this creative view of followership that has promise for future leadership studies.

The diverse forms of followership parallel some of the insights into leadership that I discussed in distinguishing leadership, management, and expertise. Table 10.2 illustrates these parallels. If the problem is known and fixable, the required action is expertise; followership, therefore, is thoughtful obedience to any advice that is given. Pilots flying in unison know that mastery demands following the lead of the front pilot. Obedience is not appropriate, but technical excellence is. If a problem is partially known and the

Table 10.2. Reflective Followership's Diverse Responses.

Problem	Solution	Action	Followership Response
Known	Known	Expertise	Thoughtful obedience
Partially known	Partially known	Management	Functional team membership
Unknown yet felt and believed	Unknown	Leadership	Cocreation

solution is only partially known, the required action is management of the structures that can cope with the situation. Followership thus becomes membership in a functional team. Each team member fulfills his or her complementary task to bring about the desired outcomes.

In the third scenario the problem is unknown, although deeply believed and felt. Therefore, the solution is also unknown. What is required is leadership, and followership now becomes cocreation, as leaders and followers together establish a vision. Where there is total obedience, neither leadership nor followership is present.

Leadership raises the question of what is really going on, and leaders together seek to give definition to the problem or issue. Neither leaders nor followers begin with answers; they struggle with the question and together propose directions and solutions from the diversity of perspectives covered by the Action Wheel. At the beginning of this section, I said that I had been asked what I would teach in a course on followership that I would not teach in a course on leadership. Once when I proposed this question to seminar participants, an undergraduate student, Scott Marquardt, presented the insight that "followers choose their leaders, leaders do not choose their followers." He would teach the "discipline of choosing." Perhaps convening an institute of followership is the right idea. Imagine a movement of followers demanding, requiring, and expecting authentic action leadership. Instead of witnessing leadership heroics, we could experience the wonderful paradox of followers leading.

Robert Kelley (1992) is already opening a line of inquiry into followership. Suggesting that it is followership that holds "the keys to understanding organizational success" (p. 13), Kelley outlines ten steps to "courageous conscience" for followers:

1. Be proactive.
2. Gather your facts.
3. Before taking a stand, seek wise counsel.
4. Build your fortitude.
5. Work within the system.
6. Frame your position so it will be heard.
7. Educate others on how your view serves their best interests.
8. Take collective action.
9. If you meet leader resistance, seek higher authority.
10. Have the financial and emotional cushions to exercise other alternatives [pp. 185–197].

In Kelley's view, and mine, followership is not the opposite of leadership. Lack of creative engagement is the opposite of both leadership and followership.

Leadership: Taught or Learned

Why do some people lead, some follow, and some watch from the sidelines? Is the reason a personal trait, a situational challenge, a role expectation, personal or collective interest, quickened vision, and/or ethical outrage? The hard truth of the matter is that we do not know. The variables are many, the theories conflicting, and the empirical research meager. Burns's comprehensive review (1978) of the psychological, social, and political dimensions of leadership yields no firm conclusion. Many mothers and fathers have had children killed by drunk drivers, yet it was Candy Lightner who founded Mothers Against Drunk Drivers (MADD). Many older citizens have been discriminated against, yet it was Maggie Kuhn who founded the Gray Panthers. All slaves were oppressed, yet it was Harriet Tubman, an escaped slave herself, who risked her life leading others to freedom on the Underground Railroad. Nevertheless, it is amazing how many people respond to the call of authenticity.

In leadership education circles, a refrain echoes: leadership cannot be taught; it can be learned. Is this just a more acceptable version of the "leaders are born not made" refrain? Or is it an acknowledgment that educators really do not know how to educate leaders because no one knows how to predict human responsiveness to events? Perhaps the learning/teaching distinction makes a different point. Teaching involves theory; learning requires doing. Thus, leadership is learned by reflection on action rather than taught in the classroom. Or, perhaps, the distinction admits that leadership requires courage and courage is unexplainable because it is *sui generis.*

I am not impressed with the born/made distinction. A propensity for left- or right-handedness does not signal a knowledge of writing. What I possess as part of my existence must be enhanced by education. There is some merit to the concern that not enough is known for us to be good leadership educators. Research, however, is possible, to figure out what works and what doesn't. We can even learn more about how to predict human responses. The idea that theory and practice are separate ignores the well-tested teaching method of reflection on practice. To set up a real-life experience and reflect on it *is* teaching leadership.

I am most intrigued by the question of leadership's need for courage. I agree with Winston Churchill's view that courage may be the most important human virtue because without courage none of the other virtues is likely to exist. Courage can be advocated, described, and discussed, but can it be taught? I'm inclined, at this point, to think that it cannot be taught. I believe that courage is the response to the call of authenticity, and that courage reinforces itself as it participates in authenticity. Is leadership taught or learned? Maybe it is neither and both.

Courage is central to the spiritual view of leadership and will be discussed fully in Chapter Eleven. But, first, let me share this passage from *McGuffey Readers* (McGuffey, [1844] 1973):

Mr. Phantom: Sir, persons of large views will be on the watch for great occasions to prove their benevolence.

Mr. Goodman: Yes, sir; but if they are so distant that they cannot reach them, or so vast that they cannot grasp them, they may let a thousand little, snug, kind, good actions slip through their fingers in the meanwhile; and so, between the great things that they *cannot* do, and the little things that they *will not* do, life passes and nothing will be done.

Leadership lives in the little as well as the great places. It lives where anyone or any group has the courage to call forth authentic action in the commons. What then does it take to lead? That is the message of the seventh view of leadership, which embraces the first six that I have discussed and moves us to a deeper engagement with life.

Summary

The three traditional and three provocative schools of leadership can be framed by the Action Wheel to bring out the many different aspects of authentic action. With this information, leadership programs can be designed to fit specific needs. Positional leadership, management, and technical expertise can be distinguished from each other; nevertheless, when authenticity is required, leadership is also required in all three of these roles. Followership can be shown to be essential to leadership, not as its opposite but as its essential and equal partner in framing issues, choosing metaphors, creating visions for answers, and using power appropriately.

Yet those of us involved in leadership education still do not know how to teach the essence of leadership, nor have we clearly identified that essence. I have said that leadership frames issues and calls forth authentic action in the commons, and I have defined action, the categories of issues, and authenticity, yet there is one more major view of leadership to be discussed—the seventh view that embraces all the other views.

PART FOUR

A SEVENTH VIEW
OF LEADERSHIP

Chapter Eleven

On Knowing and Living Leadership

I set out to rethink leadership, to construct a comprehensive framework of authentic action that both recognized, embraced, and critiqued other perspectives, yet offered a unique perspective of its own. Furthermore, the new framework for leadership had to be intellectually and morally justifiable while simultaneously being practical.

I began with leadership as an enigma; I end by puzzling about people as an enigma. The leadership inquiry challenges us to examine our most personal selves and relationships.

Five questions guide the next part of the inquiry:

- How do we recognize and embody leadership when it is defined as the courage to call forth authentic action in the commons?
- What undermines leadership?
- What quickens leadership?
- Where does leadership act?
- What supports and renews leadership?

The first question will be addressed in this chapter; the remaining questions will shape Chapters Twelve and Thirteen. The first question is epistemological: How do we *know* that leadership is present? The last four questions examine the relationship between leadership and fear, courage, the common good, and spirituality.

Recognizing Leadership as Authentic Action

In previous chapters, I have explored and proposed numerous ethical, visionary, and political criteria that help us to know when authentic action is present. I have defined authenticity. Yet if leadership is a subset not only of action but of authentic action, then at some point we all will address the problem of making judgments about authentic action, and what kind of *confidence* can we have that we can recognize authentic action in others and in ourselves?

I have already explored the difficulties of gross relativism and its self-contradiction. If there is no authenticity, then gross relativism itself cannot be authentically proposed as a concept. However, this tidy theoretical point is of little assistance in the everyday world. We need criteria that will judge whether or not any particular truth claim is viable. Ralph Brauer, a colleague of mine, pinpoints the true issue. I stated earlier that Hitler was not authentic and, therefore, not a leader. Brauer, however, makes the following point:

> As for true to self, true to world, who can say Hitler was not true to himself? It is also easy to say, with a perspective of hindsight, that he was not true to the world. But several million people thought that he was in 1932. In fact, that was a large part of his appeal— he gave them a "model" which they took as being true to the world. When he talked of a "Jewish conspiracy," he said, "Look at who owns the banks or major businesses"—and people believed him. It was the classic paranoia paradigm which, as Richard Hofstadter so perceptively pointed out, many people have found and still do find appealing. If it takes hindsight to definitely determine the world, how do you do it now,

in this environment when nothing is what it seems?
[R. Brauer, letter to the author, 1989]

In a much lighter vein, Brauer relates the following story:

Recently, I was driving home and saw a large crowd
of cars parked along the road near a swamp. There
must have been at least a dozen police and sheriff's
cars, lights flashing, as well as several vans from local
television stations. Some people had cameras and bi-
noculars. As I drove by I saw a group of men emerge
from the street by the edge of the swamp. They were
carrying something that looked like a body. Imagine
my surprise when I found out on TV that night that
what they had been carrying was a bear. Why had I
been programmed to "see a body"? Part of it, of
course, is all the news reports we see about crime. Part
of it may have been my own morbid curiosity. Part of
it may have been that not in my wildest dreams would
I have expected a bear. As old northern Minnesotans,
we just don't get that excited about bears. What was
true and what was real? The bear or the body? At the
time? Or later when I saw the TV report? What if I had
never seen the TV report? [R. Brauer, letter to the author, 1989]

The Hitler theme, first raised by Burns, has accompanied us
throughout this text. It has been one constant referent point to
struggle with what is and is not leadership. I will return to it after
developing the criteria of authenticity. The bear example provides
a different slant on the issue. How can we know whether we are
trapped in ignorance? A discussion of the bear case will conclude
this section.

The Seven C's of Authenticity

Even though we cannot have perfect knowledge, I suggest that there
are seven criteria we can use to judge the reliability of our partial

knowledge: correspondence, consistency, coherence, concealment, conveyance, comprehensiveness, and convergence.

Correspondence

Authenticity, as I said earlier, is different from sincerity. Sincerity is good intentions; authenticity is the embodiment of intentions in the world. An act is minimally authentic if it exists, if some behavior or fact is either actually or potentially available to inspection through our senses. Action is anchored in real space and real time, and it has real effect and real substance; it shows up. Minimally then, we can say an action is authentic when we experience a correspondence between the idea of the act and some actually or potentially manifested behavior.

Consistency

Capriciousness in action is no more intelligible than capriciousness in language. We cannot assign any meaning we like to a word, nor can we assign authenticity to any action we like. If I say I am going to build a house myself and possess no knowledge of home building or construction tools, I am inconsistent. Building a house by myself entails knowledge and use of tools. If the entailment does not follow, my claim sinks into unintelligibility. Therefore, this criterion investigates resources.

When the United Auto Workers pioneer in the union movement and at the same time resist unionization by their own employees, that resistance is inconsistent and therefore inauthentic. When Eastern bloc nations demanded freedom for themselves yet refused freedom within their own borders, they were inconsistent and inauthentic. As part of its marketing, the Prodigy program for home computers offered an unlimited use of its bulletin board feature. Purchasers could drop messages to each other without restriction. After Prodigy increased its rates, system users put messages on the free bulletin board to organize resistance. Prodigy then laid out the rule that any messages could be posted except those that resisted cost increases. This too is an inconsistency.

Most judgments of the authenticity of an action end here.

Inconsistency often is the issue. Calls to walk one's talk, match feet and lips, are essentially calls to overcome inconsistency. However, when we are looking for leadership that calls forth courage in the commons, these two criteria of correspondence and consistency only set the stage. They do not exhaust the benchmarks for authentic action.

Coherence

Coherence, the third C, links action to other actions. It asks questions about structure. It tests for a relationship with other authentic actions and asks whether the particular action functions in concert with those other actions. Policymakers often fall prey to lack of coherence. A policy made to solve one problem often unintentionally ignores a related but contradictory policy. For example, forceful policies to fight crime and drugs collide with policies on civil rights and liberties. Each action exists and is consistent with its own assumptions but is not coherently linked to other actions. Coherence requires that each action be viewed communally rather than independently. It focuses on possibilities for synergy and creative options.

Thus, correspondence between idea and concrete presence anchors action, consistency entails matching claims about action with its manifestation, and coherence connects one internally consistent action to another.

Concealment

Every action has a downside that can be destructive. The criterion of concealment asks questions about power, because preoccupation with an action's justification may not reveal that action's full impact. The public face of the action conceals the ambiguities, profundities, and contradictions that often attend action and may open up new insight. But in the heat of conflict or the rush to convince someone, we can easily fool ourselves that we have grasped the whole action, when, in fact, we have concealed a part of it from others and from ourselves by a selective preoccupation and self-serving rationalization.

Insofar as it is true, the adage that in politics there are no permanent friends, only coalitions of interest, raises serious issues for authentic action. As interests shift, the assumption is that the past plays no role in the future, as if interests were distinct and we could go from one to another with no memory of past involvements. Authenticity does not oppose shifting alliances. It expects them and understands them as sources of creativity and innovation. However, authenticity does demand that we recognize the role of the past and the consequences for the future of our shifts. For example, can former Panamanian president Manuel Noriega authentically be an ally one day and an accused criminal the next? When our actions may have unintended consequences that we should know about but do not want to address, we are not being authentic.

Conveyance

An action can be inauthentic even after its hidden sides are revealed. However, it becomes increasingly arduous to find that inauthenticity. The fifth C, conveyance, asks if the thought and the action, as they couple together, open up rather than close future thought and action. Does the action convey itself and the whole human enterprise forward, in a kind of self-regeneration? In short, What is the action's mission?

From this perspective, authentic action is defined as adding to and deepening the human journey. Conveyance makes the journey possible because the action opens itself to other action, not only to express its own authenticity but to appreciate the authenticity of the other. When Senge (1990) talks about dialogical action, he is essentially meeting the criterion of conveyance. We do not wait for our turn to talk; rather, we engage in the listening and understanding that cross boundaries and enter into the life, space, and experience of the other. Dialogue, through storytelling, is the embodiment of the conveyance criterion of authenticity.

Comprehensiveness

Conveyance opens action to the other; comprehensiveness expands the frame that incorporates the action. Comprehensiveness is concerned with meaning; it embraces differences and opens dialogues. It rejoices in plurality and takes ownership of its own shadow. However, the shadow is deeper than that concealed in political action. Comprehensiveness embraces even irrational fears. It looks both out and in, forward and backward, probing as totally as it can what is really going on.

Comprehensiveness is the most inclusive quality of meaning. It seeks to add depth of insight, celebrate wisdom, and in its creation of meaning, affirm the joy and tragedy of existence.

These six criteria are benchmarks for judging authentic action. They have been at work throughout this book, operating behind the scenes as I have discussed ethics, metaphors, and power, as well as structure, resources, and existence. They are present as people assess social movements in Poland, China, the former U.S.S.R., and the United States. They are present as organizations actively build quality-based activities. They are present in face-to-face dialogues. Table 11.1 displays the criteria in relation to the Action Wheel.

Each of the criteria is necessary to a full recognition of authentic action. However, each of the six also points toward a seventh measure.

Convergence

Convergence is the seventh criterion of authenticity, implicit in the other six, transcending each of them. It ends one inquiry and opens

Table 11.1. Six Criteria of Authentic Action Framed by the Action Wheel.

Generic Features of Action	Criteria of Authentic Action	Result
Meaning	Comprehensiveness	Expands
Mission	Conveyance	Opens
Power	Concealment	Hides
Structure	Coherence	Reveals
Resources	Consistency	Connects
Existence	Correspondence	Anchors

a new one. According to Webster's Third New International Dictionary, *convergence* means "moving toward union or uniformity." It suggests the many seeking the one, which is a concept at the heart of great truths. Compelling metaphors that emphasize convergence bridge differences by seeking common ground. Martin Luther King, Jr.'s "I Have A Dream" speech and Abraham Lincoln's inaugural address both have this quality, which is why we revere these leaders.

Convergent thinking is powerfully authentic because it is open-ended enough that each of us can connect its inferences with our own experiences. Franklin Roosevelt's memorable declaration that we have "nothing to fear but fear itself" had the quality of convergence. All who heard understood. They not only understood their individual experiences of the cruelties and uncertainties of the Great Depression but they also understood that their president understood them and was prepared to act on that understanding, not out of panic but out of compassion and responsibility. Roosevelt's language reached beyond each individual who heard it to something all listeners could embrace. Disparate lives came together. People found a basis of unity without uniformity.

Even Ralph Stacey, who questions the value of mission statements and other forms of organizational agreements, proposes a vision of convergence—complex learning in a complex organization (Stacey, 1992, p. 182). He writes that successful companies "will recognize that open-ended change removes all the conditions required for the practice of planning and ideological modes of control and development, they will abandon all attempts at long-range planning and envisioning" (p. 168). He is, in fact, laying before us an extremely energizing vision of life in a time of chaos. His sense of the new convergence is creativity, triggered by multiple centers of action. Again, the issue of the one and the many surfaces. Stacey emphasizes the many while challenging the one, yet cannot escape his own proposal for a new agreement.

Stacey's viewpoint supports the idea that leadership is not merely a process that imposes visions on others but, instead, proposes a future that grows out of continual engagement with the world. The more perspectives we seek out, the more our disparate lives can be brought together in mutual understanding, the greater our sense of convergence and the more we experience leadership.

Thus, convergence is both the end and the means of authenticity. It is the telos of human inquiry. It embodies and transcends current historical experience. It is the search for the one and the many that transcends the many in the search for the one.

Applying the Criteria of Authenticity

The seven criteria supply the answer to my colleague's observations about Hitler. Certainly Hitler existed. He was and still is, through film and written records, an observable reality. I could also make a case that Hitler was internally consistent. *Mein Kampf,* written prior to his rise to political dominance, staked out his vision. Furthermore, given certain assumptions, I could argue that he met the criterion of coherence. While deeply racist, his views of the world and of Germany in particular were supported by much of German culture. So on three counts, it could be plausibly argued that Hitler was authentic.

However, the next four criteria counter the argument. Burns's critique of Hitler stresses the fourth criterion, concealment. Hitler was an oppressive tyrant who abused power and concealed aggression by blaming the victims of his abuse. He also violated the criterion of conveyance. By assuming that his and his nation's journey were the only ones worth pursuing and by severing communication with other nations, Hitler imposed a doomed future on Germany.

Now we come to the criterion of comprehensiveness, which deserves extra attention because it is so central to the seventh view of leadership. Comprehensiveness calls us to embrace our own fears. Earlier, I described Jung's view that we have a shadow part of ourselves that we typically deny, projecting its qualities onto others. Philp (1958), summarizing Jung's view, says this projection is "the way in which the majority of mankind obtains relief from its shadows. This is what frequently happens when a nation or an individual believes that the Communist, the Jew, the Capitalist, or some other projected figure, is the source of all evil" (pp. 93–94).

What happens when we recognize comprehensiveness as a fundamental quality of existence? What happens when we face the shadow?

There must be a perfect readiness to face all that one is and this takes great courage. It is a task which we ordinarily shirk and prefer instead to hide behind a mass of projections and rationalizations and the mask of some carefully chosen and stubbornly held persona. As Jung expressed it: ". . . Acceptance of oneself is the essence of the moral problem and the acid test of one's whole outlook on life. That I feed the beggar, that I forgive an insult, that I love my enemy in the name of Christ—all these are undoubtedly great virtues. What I do unto the least of my brethren, that I do unto Christ. But what if I should discover that the last amongst them all, the poorest of all beggars, the most impudent of all offenders, yea the very fiend himself—that these are within me, and that I myself stand in need of the alms of my own kindness, that I myself am the enemy who must be loved—what then? Then, as a rule, the whole truth of Christianity is reversed: there is then no more talk of love and long-suffering; we say to the brother within us 'raca' and condemn and rage against ourselves" [pp. 95-96].

Burns's analysis of Hitler as a tyrant not a leader, while a courageous statement in contemporary leadership studies, does not, I believe, plumb the depths of the issue. Hitler was more than a tyrant. By acting to project an entire nation's fears onto the Jewish people, he represented the demonic. Some of what Hitler tapped resides in each of us and our own cultures. No one is immune. The inauthentic within and the inauthentic without are constant dangers, alienating us from ourselves and from others. The U.S. Government slaughters Indians; we focus on *Custer's* last stand. Our memory of the Mexican War is to celebrate the Alamo. Hitler is not just Them; he is a part of Us. To call him a tyrant frees us too easily from ourselves and our own participation in destructive living.

In response to Brauer's concern about the bear, suppose Brauer had not seen the television program. He would have been ignorant of the truth, and he would have assumed, based on his own judgment, that a body was in the bag.

Our ever present reality of not knowing enough does not undermine our need for authenticity; however, it does caution against premature harsh judgment, condemnation, and self-righteous surety. Our knowledge that our knowledge is always partial should tell us to support a gentle authenticity. We should approach authenticity by listening and being open to the new, actions that replace speaking and being closed to the new. Dialogue should replace discussion as a primary mode of engagement (Senge, 1990, p. 247).

Increasing Our Knowledge

Two events inform the process of listening and being open. The first is *bumping* (an event I have mentioned before); the second is *pacing*. Bumping frees us from our ethnocentrism. We are not born with knowledge of the world; therefore, we are all raised ethnocentrically. If we never experience ideas, or events, that are different from those with which we were first made familiar, our future will be forever locked into the mold of our past. However, most people in a rapidly changing world experience bumps, contrasts that raise doubt and often generate new knowledge and new action.

A simple example of bumping is my experience as a young student at Cornell University. In the dormitory dining room, I was given a plate of long white spindly stuff with red sauce dumped in the center. What is that? I wondered. Spaghetti, you say. But real spaghetti, for me, was canned Franco-American. It was all red, chopped up, and looked as though it had already been eaten once. I looked at the plate and thought that the staff must have really been rushed if they didn't have time to spread the red sauce around and cut it up. But thank goodness for diversity. Without it, I would never have discovered good spaghetti.

My ethnocentrism was exposed when it bumped up against a difference. I was true to myself, and thought I was true to the world, but I found I had a better option. My personal center of authenticity discovered a deeper worldly authenticity. If someone had suggested that I go inside to get in touch with real spaghettiness, without experiencing it firsthand, my experience would have produced only more Franco-American. Only by bumping against a real world difference could I learn about myself and reveal my ignorance to myself. A more complicated example of bumping is the experience I described earlier of having my perspective on racism questioned by Reverend Douglas Fitch. This bump made me seek out many more bumps, as I undertook a journey to expand my understanding of the issue of racism and the roles all of us play in that issue.

When a new situation faces us, our first response is to fit the new into the old. We back into the future, bringing our history with us. New insight is aligned with old understandings. Only when the new resists the old are we challenged to discover new possibilities. We then participate in a new inquiry. We have discovered a new dimension of authenticity.

Knowledge, then, is initiated by contrast and doubt. Whether we examine Plato's dialogical bump with universal forms, Aristotle's problematic bump with social diversity, the sophists' intentional bump with themselves, Democritus's empirical bump with raw experience, or a faithful person's bump with his or her God, the one commonality is contrast. If there is no contrast, there is no perception. Just as a blackout or a whiteout precludes any sight of differences, so, too, knowledge that appears to have no edges supplies no incentive for us to escape our own envelope of meaning. Moreover, like any metaphor, bumping carries many connotations, and one of these connotations is roughness or forcefulness. A bump is a *push* that *knocks* us out of our intended path. Therefore, while bumping is a necessary experience, it may often be a startling or even painful one.

Bumping opens the door; it does not carry us forward on the path of knowledge. Thus, we need the concept of pacing. I first heard of it in the context of neurolinguistic programming. To pace someone is to participate in their patterns of movement while slowly altering those patterns and leading the person toward a different, and ideally more healthy, pace. Bumping and pacing are complementary. Through bumping, we can learn the new; through pacing, we can confirm the new over time. If we experience a new insight, that insight can be tested as someone else enters into our thinking, working with us to explore its traps and promises.

In terms of our authenticity, bumping presents a new choice to us, pacing checks out that choice against the criterion of convergence. Leadership, therefore, bumps and paces. It stimulates fresh insight, yet is empathetic to others, humble in its discovery process. Arrogance and self-righteousness find no home in leadership because each undermines leadership's creative journey. Authentic persons, suggests Martin (1986), "would be committed seekers after truth rather than discoverers of any particular truths. And they would be persons who shape their self-identities on the basis of that concern for truth" (p. 78).

An example from a colloquium on teaching ethics illustrates the reality of bumping and the need for pacing. One of the participants related a story of what she considered to be successful teaching in an introductory undergraduate ethics course intended to engage students in serious inquiry into four contemporary moral problems, to get them to realize that they could do careful analysis of ethical dilemmas, and to build a climate of trust to support the inquiry and debate. The particular ethical conclusion a student might reach was less important than the disciplined process the student used to arrive there. In this class, two twenty-year-old suburbanites, who had been lifelong friends, came up to the professor after a class discussion on abortion to report that, prior to the discussion, one of them had been for and the other against abortion, but they had never discussed this critical moral issue. After the debate, they had reversed positions. The professor felt she had succeeded with these two students because they had addressed and reasoned carefully about an important issue.

However, the professor had also had a failure. One of her students was a deeply committed fundamentalist who believed that abortion was an abomination. He had made his views known to the class, stirring such interest that other students wrote unsolicited papers in rebuttal. The professor was thrilled by this level of student engagement. Shortly after the issue surfaced, however, the fundamentalist quit the course. The professor thought she had failed him and the class, and the class felt cheated by his departure.

The subsequent colloquium debate centered on how a university that is committed to reasoning and tolerance for diversity should deal with a person who is "extreme" in the view of others and who will not participate in the reasoning process, as that process is defined by the university's standards. The fundamentalist believed none of the readings reflected his particular view, and he left. The ethics professor believed the readings represented a diversity of "rational" views. With authentic concern for this student's intellectual well-being, she asked how she could have done a better job.

Solutions flew around the room: Ask the class before it begins if there are any fundamentalists present—if there is only one, request that person bring a buddy to class for support. (This proposal sent a civil libertarian shudder down the spine of one person who imagined the irate calls that would come to the university protesting the invasion of a student's personal beliefs.) Increase personal contact through conferences, to demonstrate respect and caring. Encourage class members to try to understand each other by asking them to script viewpoints. Don't focus them on trying to convert each other.

The discussion took an important turn when another professor reflected on his own teaching. He said he now laid out his own view at the beginning of a course, so that the students would know his perspective. Another professor asked how teachers can build an inclusive community if they still believe certain views to be dead wrong. She, for example, believed that homophobia was an evil on a par with racism and sexism. She did not tolerate homophobia in her classes even though she also believed that a community should include a diversity of perspectives. Perhaps, we are all fundamentalists, someone observed. Just pick your nonnegotiable absolute. Is community possible among a community of differing fundamentalists? This view reached the heart of the matter. Bumping had exploded in the professor's class when abortion was the issue, yet there had been no pacing. The ethics professor had sought to include the fundamentalist student on the professor's terms. The student most likely sensed that the professor's real mission was to get him to doubt, a mission he did not accept on this issue.

What would have happened if the professor had admitted that she had her own fundamentalist beliefs, and had thus sought a point of shared experience that cut across the issue? Suppose she acknowledged one of her own nonnegotiable convictions?

This sharing approach requires courage because it demands a heightened self-critical capacity and a willingness to admit that total flexibility is a myth. We all have fundamentalist sides. A nonnegotiable belief in the sanctity of reason or the importance of individualism is as fundamentalist in respect to the conviction with which it is held as is an unalterable belief in the wrongness of abortion.

In effect, the ethics professor had refused to accept the fundamentalist challenge as a bump for self-insight, an opportunity to transcend the issue of abortion and to examine human beings in a community of other human beings. Instead, the professor became the powerful up, and the student became the powerless down. Ethically, the greater responsibility rested with the professor. Although she appeared open, the student may have sensed her closure, which was not about abortion but about fundamentalist views as a legitimate category of thought. The student, perhaps fearful of the professor and his own doubts, and believing that his view was not respected, left.

The class had the appearance but not the reality of being open. In Etzioni's terms, the underlying conditions were alienating. The fundamentalist also triggered a crisis of leadership in the community of scholars represented at the colloquium. He was not the problem. The problem rested in the character and nature of the community itself, which was not initiating and building authentic action in the commons.

With pacing, dialogue in the class and the colloquium might have been possible. Then authenticity, in its richness, could literally and metaphorically have come into play.

Summary

The seven criteria that identify authentic action are correspondence, consistency, coherence, concealment, conveyance, comprehensiveness, and most importantly, convergence. These are also the criteria that help us to live out authentic action in our own lives. However, leadership is not reducible to authentic action alone. As the last example illustrated, acting authentically requires courage, coping with fear, a sense of the common good, and hope. Leadership takes authentic action and marries it to courage. What this means is the subject of the next chapter.

Chapter Twelve

Fear and Courage: Leadership in the Commons

Fear extinguishes leadership. Courage ignites leadership. In the commons, we secure safe places for leadership to face fear and discern the common good. This chapter explores fear and courage and defines the spaces we hold in common and the good that arises from these shared spaces.

Fear

If, as human beings, we are called upon and expected to be authentic, why are we often not authentic? What causes us to replace our deepest and best inclinations and intentions with our worst actions? What blocks sincerity from becoming authenticity? What corrupts leadership? My search for an answer to these questions took me far beyond where I expected to go, and the conclusions I have come to have transformed my understanding of leadership and myself.

Many of my arguments, especially those surrounding authenticity, are rooted in a comprehensive notion of rationality. However, this rationality is not technically oriented. It goes beyond means to a nonrational end. Although my argument for authenticity as both presupposition and prerequisite is based on the ideas of non-contradiction and entailment, both of which are rational notions, and although it may thus appear that my view of leadership proposes a purely optimistic, super-rational view of human nature and leadership, I have also reflected my and others' underlying restiveness with logic detached from passion and idealism disconnected from the starkness of pain in everyday life. As I have reiterated—justifiably, I believe—we can easily see signs of hope and the promise for peace and well-being around the world, but we can also see that terror and pain still mark the global landscape. These phenomena live side by side. Thus, leadership, if it is to be authentic, must embody the highs and lows, the breadths and depths of the human spirit.

What is it then that distorts and masks our perception of the true and the real? Here are some of the many answers that are typically offered: It is our aggressive nature; we are playing out the survival of the fittest. It is uncontrolled greed, and monopolies, especially government, unions, and organized groups. It is personal addictions and dysfunctional systems infecting the community. It is pride, political aggression, and opportunism. It is ignorance and disinformation. It is profound loss of identity and alienation from others and even from God.

We have heard these answers before. Each reflects one of the features of action. But there is another answer, often unheard, but when heard, so energizing and terrifying that other voices quake, an answer so amazing that it profoundly transforms any examination of leadership. This answer is that the cause of our inauthenticity is fear—specifically, fear in and of ourselves.

Henri Nouwen (1986) believes that "the negative power of fear . . . has invaded every part of our being to such a degree that we no longer know what a life without fear would feel like" (p. 15). Of course, not all fear is destructive. Some fear is useful, to keep us out of harm's way. It is appropriate that we teach children to fear cars at street crossings, so that they will look both ways before crossing the road. Also, there are fearsome aspects to life—torture, rape, murder, and other abuses of power. Thus, fear in itself is not a problem. It becomes a problem only when it is permitted to run rampant through our lives—unacknowledged, unnamed, untamed, and unembraced. Rampant unchecked fear leads us to substitute inauthenticity for authenticity and most importantly *to become what we most fear.*

Let me illustrate, using the six metaphors as my reference point (see Table 12.1). If we fear death, the destruction of our natural gifts, we hunker down rather than reach out. Cornered, we revert to our most base nature, initiating a preemptive strike. It is survival of the fittest. Attack or be eliminated.

If we fear failure, the destruction of our utility in the market, we lose our personal center. We surround ourselves with material possessions, hoping our accumulation of objects proves our success. We become objects to ourselves, and we become objectified, we treat others as objects, also. We say "They must be somebody; look at their possessions." Through greed, we seek protection from the vicissitudes of the market, hoping to reach a safe haven of respect and to avoid being thought useless. Our fear drives us to succeed in a way that makes us fail our full potential.

If we fear isolation and rejection from a social body, we caretake. However, our apparent love and concern masks a false sense of belonging. We present the appearance of connectedness, without

Table 12.1. Fears That Extinguish Leadership
Framed by the Action Wheel.

Generic Features of Action	Metaphors	Object of Fear	Result of Unchecked Fear
Meaning	Art	Disorientation	Maintain cynical orientation
Mission	Journey	Lack of direction	Claim self-righteous surety
Power	Up versus down	Victimization	Victimize others
Structure	Body	Isolation and rejection	Insincerely caretake
Resources	Market	Failure	Build external identity
Existence	Gift	Elimination	Mount preemptive attacks

the vitality and nurturance of true connectedness. We perpetuate addictive selves, families, organizations, and societies. Dysfunction becomes normal and social sickness prevails.

If we fear victimization by oppressive ups, we imitate the ups when we get into power. We victimize downs as a way of convincing ourselves that we will never be downs again. The way this game is played is to remain an up by whatever means necessary, because "we deserve to be ups." Arrogance and oppression clasp hands in a unified front of tyranny.

If we fear loss of direction, a distortion of our journey, we trigger a self-righteous surety. We cease to worry about disinformation as our fear instills personal and collective ignorance. Life is simplified into good and evil, right and wrong. As in the Potemkin villages, ambiguity is hidden away behind painted scenery so the journeyer is spared having to look at the undesirable conditions of reality. Actual ambiguity is not an acceptable sight on such a narrowly crafted journey.

Finally, if we fear fundamental disorientation, a destruction of our lives as art and of our inventiveness at discovering and creating meaning, we experience profound alienation and cynicism. Life becomes flat. We cease to maintain and validate our ethical sensibility. Our shadow, the ever-present self we would deny, takes charge. When our eroded life confronts other lives, it makes little difference whether we affirm or deny them, or ourselves for that matter.

Primordial Fear

For quite a while I was satisfied, and a bit smug, with the critical insight that we become what we fear. Yet something still evaded my understanding, because there is a seventh perspective on fear that creates havoc within the human spirit and must be faced before we can be released for authentic action. I gained a fundamental insight into this seventh perspective on fear from Schwager's discussion (1978) of the ideas of René Girard, an internationally renowned literary critic. Girard's thinking helped me explain to myself the primordial mechanisms of rage, anger, and fear that accounted for both violence and unity in so-called primitive societies, and it opened a window for me onto contemporary society. He went beyond an analysis of shadow and sought to explain why we have shadows and whether they are necessary.

Schwager's interpretation of Girard confronted my ideas of courage, spirituality, and hope, for it probed to the question at the heart of the human condition: Is violence a necessary part of human life? What both Girard and Schwager proposed linked meaning back to existence and grounded hope in a radically different interpretation of spirituality.

Girard set out to account for violence and peace. Asking himself whether individuals ever really put the common good before their private good, and whether they did not "often act against their obvious self interest," Girard became convinced that we are not normally reasonable, autonomous beings, but are, in contrast, "continuously subject to blind passion" (Schwager, 1978, pp. 1–2).

Girard examines studies of primitive societies in which religion was central in order to learn what experiences make human beings "submit with sacred awe to certain concepts and rituals" (p. 2). Like Joseph Campbell (Campbell and Moyers, 1988), Girard is struck by the commonality of structures underlying the vast diversity of sacrificial acts and rites and the vastly diverse religious beliefs that are the proximate cause of these rites.

Girard's pivotal insight is that anger, rage, and fear, on the one hand, and sacrifice, on the other, are connected. There are several steps to his argument. First, "Men and women are creatures of passions. They are too easily overcome by rage and anger. But angry human beings resemble one another closely, no matter what culture or what religion they belong to. They have almost identical psychological and physiological reactions. Rage in particular makes all human beings blind in the same way and leads them to accuse their enemy of all that is evil" (Schwager, 1978, p. 3). Here, Girard aligns himself with the psychoanalytic tradition, part of which I described earlier when discussing Jung's concept of the shadow. Yet Girard parts significantly from Freud, who sought to link hidden passions to sexuality. Girard argues that this connection does not make sense, because sexuality is very public in tribal life. The nature of anger, however, is concealed from an angry person because "anger is lured toward the object of its arousal" (p. 4). Indeed, anger does not even have to be projected onto an enemy; it can be displaced onto a chance person or object, creating an enemy at will.

Second, in contrast to the lower animals, we seem to have no built-in restraint to our rage. Rarely do stronger animals kill the weaker. The weaker signifies its harmlessness and humbly moves out of harm's way. Not so with us as a species. We can all too readily kill in anger. In modern society, we have law, police, the courts as curbing mechanisms. Primitive societies, says Girard, had sacrificial rituals.

Anger is powerful, but since it is also masked, it can easily be manipulated, even tricked. A tribe could "seize upon surrogate victims," thereby appeasing the fury—the enemy within—by tossing "him a morsel that [served] to satisfy his raging hunger" (p. 5). In this way, the ritual sacrifices of tribes deflect passion, neutralize dangerous powers, and protect people from mutual destruction. Intriguingly, human sacrifices were never chosen from the tribe making the sacrifice. Because the purpose of the sacrifice was to restore harmony to the community, only the sacrifice of others, of Them by Us, could break the chain of violence triggering more violence. By projecting violence outward, the community could be preserved and thrive.

For Girard, this dynamic is also the core of the tragic form in contemporary fiction. A community is threatened, heroes appear, "to overcome the dangerous situation and to help reinstate justice." But what happens? Each "saviour" is implicated and tangled in the controversy he or she is supposed to save. Finally, all clear distinctions between hero and villain blur. "Sooner or later all are invariably overcome by passion and irrationality" (p. 7). The portrayal is one that people can find "distasteful" because it says "that the 'reasons' on both sides of a dispute are equally valid—which is to say that *violence operates without reason*" (p. 8).

The third step in Girard's argument is his answer to the question of why violence spreads so easily. That answer is *imitation,* or what Girard calls *mimesis*. His analysis posits a triangular relationship between the desiring hero, the model who is simultaneously a rival, and the person desired (p. 9). In contrast to Freud, who thought that desire must have an object, Girard, following the novelist Dostoyevsky, suggests that the content for the desire comes from some model that a desiring person imitates. Thus, "the desire of the model designates for one's own desire what is desirable" (p. 9).

The issue is complicated because the problem of imitation is not exhausted by the fact that it leads to conflict. "The rival is also a role model" and "the role model becomes a rival. . . . Since desire always imitates another desire that serves as its role model, it wishes for the latter's success but at the same time fights against it because the rival longs for the same object. This desire can increase to such an extent that the model becomes idol, and archenemy all in one" (p. 11).

If we tend to become hostile "opponents," our harmony and community are anything but secured. Violence stands at the threshold, ready to strike. How then are peace and tranquility possible? What has to happen for there to be some profound resolution to the conflict? In primitive communities, as I have described, sacrificial rituals and "sacred awe" hold "all dangerous desires at bay; taboos have the effect that certain limits are almost never transgressed" (p. 15). However, when the sacred and the profane in a society are totally severed and sacred awe and sacrificial rites are no longer celebrated and no longer generate release, then order among individuals unravels. Persons who are imitating each other blame each other; the rival becomes the paradigm of evil and appears as a true monster (p. 15). Thus the breakdown of sacred awe releases violence.

Girard believes that the sacrifices and sacred awe that break this chain of violence also spring from imitation. They imitate the sacrifice of an original *scapegoat*. In other words, violence recommends its own imitation. Violence that is disuniting the community is collectively transferred upon a "chance victim"; the community is again "united against the victim," expels the "evildoer," and kills him or her (p. 19). The "accidental victim still bears the onus of monstrous evil but at the same time exudes the aura of a super human savior" (p. 19). The cursed and the blessed, the repulsive and the attractive, and the ugly and the radiant are united. "The expelled victim causes fear and at the same time brings salvation. [People] experience this as sacred and remain ignorant of the fact that their own collective transfer sanctified the victim" (p. 20).

Girard maintains that what makes something sacred is its connection to violence rooted in fear of the other. Rivalries and conflict destroy communities, but in each tribe, a scapegoating event occurred that relieved rivalry and violence. For early tribal groups, ritual sacrifices became the unconscious mechanism for repeating this original effective scapegoating event. These rituals and symbols protected the community from the other. The pattern carries on to this day in ritual and worship services throughout the world. The "notion that some godhead accepts the sacrifice and blesses the sacrificing community," writes Schwager, "is the mythological expression of the fact that aggression is once again channeled to the outside and peace is secured" (p. 22). When violence is transferred from inside to outside the community, a sharp divide is drawn between the pacified inside social space and the threatening, fascinating domain of the sacred (p. 23).

Virtually all peoples have stories that tell how a cult hero was killed and how he rose to a new life and brought blessing to the community. While many scholars have seen the dying and rising theme as a response to the seasonal rhythms of nature, Girard observes that the same dying and rising motifs occur in regions that are fruitful year round. In addition, the hero's death is usually a violent one, or at least threatens to be violent. Thus, the explanation of the imitation of nature does not fit. Girard's proposal is more profound and is applicable to modern societies as well as the primitive world.

I have reported Girard's view in some detail because it is only in relatively peaceful space that people can build toward a peaceful future. Selves and communities may, as I said earlier, recoil at the explosive force of nature yet also be attracted by its unrestrained energy. Yet it is not nature that triggers our violence. It is we ourselves, individuals and communities yielding to an uncontrollable, devastating, primordial fear of rampant violence. In modern societies claiming to be civilized, this primordial fear recedes from public consciousness. In its place, fear is rationalized to maintain social acceptability. However, when our fear is about to be exposed, then we quickly project that fear onto the other and falsely justify acting violently toward the other as a protection of our societal and personal well-being. We imitate that which we fear, out of fear, and this fear becomes our shadow.

Rationalized Fear

Yet imitation also spawns hope; recognizing our rationalization is one step to authentic peace. Few people willingly expose their unethical actions. We prefer to believe that we are the embodiment of virtue. Thus, we experience the disconnection between our professed beliefs and our actions only dimly, at best. The greater the threat of exposure, the tighter our grip on rationalization. Among the strongest of these personal and collective rationalizations are the following:

Unethical Actions	*Rationalizations*
Abdication	They are not involved so ignore them.
Apathy	They are not worthy so avoid them.
Oppression	They are not ready so control them.
Social sickness	They are not healthy so fix them.
Discrimination	They are not useful so discard them.
Genocide	They are not human so eliminate them.

Leadership admits and names the fear. It admits and names the rationalization. It dips into the hidden recesses of life, into the shadows, and faces the fear. Leadership admits that the other is the same as ourselves, in both its soaring greatness and its struggling debasement, because when we deny the claim of the other on ourselves, we set the conditions for self-destruction. Thus, as I suggested earlier, when we declare that the other is not useful, we become undesirable objects. When we declare that the other is not healthy, we become sick. We become what we fear.

Listen as the same story is told mythically about the daughters of Copper Woman confronting Sisiutl:

There are rocks on the coast, which, like the trees, seem corkscrewed, seem to twist upon themselves, as if in agony. Whirlpools and riptides are the same, only different. All because they have seen Sisiutl and tried seeing Sisiutl and tried to flee.

Sisiutl, the fearsome monster of the sea. Sisiutl who sees from front and back. Sisiutl the soul searcher. Sisiutl whose familiars are often known as stlacun, the vision people, those who ride on the wind and bring dreams, stlacun who search out the chosen those who would see beyond the externals.

[Sisiutl] seeks those who cannot control their fear, who do not have a Truth. Fearful is he and terrifying. . . . When you see Sisiutl you must stand and face him, face the horror. Face the fear. If you break faith with what you know, if you try to flee, Sisiutl will blow both mouths at once and you will begin spinning. . . .

When you face Sisiutl the terrifying, and know you are frightened; stand firm. There is no shame in being frightened, only a fool would not be afraid of Sisiutl the horror. . . . Before the twin mouths of Sisiutl can fasten on your face and steal your soul, each head must turn toward you. When this happens, Sisiutl will see his own face. Who sees of the other half of self sees truth [Cameron, 1988, p. 44].

At the most radical level, leadership abides no naïveté. It knows its own foibles, its own potential for destruction. It acts from clarity, and it knows and lives into and toward an enduring, thriving, hope-filled future. It asks, Are scapegoats necessary? Is there not another mode of being engaged in the world?

Courage

Courage ignites leadership. It unites logic and life, propelling authentic action into the past, the present, and the future. Retrospectively, courage quickens authentic renderings of history and resists self-serving justifications or recriminations. It propels us to ask, What really went on? In the present, courage sparks energy, asking, What is really going on? It challenges those who disguise truth to expose the mask and face reality as it is. And courage invites a common exploration of the future. It challenges us to search for common good amongst the diversity of perspectives available to us. It searches for unity without uniformity. Courage takes us through the transition from authenticity as concept to authenticity as embodiment.

Logic Engaging Life

Previously, I gave a logical answer to the question, Why be authentic? It is self-contradictory not to be authentic. Conceptually, authenticity is reflexive, true to itself. The logic of authenticity's existence captures even those most forcefully seeking to break its hold. Yet logic divorced from life is form devoid of substance, the principle of life disconnected from life as it is lived. It is courage that energizes life in the real world, in real time. Courage cannot be disembodied. Its essential quality is to induce action, engagement, and participation. In part, therefore, it is power, but power linked with noble means and noble ends. We may be able to have courage without leadership; however, there is no leadership without courage.

Courage, like leadership, is an honorific action. It is exalted in public with awards and recognition. While not itself the end, or mission, of action, it is always committed to an end. And just as it is popular to argue that the end justifies the means, it can also be appropriately argued that the means determine the end. Mahatma Gandhi continually reminded the world that nonviolent ends cannot be achieved by violent means. Neither can authentic ends be achieved by inauthentic means. Means and ends are interdependent, relational, and reciprocal. Thus, courage is not only an honorific term, it is also an ethical term. It invites reflection, not only on the great acts but also on the little acts of everyday life. It invites reflection on both life's appearance and its reality. Logic answers the question of why we should be authentic, with a logical argument; courage lives out the answer.

Courage is central to leadership, but it is virtually ignored in leadership studies and general studies of human action. Modern theorists have given free will a near deathblow. In a world informed by B. F. Skinner, Freud, and Marx, human will has receded into the backwater of consideration, trapped by a pervading determinism. When will was dismissed as irrelevant to human action, courage's dismissal was not far behind. Nevertheless, will and courage refuse to be buried. In leadership studies, their time to be resuscitated as central categories has come.

Defining Courage

A small start can be found in Peter Koestenbaum's *Leadership: The Inner Side of Greatness* (1991). He defines courage as "action with sustained initiative" (p. 7). However, that is not enough. Courage is a more complex concept. Aristotle offers a richer idea. For Aristotle, courage stands between rashness and cowardliness. A rash person fears nothing, pretending to be courageous even in the face of disease and war, when fear is appropriate. A cowardly person fears everything, even inappropriate things such as friends and loved ones. Courage is the mean between these extremes, and courage is directed toward noble ends (McKeon, 1941, pp. 976–977). Aristotle's reflections on six expressions of courage form a base for further definitions.

Courage Transcends Ritual. Courage is internal, embodied in our inner beings. It is not reducible to a ritual or habit that prescribes sets of actions based on past performance. Nor does it rest solely on past successes. Ritualized behavior can lull us into a state of sanguinity, dulling our need to reflect afresh and be open to engage the unknown or novel. When new conditions threaten the security of old patterns, courage may falter in the face of the new, thereby exposing itself as pseudo-courage. A set of tested recipes from the past is no guarantee of courage in the present. Who is more courageous, someone who speaks out on a controversial issue mechanically and predictably, someone who does it for the first time, or someone who reflectively and creatively engages the issue repeatedly, yet freshly?

Courage Transcends Ignorance and Danger. Courage is often confused with danger or is equated with daring and impulse. In this light, it is not the new or the novel that exposes pseudo-courage; it is lack of attention to likely results. Daring looks like courage. But is there not a significant difference between someone who knows the danger and still acts and someone who rushes in blindly? Terry Waite knew the risks when he went to Beirut to negotiate the release of hostages, but he acted anyway. Harriet Tubman knew the risks of helping escaped slaves, but she acted anyway. Action upon reflection adds a seriousness to courage that impulse fails to demonstrate.

Courage Transcends Job and Institutional Requirements. Awards for courage are often tied to job performance. Firefighters risk their own safety to rescue children. Police endanger themselves in high-speed car chases. Nurses initiate lifesaving procedures on patients, fighting against losing odds. These acts are laudatory and deserve any public gratitude they receive. But is it more courageous for a person to act within a system of supports or to stand alone, challenging an oppressive system? A police officer in a shootout and a student facing armed police in Tiananmen Square both face severe threats to their lives. Both are courageous. But is there not a qualitative difference between a police officer whose job requires and supports courageous action and a protestor who faces a menacing oppressive force without institutional supports?

Courage Transcends Passion. Courageous persons are passionate, but not all passionate persons are courageous. "Lust," writes Aristotle, "makes adulterers do many daring things" (McKeon, 1941, p. 978). Daring called forth by passion is neither reflective nor necessarily called by a noble end. Courage is more than power, or energy, rooted in feeling. Courage is that which requires both passion *and* reflection. Is there not a significant difference between the angry person who reflectively directs anger toward constructive ends and the angry person who strikes out to punish without reflection?

Courage Transcends Utility. When ends are negotiable, means are negotiable. Courage questions easy negotiability. A cost-benefit analysis of a noble end undermines courage's resolve. Are not some ends sufficiently noble to be beyond calculation? Is there not a significant difference between the scientist who risks his or her repu-

tation by proposing a new theory and the scientist who calculates
the merits of telling the truth against the personal gains from
simply keeping quiet? And when there are profound and perplexing
conflicts of worthy ends, does not courage resist a trade-off? Courage
strives toward a deeper synthesis. Courage is that which challenges
utility as the final arbiter of ends.

Courage Transcends Pleasure. Courage, suggests Aristotle, is
drawn forth by pain, because "it is harder to face what is painful
than to abstain from what is pleasant" (McKeon, 1941, p. 979).
Thus, courage is what faces and embraces the most difficult. Even
though a mission is noble, the pain associated with embodying that
mission may be severe, even life-threatening. Courage gives us the
power to withstand that pain.

In the aggregate, then, courage confronts the fear of the new
and the unexpected, the fear of eminent danger, the fear of institutional isolation and separation, the fear of unrestrained passion, the
fear of negotiable ends, or missions, and the fear of difficulty and
pain. *Courage acknowledges, embraces, and transforms primordial
fear as it presses sincerity into authenticity.* Most profoundly, courage emboldens us to face ourselves, acknowledging that the fear that
separates us from each other is our own creation and that unity is
possible, in real time and space.

At the same time, courage expresses itself differently in each
leadership perspective and each corresponding metaphor for understanding life. When we view life as a gift, courage is that which
separates fact from fear. It directs us to base our action on the possibility of peace rather than the necessity of violence. When we view
life as a market, courage evaluates our resources. It believes that
inner worth transcends externals such as status and success and
recognizes that other individuals and groups are deeply connected
to us. When we analyze what is going on in the social body or
system, we require courage to free us from caretaking, impel us to
clarify our own interests, and help us be comfortable when we are
alone with our inner selves. When we weigh our relationships from
an ups versus downs perspective, it is courage that releases us from
controlling our environment and relationships. It challenges us to

care, and to eschew aggression and deviousness. When we look at our lives' journeys, courage quickens our openness to others, affirming them and ourselves as partners and responsible contributors to society's well-being. Finally, when we shape our lives as art, we need courage to acknowledge our contributions and to accept ambiguity and chaos as gifts that will eventually lead to profounder understandings of ourselves and the world.

In all these ways, courage ignites leadership, propelling us beyond our comfort zones, to know, experience, and act on what is really possible and worthy. It moves us clockwise on the Action Wheel.

Leadership Stories—Courage in Action

Anyone, anywhere can be courageous. A family huddles in the living room. Only the father is absent. He is an alcoholic, and the family is deciding whether to intervene and send him to treatment. Each member of the family is scared; each is convinced the action is the right thing to do, but at first, no one speaks. At last one person says, "Dad is sick, he needs us, we have to act for him and for us." They decide to intervene.

A close-knit family is gathered around a holiday dinner table. The spirit is festive, the food ample, and brother Bill, a hilarious storyteller, begins to regale the family with jokes and incidents he has heard at work. Laughter abounds, but when Bill tells an ethnic joke, another brother finds he cannot laugh. The joke is demeaning. He asks himself if he should speak up, risk the family's ire, and break the gala mood or remain silent, compromising his deep values. He takes a deep breath and speaks up. The spirit is dampened; however, the demeaning storytelling ceases.

Lou, a quiet, reserved, and very private person, has been challenged by a leadership seminar to engage more vigorously in life. A black, she lives in a predominantly white metropolitan suburb. With great trepidation, she decides to run for the state senate. Frightened, yet supported by friends and colleagues, she ventures forth and loses, but she decides to run again in the next election.

Jorge is Cuban and gay. A community activist and well-respected citizen, he has not declared his sexual orientation and fears exposure. His family and his Cuban male colleagues, who engage in sexist talk and behavior, do not know his secret, but his three closest friends, who are also Cuban, know he is gay and support him. When the governor selects him to head a blue-ribbon committee, he fears public disclosure more than ever. One of his good friends counsels with him, urging him to go public. After many sleepless nights, Jorge follows the friend's advice. His colleagues reject him, his family, after much struggle, stands with him, and the governor follows through on the appointment. Jorge serves with distinction.

Rochelle is president of her local Parent-Teacher Association. The predominantly white school is under court order to integrate, but the white parents and administrators are adamantly opposed. Rochelle, with three children in the school system, supports the order. Time after time, she challenges the administration and parents to look toward the future with new eyes and to be open to the promise contained in multicultural education. She is rebuffed and loses the next election. However, she remains in the neighborhood as a voice of hope as the system is coerced into change.

We usually hear only the stories of exceptional courage that attract the media and the historians—the stories of such people as Cesar Chavez, Chief Joseph, Bishop Tutu, Nelson Mandela, Harriet Tubman, Florence Nightingale, Eleanor Roosevelt, Mother Teresa, Martin Luther King, Jr., or Thomas Jefferson. Each of these individuals is noble and deserving of the attention and praise given to him or her. Yet attention to figures whose courage attracts publicity should not rule out attention to less publicized acts of courage. In families, in hamlets and neighborhoods, in public meetings, behind the scenes in social movements, all kinds of people act courageously every day. It is these courageous little acts that eventually make big acts possible. Rosa Parks's refusal to change her seat on the bus galvanized a movement, inspiring a vast courageous response from others.

Can Courage Be Taught or Learned?

This question is the corollary to my question of whether leadership can be either taught or learned. The answer I gave then can be explained more completely now.

At the most fundamental level, courage, hence leadership, can be neither taught nor learned—*it is experienced.* It is lived in response to events and the times, quickened as responsible action in the face of experienced inauthenticity. Courage is created out of itself in a spontaneous relational act. We can recognize it, describe it, discern it; we cannot predictably induce it. It is its own generator. Nor is it cumulative. One act of courage does not make the next one easier or more likely, because the nature of the courageous act must evolve as that which calls it forth evolves. A habit of courage ceases to contain courage. Courage lives on a frontier of risk, not in the comfort of the familiar.

What then do my colleagues and I teach in the Reflective Leadership Center if we understand courage as an essential component of leadership? If we cannot address courage directly, how can we deal with it in leadership courses? Using the Action Wheel as a guide, I use seven strategies, not to produce courage, but rather to give opportunities to understand courage and courageous action. Since courage arises in response to the world, at best we can offer situations for that response. As would be expected, people respond in diverse ways.

The first strategy is to engage in a discussion of courage. What do you think it is, how does it work, who have you known who you think is courageous? I introduce Aristotle's perspectives on courage and explore his ideas of counterfeit and real courage. Second, participants are invited to tell stories about their own acts of courage. They become resources to themselves about the nature and dynamics of courage as they have experienced it.

Third, all participants are invited to write out an *exit card.* This device is based on a paradox: we can only stay freely if we can leave. System entrapment, through either rules or false expectations of others and oneself, undermines courage. Participants who feel imprisoned in a system undermine authentic participation. A member of an organization who has accepted the conventional system boundaries as fixed and immovable will not see options for courage even if they present themselves. Courage, by its nature, challenges boundaries to test their resilience and appropriateness. The exit card is not suggested as a way out. It offers the option of saying no so that one can definitively say yes to the system. Rather than undermine commitment to a system, the exit card guarantees authentic commitment.

Fourth, we construct courage boundary experiences. Sometimes they take the form of Outward Bound–type challenges: climbing mountains, going on solo trips for personal reflection, wire walking, or climbing a rock face. Other times they involve challenges that are personalized to meet individual comfort zones. For example, speaking affirmatively for five minutes about oneself can be more threatening for some people than climbing a rock wall. In all these cases, people are presented with opportunities to act first, then reflect on their actions later.

Fifth, I encourage imagining oneself as courageous. Using the techniques of guided imagery and other intuitive devices from visionary leadership, participants are asked to write scenarios about themselves as people of courage. How would they like to be remembered as courageous people after they die? Could they imagine a courageous way to address obstacles that they are currently facing?

Sixth, we explore fear as the deterrent to courage in two ways. First, I show *The Abilene Paradox* (1991), a film based on Jerry Harvey's book *The Abilene Paradox: The Mismanagement of Agreement* (1974), which vividly illustrates what happens when hidden agreements that no one has the courage to challenge take us where no one wants to go. Second, we explore the shadow self using Charles Bates's *Pigs Eat Wolves* (1991), an extremely insightful interpretation of the fairy tale "The Three Little Pigs." The wolf, who the little pigs are taught to fear by the mother pig, must eventually become their teacher and partner as they develop into mature characters. As participants understand their own "mother pig" messages of good and evil, then journey with the little pigs as they seek wisdom, they are challenged to face their own fears not as something outside of themselves, but as fears within themselves. They are then invited to name, acknowledge, and own their own fears rather than project them onto others. Of all the exercises I offer, this one is the most profound. Most people do not take the time to think of their fears, or when they do, they do not see them as their teachers.

Finally, throughout these exercises of discovery I structure occasions for participants to confront their own inauthenticity in the midst of their deeper authenticity. I endeavor to create the twin conditions for leadership: a deep, disquieting sense of self and world juxtaposed with a better and believable future. Does all of this activity induce courage? Sometimes. But that is not the ultimate goal. Rather, we are preparing people for leadership. If it happens in our midst, so much the better.

Racism—A Case in Point

As I review what I and others were doing to combat racism during the 1970s (see Chapter Eight), the primary task seemed to be to get whites to accept the fact of white racism. The task was not to explain why there was white racism, or racism on the part of any dominant color group, for that matter. Rather it was to push whites to take responsibility for white racism. Those early efforts persist today. Yet the more I wrestle with racism, the more I believe that the primary task is understanding what is really going on. Even after racism is accepted as real, and owned by whites as well as everyone else, we still have not identified racism's cause and the reason for its persistence.

If we accepted that we knew what racism was, we could fix it. If we accepted that we knew how to manage it, we could manage it. It is because we have not accepted that we know both problem and solution that racism and discrimination of all kinds are our contemporary leadership challenges. I have already discussed some of the popular explanations for racism's persistence. People practice racism because they believe they are superior, they believe in skill differentials, they believe others have been poorly socialized, they believe they must oppress and exploit to maintain their status, or they are ethnocentric. But there is another explanation that encompasses all these, one that requires us to take the shadow self that is in the background of our lives and bring it to the foreground.

In the exigencies of daily living, the primordial fear resides as background noise, present but garbled. Often, we can shut it out. Occasionally, however, some event reveals an underlying truth. We open ourselves to authenticity's prodding, and we experience primordial fear surfacing in all its viciousness. The background bursts into the foreground. One such event was the now infamous "Willie

Horton" television advertisement used in George Bush's successful presidential campaign. The ad, claiming that presidential candidate Michael Dukakis was soft on crime, described how a black male committed a rape when he was released on parole. While the episode described was literally true, it was widely believed that the ad's effect was based on its appeal to the primordial fear of the other, who is perceived to threaten white reality. The ad allowed whites to seize upon Horton as a scapegoat and to feel unity in their opposition to his color, his violence, his sexual crime. The ad triggered a flash point—Us versus Them—and the vivid fear and expulsion of fear that accompanies the sacrificed scapegoat was rehearsed one more time. In some ways the ad was a gift. Not often does such a clear window open on the deeper realities of life. We were able to witness the shadow at work. And what did we see? Imitation. Whites saw one of their potentials mirrored in Horton. They tasted the primordial fear, the originator of violence.

Winthrop Jordan (1968) offered a similar analysis of racism during a speech in which he argued that racial conflicts were crystallized by the old saying, "If you've got the money, honey, I've got the time." Time, sex, and money divide blacks and whites. Whites fear that blacks spend all three, yet white-controlled society rewards such spending. Even though that society *says* to save time, sex, and money, it is *organized* to exploit all three. Therefore, in blacks, whites can see themselves and then deny what they see, claiming it as the other. The United States is one of the most violent countries of the industrialized world, if not the most violent. We have more prisoners in jails than South Africa. Our murder rate is outrageous. And the majority whites have a scapegoat—people of color. And, so, whites live out an unjustifiable fear.

Yet there is hope. Racism is not destiny. The vicious cycle of fear can be broken. But only by leading toward the fear, admitting the fear, and taking responsibility for the fear is profound hope possible. The We that embraces us all can be discovered if the monster of racism that divides Us from Them is courageously and faithfully acknowledged, embraced, and transcended. Girard is right—there are no pure heroes and no pure villains. Once loosed, primordial fear rips through all communities, all countries, all selves.

The Commons

Leadership occurs in the commons, safe places in which leadership faces fear and discerns the common good. A common place may be as small as a face-to-face dialogue or as large as the globe, but through it, leadership steps into the world of public scrutiny. Even the prophet who has few, if any, followers requires shared space. Shared space, however, is not initially value free or safe. It is the ethics of authenticity that transforms a common space into a common good, creating safe places for action.

In the commons, leadership presses for convergence amid great diversity, searching for bonds that protect and enhance the very diversity that threatens the possibility of the commons. In the commons, pluralism endures and thrives. Courage challenges the fear of diversity that can destroy the commons; thus, leadership offers hope that in our commons we can discover and live toward the common good.

The commons and their implied common goods can be defined through the generic features of action and the accompanying metaphors.

Dwelling Commons: Shared Physical Spaces

These commons include such diverse places as the Boston commons, game sanctuaries, foreign embassies, religious buildings or sacred shrines, and many general gathering places. They also include international commons: outer space, Antarctica, and much of the world's oceans. These are geographic commons, the physical homes of authentic action. At their most expansive, they include the global commons and the universal commons. Geographic commons are both ecologically and ecumenically real and push for their own security and survival. Without shared physical space, diversity practices genocide; the world falls prey to annihilation and violence.

Market Commons: Shared Exchange Spaces

Any places where two people, organizations, or nations exchange goods or services constitute exchange, or market, commons. To

258 Authentic Leadership: Courage in Action

work, exchange commons have to be free of restraint and open to accurate information flow. Contracts made here are rightfully expected to be kept. The common good extends beyond survival to maximization of choice. Each entity must be free to decide its own individual future, without hindrance from others, while simultaneously guaranteeing the freedom of others to do likewise. The summation of choices declares a society's practice of this common good.

Community Commons: Shared Bonding Spaces

These are sociological spaces, where trades and bargains are nurtured by a deep commitment to cooperative community development. Repairs of the material excesses of market exchanges occur in these community spaces. Sustainability replaces summation of choices as the definition of the common good. If changes threaten the sustainability of a family, community, or the globe itself, those claiming bonding space will take appropriate action. Sustainability is self-renewing and self-generating. Interdependence within these commons develops bonds among people that make them parts of the larger whole.

Political Commons: Shared Interest Spaces

Disparate groups unite to accomplish shared interest in these political commons. Conflict among interests drives the process. If appeals to sustainability smother legitimate interests, sustainability becomes inauthentic. The common good in these commons is collective self-determination. Claiming opportunities, even creating them, marks these political commons.

Idea Commons: Shared Vision Spaces

Dreams and hopes shared and acted upon characterize vision spaces. Physical place recedes in importance. Shared views cross arbitrary boundaries of place and politics. Science, art, and religion intersect and overlap as journeys blend. The common good in these idea commons is the enhancement of the world with transformed interests that point toward a new unity.

Art Commons: Shared Creativity Spaces

Boundaries of physical space fall away when art commons are constructed. Reflection surrounds these art commons, probing, inquiring, and asking previously unasked questions. The common good is synergy. Playful explorations, new connections, and fresh insights mark life in shared creative spaces.

Leadership endures and thrives in the six commons as a common good comes alive in each. When leadership acts upon the common goods of survival, summation, sustainability, self-determination, shared vision, and synergy, they point toward hope.

Summary

We exist between fear and hope. We may fear for our existence, material success, social roles, power, mission, or meaning. If our fear becomes overwhelming, we will build barriers that prevent us from having to face the fear but that also cut us off from authenticity. We then become what we feared to become.

We have an even deeper fear, which is the fear of our own violence. We buy apparent freedom from that internal violence by committing external violence, projecting the object of our fear onto others.

To face our fears, we need, at the least, courage. Courage helps us acknowledge, embrace, and transform our fear into authentic action. Leaders at all levels of society can possess this courage. It is formed in the commons, the shared spaces in which we come together and work for a common good. In these spaces we are open to courage's voice.

I have defined six of these commons, but there is one more, which helps us find more than courage. This seventh common space is the spiritual commons. In this commons, spirituality and authenticity address our primordial fear, revealing that violence no longer need prevail. For those living in authenticity, primordial violence can be and is being transformed by the spirit. Scapegoats are not necessary. The final chapter addresses the issue of leadership, spirituality, and hope.

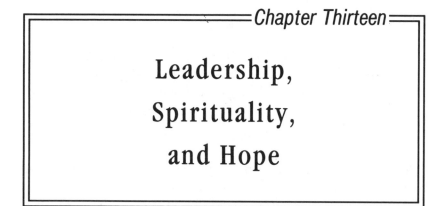

Chapter Thirteen

Leadership,
Spirituality,
and Hope

Leadership brings no answer to the table. It does come with questions and a disturbing sense of unease. Leadership is triggered by an unnerving experience of disconnection and inauthenticity. Leadership uses all its framing tools yet still faces the dilemma of action. It confronts an abyss of unknown consequences and obligations in any action it does take. The ripple effects of action are so vast and complex that no computer or cost-benefit analysis can totally analyze them. Duties often conflict; ethical choices are usually not made between right and wrong or good and bad but between conflicting rights and goods. Yet in spite of these daunting realities, leadership lays claim to its responsibility. It must act, and something must undergird that action.

"From whence cometh our help?" asks the Psalmist. That question is usually reserved for the most private moments of personal struggle. Yet today, this very personal question is often raised in secular public places. Private doubts and worries are entering public discourse outside the bounds of traditional religions. Matters of the spirit and issues of authentic power and character are breaking the confines of their normal channels.

In conducting seminars for business, health care, and government groups, I have found that when I open the question of deep faith there is great desire to discuss this intimate issue. Indeed, Gary Zukav (1989) articulates the need to get to the heart of the matter by connecting a deep, transcendent authenticity to action. He contends that "each of us is now being drawn, in one way or another, to that same great vision. It is more than a vision, it is an emerging force. It is the next step in our evolutionary journey. Humanity, the human species, is longing now to touch that force, . . . which longs to transcend religiosity and spirituality and assume the position of authentic power" (p. 13). M. Scott Peck (1988), who has traversed this territory of the human spirit, has helped many people deepen their engagement with life.

Consultant Peter Vaill (1991) believes it a "scandal" that fear, courage, and hope and other issues of spirituality are not discussed more as part of businesspeople's education. "I am genuinely embarrassed for myself and my colleagues," he says, "that we should, by and large, be leaving these deep questions of executive character unaddressed all the while calling for vision, vitality, and spirit in western organizations" (pp. 3–4). Vaill focuses on the question of character, rather than on ethical principles, vision, or empowerment. Implicit in his analysis is a sense of authenticity as concrete, lived reality rather than as an abstract vision. To restrain leaders from employing leadership tools as manipulative devices, leadership must be rooted in authentic being. Being undergirds doing.

The current discussion of spirituality as an issue for business does not seem to be propelled by concerns of personal faith traditions or past faith. It seems rather to be aroused by the pervasive problem of disconnection. Vaill has a similar view. He does not feel that "spiritual emptiness" is the problem. Instead, there is a "problem of a *disconnect* between what the executive is feeling and what kind of a person the organization apparently needs as a leader and what kind of a contribution that person needs to make. We have so thoroughly technicalized and intellectualized the job of organizational leader that there is no place for the real passions and pains that men and women in these jobs feel" [emphasis added]. Vaill recalls Carl Rogers's concern over "incongruence." According to Vaill, Rogers looked at the "degree of match/mismatch between three things: A person's total experience of a situation, the parts of it which are allowed into awareness, and what is actually overtly communicated to others." Vaill thinks "we are possibly in a situation where the real feelings top managers have about themselves, their organizations, and their stakeholders are being systematically suppressed and distorted and ignored in favor of maintaining a front called 'executive'" (pp. 8–10).

I believe that what Vaill rightly identifies as the experience of disconnection also lies behind the popularity of Rabbi Kushner's account of bad things happening to good people. Kushner's work struck a public nerve as he described the private struggles of many people plagued by injustice, betrayal, and deception. Just as bad things happen to good people, good intentions sometimes produce bad results, and bad intentions sometimes produce good results. Loyalty to one person can mean betrayal to another. Novelist John le Carré uses the spy genre to confront similar moral dilemmas with insight and empathy.

These ultimate concerns about life and destiny necessitate a new connection between spirituality and leadership, a connection that can respond to our disconnection. To make this connection and build a comprehensive leadership perspective, I must go beyond meaning and ethics into the question of hope.

Authentic Spirituality

Authentic spirituality can be viewed from a diversity of perspectives. Some are profound; some are hawked by charlatans and exploiters. We have seen how both Zukav and Vaill are themselves nervous about the notion of spirituality. Once again, the features of action and their metaphors can be used to distinguish six perspectives of spirituality. Each has an authentic view of spirituality, yet each is also open to distortion and inauthenticity. Because I know the most about Christianity, most of my examples come from that tradition. However, I believe the principles expressed here are generalizable to other spiritual traditions. It is my intention to be inclusive, not exclusive.

Spirituality: Fundamental Traditionalist

At its most authentic, this perspective is legitimated by a sacred text and embodies historically tested wisdom. For example, Oswald Sanders (1980) distinguishes between "natural leadership" and "spiritual leadership."

Natural	*Spiritual*
Self-confident	Confident in God
Knows men	Also knows god
Makes own decisions	Seeks to find God's will
Ambitious	Self-effacing
Originates own methods	Finds and follows God's methods
Enjoys commanding others	Delights to obey God
Motivated by personal considerations	Motivated by love for God and man
Independent	God-dependent [p. 13]

Sanders supports his spiritual view of leadership with insights from the Bible. Thus, questions raised by leadership find answers in scripture.

At its most inauthentic, this tradition of fundamental spirituality excludes others and controls outcomes. Zealots take over, authoritarianism and absolutism overcome scriptural authority, and the gift of leadership turns into a nonreflective supremacy of belief. Rather than opening the door to a profound dialogue, this inauthentic view slams shut the door of inquiry.

Spirituality: Refreshment of the Spirit

I believe that Billy Graham's ministry embodies an example of this view of spirituality in its authentic form. The Holy Spirit, entering an individual's life, refreshes and renews the spirit. This spiritual resource quickens life, saves the soul, and offers new possibilities for eternal life. Leadership lives through the spirit, drinks of the holy waters of hope, and frees the captives, says this view.

At its most inauthentic, this view equates the offerings of the Holy Spirit with material success, exploiting the fear of failure and advocating a radical individualism at the expense of a community of believers. It offers pseudo-hope, reducing faith to consumerism and marketing spirituality as a commodity.

Spirituality: A Sense of Community

From this perspective, selves are social, and spirituality is communal. In earlier Catholic thought, community was a basic principle upon which natural law rested. In many mainstream Christian denominations with temporal positional leaders, the concept of the church and its members as the body of Christ encourages the faithful to live within the community structures, accept community norms and values, and participate in a healing, health-giving community of believers. Leadership, therefore, is expertise that administers to the community's spiritual needs.

At its most authentic, this spirituality encourages and heals the outcast as he or she becomes part of a vital, healthy, functional body. At its most inauthentic, the communal body exists in a straightjacket of conformity, expects lockstep obedience, resists political pressure for the inclusion of the oppressed, thwarts creativity, resists new thought, and ossifies a flexible organization into a rigid skeleton of formal beliefs, rules and regulations, and norms of social conduct.

Spirituality: Liberation

Struggles for liberation test and ground this perspective of spirituality. Earlier, I described Latin American liberation theology, which "does not start with existing theologies but with the real and concrete totality of what is taking place. It starts with 'praxis'—with passionate and committed involvement with the struggle for liberation. It is a dialectical reflection: reflecting on practice in the light of faith and on faith in the light of practice. Theology is therefore the 'second movement,' after involvement. Moreover, this involvement has a clear bias: the perspective of the poor and oppressed" (Lebacqz, 1986, p. 101). Authentic liberation spirituality requires action on behalf of and with the oppressed. To be faithful is to be engaged, to do justice for our neighbor. Love and justice unite in liberating action that mediates God's action in the world.

Some of the literature on women's spirituality reflects a similar call to liberation from male domination. As Sandra Schneiders (1986) puts it, the feminist movement "has established the fact that Western society, including the Christian church, is male dominated. Some are convinced that this state of affairs corresponds to the divine plan of God. Others, both men and women, are convinced that the God of Judeo-Christian revelation calls us to liberate ourselves and one another from what can only be called the shackles of sexism, as we are to liberate ourselves from racism, anti-Semitism, and every other form of human oppression" (p. 31).

At its most authentic, liberation leadership empowers the downs themselves, helping them release themselves from years of collective bondage. Leadership participates in and rejoices in the moments of liberation.

At their most inauthentic, liberation perspectives mask a deep contradiction by continually limiting options to an up versus down perspective. Owing to this limited framing, downs are defined only through their power relationship with ups. All too often, "liberated" downs repeat and mimic the world of the ups they have replaced.

Spirituality: The Path

Spirituality from this perspective invites us to travel with God or the spirit, exploring places that we might not go otherwise. A prime example of this spiritual orientation is Hagberg and Guelich's developmental model (1989) that identifies six stages of spiritual growth: the recognition of God, the life of discipleship, the productive life, the journey inward, the journey outward, and the life of love (p. 7). For these two authors, spirituality describes the way in which we live out our response to God. We have faith when we let God direct our lives, and the process of a life journey is as important as its destination (p. 17). Leadership guides the process—mentors, coaches, and suggests a direction. Spiritual gurus, who have passed much of their own journeys, question the neophyte, encouraging, supporting, challenging, and inviting the adventurer into deeper insight and wisdom.

At its most authentic, a spiritual-path orientation invites side-by-side journeys and values multiple paths toward the same destination. At its most inauthentic, it undermines the need for critical thought about the value of the differences with other people whose journeys might be a bad trip.

Spirituality: The Ultimate Answer

The search for an ultimate understanding of the meaning of life characterizes this extremely common view of spirituality. When Robert Coles (1990) investigated the spiritual life of children, he sought to discover how a child makes spiritual sense. For him, this meant discovering how different children answered such questions as, Why, ultimately, does the world behave as it does? What is the meaning of events? Who are we on this earth? And does the way we answer that question make a difference in our daily lives? Robert Bly (1990) takes a similar tack when he proposes that men explore "the wild man," who can reconnect them to the earth (p. 249).

At its most authentic, this perspective offers profound insight into the ways we find meaning for ourselves when faced with questions for which no answer is possible. At its most inauthentic, it offers simple, palpable answers in place of the paradoxical and contradictory pain-filled realities of everyday living. These simplified answers flatten the spiritual landscape, hiding its heights and chasms, hope and despair, and all the ever-present dangers of a world that resists comprehensive clarity.

Spirituality: A Seventh View

The six ways in which spirituality and leadership exist outside the bounds of personal life or traditional religious traditions suggest a typology of authentic and inauthentic expressions of spirituality. The task that remains is to define authentic spirituality as it can be understood when leadership itself is spiritual. I have drawn on other writers, who have traveled further down this road than I have, to initiate the inquiry. Of particular interest for leadership studies is Welwood's analysis of genuine and counterfeit spiritual authority (1987). The characteristics of counterfeit authority are that the leader has total power to validate or negate the self-worth of the devotees and uses this power extensively, the group is held together by allegiance to a cause and an ideology, the leader keeps his or her followers in line by manipulating emotions of hope and fear, group thinking is used to knit followers together, and cult leaders are often self-styled prophets who have not studied with great teachers or undergone lengthy training or discipline themselves (pp. 285-290).

Welwood suggests that we can recognize a trustworthy teacher by distinguishing between egocentricity and being. The egocentric teacher is concerned with maintaining appearances, maintaining and validating a self-image, focusing on "I-ness" and playing to followers' sense of insecurity and inadequacy. In contrast, a teacher focused on being has a concern for discovering the truth, appreciates the world independently of its affirmation or negation of self-images, expands outward toward life, and has a basic sense of wholeness, well-being, aliveness, and intelligence (p. 291). Welwood observes that it is difficult to recognize an authentic spiritual teacher or leader because "conventional logic and reason often serve to support the ego centered approach to life," and the "logic of undermining exclusive identification with ego often appears quite scandalous to reason." Welwood quotes Kierkegaard's paradox, "the self must be broken in order to become a self," and Goethe's parallel expression of this "scandalous logic":

> I praised what is truly alive,
> What longs to be burned to death. . . .
> And so long as you haven't experienced
> This: to die and so to grow,
> You are only a troubled guest
> On the dark earth [p. 292].

Moreover, we must attend to subtle ambiguities if we are to recognize a true spiritual master, because both "the counterfeit and genuine master undermine the habitual patterns of self. Yet one does this in a way that creates bondage, while the other does it in a way that promotes liberation" (p. 292).

Welwood suggests that the most important standards for recognizing spiritual teachers are these:

> They [will] wake their students up from self-preoccupation to experience their larger, universal being. . . . They will have a deep respect for human dignity, rather than appealing to personal inadequacies and insecurities. . . . They will be willing to share the source of their authority and wisdom with students, so that their relationship will be based on real experiential understanding rather than on ideology or belief. They will allow tolerance for ambiguity and paradox, rather than insisting on absolute certitude in the "One and Only Truth." Their concern will be directed toward all people, rather than elevating a group of followers to a privileged status above their fellow humans. They will not manipulate the emotions of their students, but will appeal to their natural intelligence. They will encourage people on the path of self-knowledge through example, rather than mainly through promises of future salvation and reward. Instead of encouraging herd behavior, they will recognize the importance of people's time alone with themselves to discover what is true in a fresh and alive way. And they will themselves have undergone extensive training and practice [pp. 297–298].

Genuine teachers often focus outwardly rather than inwardly, stressing the effects of their teaching rather than the character of the teacher. The Buddha was reported to have said that worthy teaching is recognized if it helps to "reduce the three poisons of greed, hatred, and delusions in one's own life" (p. 299).

The call to authenticity is not a call to perfection; it is a call to recognize and address our counterfeit selves. Much good comes from the wounded leader, the one who acknowledges the personal and cultural shadows and seeks to embrace them. For Christians,

Jesus is the fully authentic person, the embodiment of full humanity and full spirituality in one being. The deeply faithful derive
great solace and hope from the belief and experience that sinful
selves and sinful societies are redeemable because authenticity is
possible in spite, or even because, of sin.

In contrast, some Buddhists take a different view. Welwood
reports that the great Buddhist sage Vimalakirti, to whom many
bodhisattvas came for teachings, was always sick, and when asked
about this, said: "I'm sick because all beings are sick." Writes Welwood, "In the archetype of the wounded healer, the healer can help
others only because of directly experiencing the nature of sickness
in himself or herself" (p. 299). I have drawn heavily on Welwood's
work in part because of its insightfulness, but more importantly
because it draws on different spiritual traditions than those with
which I am deeply familiar. In connecting spirituality to leadership, these criteria are crucial if the connection itself can withstand
the scrutiny of all the preceding work on authenticity.

I believe I have now assembled the criteria to judge an authentic spiritual approach. The task that remains is to link authentic action to spiritual leadership. The conclusions I come to are
rooted in my own personal exploration. Nevertheless, I believe that
the insights go beyond my personal experience.

Spirituality and Leadership

I sometimes think I was born a skeptic. I entered seminary to find
the answers to deep questions and emerged four years later with
deeper questions. Never would I have guessed that I would be concluding a volume on leadership with a discussion of spirituality.
Yet, here I am, engaged in a quest for language and experience that
will finally make sense to me. I know that the idea of joining spirituality and leadership raises a puzzle for some people. There are
those who believe the possession of ethical principles is a necessary
and sufficient condition for action. They do not need a larger horizon of meaning or spirituality to sustain, support, and critique
ethics (see Pritchard, 1991, pp. 225 ff). And there are the secularists,
who find that embracing a seventh view of leadership that requires
a spiritual foundation forces them into an inauthentic predicament.

They are expected to authentically believe what they authentically believe is untrue. If secularists do not believe in spirituality or God, then asking them to become spiritual to exhibit leadership violates their deepest sense of who they are and the way they think the world works.

My response to this challenge may not satisfy the secularists, but it is the best I can do. Since matters of faith are proposed, not imposed, and since they are not logically compelling, we dialogue about these matters. What I may see as a spiritual connection, you may not. Thus, what we do is bring mutual respect to the inquiry and explore with each other what we have in common and learn to live with the differences. I do not want to be perceived as intellectually coercing a connection between spirituality and leadership. However, I do need to share my insights as they have emerged in order to start the dialogue. Thus, my spiritual connections are rooted in faith and are confessional. They are not intended to exclude anyone, but to include everyone in a deeper, more expansive dialogue.

For me, the door into new meaning opened a crack when I understood authenticity metaphorically as the ever-present partner of all human action. The door opened totally when I understood that *God was authenticity. God was the ever-present partner of all action.* At that moment of insight, bold images from my past flooded into my mind, and connections clicked with overwhelming speed. God is many; God is one. God is many centers of authenticity, unified in a deeper authenticity, all at the same time. God is the bumping of self and world producing knowledge; God is the trigger of courage, provoking authentic action. Gift, choice, law, liberation, adventure, and creativity are in God and in us. Leadership is, finally, a spiritual pacing, embodying authenticity, embodying God. God as authenticity is at the center of the Action Wheel; God is also the horizon surrounding the Action Wheel.

Theological ideas long discarded returned to inform me. I saw clearly the difference between surrender and submission. The phrase "conforming to the image of God" flashed before me with new clarity of meaning, and I envisioned myself in partnership with God, with authenticity, admitting the inauthentic and embracing it in faith-filled action. I remember sensing being touched by action's ever-present partner calling me to be authentic. "Be perfect," the partner seemed to be saying. "Be authentic all the time, everywhere." What a terrible burden! First of all, I knew I was not authentic all the time. Second, I did not want to be authentic all the time. As a friend of mine says, "Sometimes, I just want some slosh time, some nonaccountable, nonresponsible slosh time." Yet the call persisted: "Be authentic." There seemed no escape.

And then, I remembered what it was like to taste authenticity. To get out of bed after two weeks when I came to terms with my racism. To participate in struggles of justice. To experience the challenge and forgiveness of a friend. I remembered the empowerment that flowed from clarity, the strength that flowed from admitting and moving beyond shortcomings, and the release of integrity that flowed from knowing myself and the world more profoundly. I recalled the gifts of friends and the confrontations of enemies that triggered fresh insight and spurred new action. I experienced authenticity as both judge and liberator.

Then came the transforming insight. I was not expected to be *perfect*. Organizations and communities and nations were not expected to be perfect. We are expected to be true and real. Being authentic meant admitting that I was not fully authentic. Claiming full authenticity would be a lie. Instead, I and all others are called to recognize, admit, and own the inauthentic in ourselves and the world, embrace it and transform it. Yes, we are to be ethical. Yet rational ethics does not motivate me in a profound way. My soul's engagement with the world is not captured only by rationality. Ethics does not probe the primordial nature of fear or encourage me to form partnerships and eventually embrace my "dark" side (Bates, 1991).

Earlier, I talked about Girard's ideas as viewed by Schwager (1978). When Schwager applies these ideas to the Bible, he refocuses three thousand years of traditional Jewish and Christian teachings. The God of the Old Testament is not a God of violence and retaliation; Jesus' sacrifice is not an act of appeasement of the Creator; and the suffering and death of an innocent victim is not a compensation for an offense against God. Instead, Jesus as the "necessary scapegoat" rejects all aggression and thus seeks to end the cycle of human violence. In other words, *unless we come to terms with our fundamental understanding of human nature and the processes of reality, we are not free to lead in the most profound sense.* As I wrestled with these ideas, it became apparent to me that if leadership is to build a world that is hope filled and vital, leadership must believe in the actual possibility of a nonviolent world. If leadership does not plumb to the depth of the human condition, it has not gotten to the core of human hope. Schwager (1978) says it well:

> When the word of revelation reveals the chasm in the heart, the scapegoat mechanism loses its effectiveness. It ceases to protect human beings from themselves and no longer creates oases of relative peace. The uncovering of their deep seated desire to kill forces men and women to a decision: to mutually destroy each other, or to look for a new, outside source to give them the capacity for true understanding . . . but the message of God's action does not excuse human beings from making their own efforts. . . . Rather, God's action calls them in a profound manner to their own responsibilities. God's action is meant to spur humans on to new deeds of their own [p. 167].

Schwager revealed a path to great discovery. I also remember the help I received from Joseph Campbell's work. For years, I believed that theology and philosophy and spirituality sought to answer ultimate questions: Why do the righteous suffer? Why do the innocent die? Campbell taught me that myths do not answer the question why. They invite us to engage fully in life *without answers.* Spirituality thrusts us back into life with all its hurts, paradoxes, and evils. It calls us to authentic living.

Leadership, in the spiritual view, does not expect roses; it lives with thorns. Yet it is hope filled. Authenticity is principle and experience, universal and particular, abstract and concrete, the one and the many, the true and the real, *sui generis,* and always connected.

Authenticity calls both leaders and followers to address what is real, to dream for a new, more humane future, and to embody the true and real in ourselves as we engage others. It is the *presence* of authenticity that transforms inauthenticity into authenticity. When we are rootless, authenticity offers historical grounding; when we are trapped, authenticity offers freedom; when we are unjustly treated, authenticity offers justice; when we are oppressed, authenticity offers empowerment; when we are apathetic, authenticity offers love; when we abdicate, authenticity identifies our responsibility.

Authenticity stands over against us as challenge and critique; it stands with and within us as support and possibility. Authenticity is hope filled for a very simple reason. For authenticity to be authentic it has to be embodied. That embodiment is implicit in all our relationships. It is potential and actual. It is in us and in our neighbor. And embodiment comes in surprising ways with surprising results from surprising places at surprising times. Leadership attends to and responds to the surprises as it opens itself to hidden opportunities for authentic engagement. Hope is rooted in others and ourselves because authenticity moves in and among us. Where have all the leaders gone? They are in our own midst in the millions of little acts of courage. Authenticity arouses us to face our fears and take responsibility for the true and the real in ourselves and the world.

Leadership is not a means to another end. It is not instrumental. Leadership is the action itself, and it is in the action that the many become one. It becomes essential to our character and the character of our organizations, communities, and society. We do not have to agree before we can act together. We do not have to find theoretical unity before we can join together in practical wisdom. Thus, leadership expresses being and becoming at the same time. Authenticity chooses both the means to our action and the end of our action, and in the embodiment of the action, we become what we were meant to be.

Whether we act from the deep resources of our spirit or from being grasped by external events, the joy that comes from total engagement is its own confirmation of validity. Leadership is a gift, to be unwrapped and treasured; leadership is choice, to be claimed; leadership is part of a web of interdependent actions, to be made functionally whole; leadership is participation, to be energized; leadership is adventure, to be embraced; leadership is creativity and innovation, to be playful. Leadership is total engagement offered for the well-being of the earth and all its inhabitants. For what does it profit us, says scripture, if we gain the world and lose our own souls? For what does it profit us, says authentic action, if we gain our souls and lose the world?

These are truly times to try our souls. We do indeed have miles to go before we sleep. These are also times that inspire our souls. The world becomes us. We can meet the call and make the difference expected of us as partners of the universe. The common ground in our hope is our action together, asking the difficult questions, searching for the fitting responses.

In our questioning and searching for existence, resources, structure, power, mission, meaning, and spirituality, authenticity is our partner. It is for authenticity that our actions are justified. It is toward authenticity that our actions take direction. It is by authenticity that our energy is impelled. It is through authenticity that our plans and programs are cradled and developed. It is with authenticity that our ideas and goods are selected, and it is from authenticity that our past is claimed and revisited. Finally, as we seek spirituality, it is into authenticity that our action is offered and entrusted. Through us, authenticity lives and moves and discovers its being.

Leadership lives at the intersection of the authentic and the inauthentic, tilting the world toward the authentic. Leadership is always mindful that, as we call forth authenticity, we can never forget that the conflicts and ambiguities of action reside not just in the world but also within ourselves. No one arrives with pure motives or unambiguous interests. The struggles for authenticity are within and without—the ultimate congruence of our actions is unknown. Good intentions can lead to unintended suffering. Bad intentions, at times, can produce unexpected good results. Faith in authenticity must undergird our actions. To be faithful, we must believe that any authentic act, no matter how small or seemingly insignificant, is upheld by the universe as worthy and honorable. Leadership is spiritually grounded. To lose this hope and this faith is to despair and to fall into cynicism. Leadership is indeed a noble calling worthy of our most profound commitment. For what we do, in the final analysis, rests solely on our faith that our actions in our families, communities, associations, institutions, and the world contribute to the well-being of all those we touch and serve.

The courage to remain engaged without answers drinks and

is refreshed at the wellspring of hope. For without hope, we will indeed perish in the drought of expediency, opportunism, and ignorance. Leadership is not induced heroics. Rather, it is the constant invitation to all of us to stay the course, to take the next steps on the journey, to create the future, to recognize and admit our own foibles and shortcomings. It is to take responsibility for ourselves in concert with others, seeking to create and build a global commonwealth worthy of the best that we as human beings have to offer. Anything less is not worthy of the effort. That is why leadership, at its heart, embodies authentic action.

I began this inquiry by recognizing the enigma of leadership and the diversity of leadership perspectives. I concluded by examining fear, courage, and spirituality grounded in authenticity. As leadership embodies authentic action, it breaks the terrible cycle of fear imitating fear. It opens onto a world of promise and possibility.

As we all must when investigating any part of life, I began with the diversity that confronts us at every turn in leadership studies and practice. My approach has been to let diverse voices speak and diverse behaviors express themselves, bump, and pace in a journey to find the one view of leadership among the many, while still acknowledging the many. I have sought to find unity without uniformity.

Someone will say, "I lead"; others, "We lead"; still others, "They did it through us." No matter which way we frame leadership, as we participate in it, we can all live and embody the truth into which authenticity invites us.

PART FIVE

RESOURCES
FOR LEADERS

Conflict Management

Strategies

The Action Wheel is leadership's primary tool for framing conflict. However, existing strategies for dealing with conflict can be used in conjunction with the model, as long as these existing strategies share the Action Wheel's goal of helping people to stand side by side in relationships of equality. In this resource, I present several of these helpful strategies.

Current thinking about conflict deemphasizes conflict resolution and focuses instead largely on conflict utilization. This trend is based on the observation that, while some conflicts are resolved, many important ones seem to persist. However, they can be managed and important and laudatory ends can be reached through that management.

Note. Much of the material in this resource is based on the work of Thomas Fiutak, Associate Director at the Center for Conflict and Change at the University of Minnesota. Although independently developed, his work dovetails almost completely with the authentic action framework. A number of points are drawn from Fiutak's conflict management seminar,

In addition, instead of seeking for a form of conflict therapy in which one party attempts to "fix" the other and make the other fit into some predetermined system, the current approach draws heavily on journey imagery. Leadership theorists are asking how we can create and build side-by-side partnerships, in which each partner can still claim his or her authentic interests. Two books that propose strategies that assist parties in disputes to look for overlapping interests and build mutual respect are Fisher and Brown (1988) and Fisher and Ury (1983).

A Model for Addressing Conflict Issues and Processes

Leadership's wrestling with conflict has two important procedural goals. The conflict must be dealt with rigorously. And the relationship of the involved parties must be maintained and enhanced while addressing the conflict. In other words, it is not enough to deal authentically with the substantive issue, we also must deal authentically with the *process* of addressing that issue.

One tool for dealing with both process and issue is Thomas Fiutak's model for achieving what he calls *true peace* and I would call authentic peace (Figure A.1.) On Fiutak's matrix, true peace is not the absence of conflict. It is a condition in which individual or group behavior and the environment exhibit relatively little conflict. However, if individual behavior is highly conflicted even though the environmental stimulus is low, so that the response distorts what we would expect from a given set of conditions, then a *false conflict* exists. Conversely, if the environment is fraught with

---

which was conducted in July 1990, 1991, and 1992 as part of the Legislative Staff Management Institute held at the Hubert H. Humphrey Institute, University of Minnesota. The discussion of true peace comes from "Employee Rights: A Social Constructionist and Political Economic Perspective," a paper by Walter R. Nord, professor at the Washington University School of Business, St. Louis. Nord's paper was delivered in June 1989 at the Conference on Organization Conflict coordinated by the Conflict and Change Center of the University of Minnesota. The Matrix for Diagnosing Peace and Conflict (Figure B.1) is Fiutak's adaptation of the grid proposed by Nord.

Figure A.1. Matrix for Diagnosing Peace and Conflict.

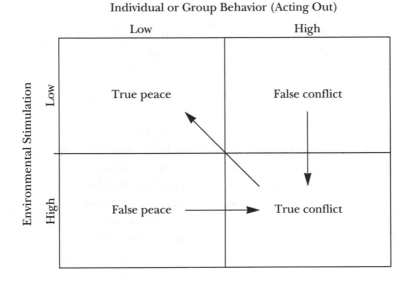

Individual or Group Behavior (Acting Out)

disputes, but those disputes are smoothed over, then a *false peace* exists.

Authentic action strives to move false conflict and false peace into *true conflict*. We cannot get to true peace from false peace or from false conflict without going through true conflict. We must create an authentic forum in which to deal with the conflict *and* to enhance the relationship. This may mean breaking one relationship, as in a divorce, in order to establish a new one.

Fiutak's work suggests that disputants believe their interests have been met when the substantive issue at stake is publicly acknowledged, the procedure to address the conflict is perceived as fair, and psychological satisfaction is felt.

Six Objectives in Conflict Management

Authentic action seeks an authentic peace, in which all parties' interests are acknowledged. Conflict resolution is marked by differ-

ent objectives. Fiutak outlines and contrasts the objectives of conflict resolution and of conflict management and utilization.

Conflict Resolution (Win/Lose)	*Conflict Management and Utilization* (Gain/Gain)
Conflict is to be resolved; it is the absence of peace.	Conflict can be utilized; managed conflict ensures peace.
Conflict is a negative aberration to be fixed/reduced/eliminated.	Conflict is a natural consequence of human interaction with both positive and negative consequences.
Resolution comes through rules. There is a right answer.	Management comes through a process that leads to multiple options.
Resolution comes through precedent and consistency.	Present and future expectations have more weight than past history.
Conflict is defined in terms of adversaries' positions.	Conflict is defined in terms of the parties' interests.
Goal is to resolve conflict primarily over the substantive issues.	Goal is to manage the conflict over issues *and* to maintain or enhance the relationship. Importance of psychological and procedural interests is recognized.

Fiutak rejects *win/win* terminology, which for years has
been the popular hallmark of successful negotiating. (For example,
see Cohen, 1980.) He prefers the term *gain/gain*. Gain/gain results

not from compromise, but from what Fiutak calls *copromotion*. In copromotion, the parties transcend the dispute. They invent new possibilities as their relationship embarks on a journey that opens them to creativity. In other words, the ongoing purpose of their journey is to live life as art, with no necessary end to either journey or art. When substance is acknowledged, procedure is fair, and psychological satisfaction is present, the ground is prepared for an expansion beyond the terms of the conflict.

Those who fear conflict will find leadership a burdensome, threatening task. However, those who see opportunity in threat will take heart at the new thinking in conflict management and utilization. Conflicts open the promise of opportunity. To utilize conflict through these tools and the Action Wheel is to mount a quest for enduring peace.

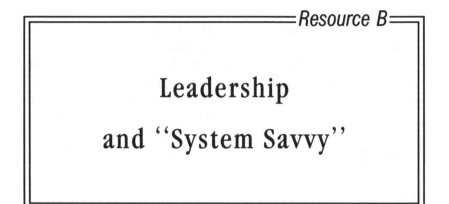

===================Resource B===

Leadership
and "System Savvy"

This resource presents my perspective on certain changes that modern leadership is encountering as it operates within structures and on the ways that authentic action can meet the challenges of these changes. It is a fact of organizational life that organizational roles legitimate authority to act. It is for this reason that I urge that we refer to the people in those roles as "positional leaders," and thereby prepare ourselves to give more thought to nonpositional leaders.

   Indeed, as our structures, especially those in the public sphere, become more and more complex, leadership faces the challenge of leading when no one is fully in charge of all aspects of a system. Think, for example, of the educational system that is formed by all this country's elementary schools, PTAs, teacher associations, school boards, and state and federal laws; or think of the complex collaborative network structures the United Nations has developed to do its work. How are these systems led?

284

Realms of Action

Bryson and Crosby (1992) open a very promising avenue of theory construction when they discuss this issue. They describe three contexts or structures of action in which leaders must be prepared to participate if they expect to produce effective action: forums, arenas, and courts. Forums are places of debate and discussion. Arenas are political decision-making contexts for stakeholders intimately involved in the action. For example, legislatures are the arenas where diverse values are shaped into unified legislative directives. The courts are the most tightly structured context of action, setting legal directives and enforcing penalties for noncompliance. Each structure contains its own dynamic rules and procedures, and it is these structures that sustain action when no one is in charge. Leaders must learn how each structure works and how it affects the issue-framing and policy-making processes.

The Action Model suggests two further realms of action: markets and the commonwealth. Markets open up the dynamics of exchanges and trade-offs in complex systems. The commonwealth expands the forums, encouraging debate and discussion about the meaning of the common good. Figure B.1 illustrates the relationship of the realms of action to the Action Wheel, showing the leadership issue that is at stake in each realm.

Figure B.1. Realms of Action Framed by the Action Wheel.

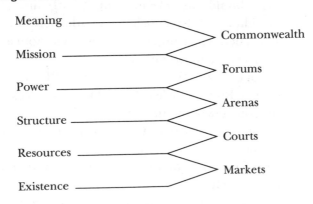

Ten Suggestions from Successful Cooperative Ventures

In part, Bryson and Crosby's work was inspired by Harlan Cleveland's description of our current situation as "a nobody-in-charge society." Cleveland and Geri Joseph, former Ambassador to the Netherlands, plus a number of graduate students, have also studied successful international cooperation in order to identify the structures and processes that sustain action when responsibility is widely shared and no one has total responsibility to make decisions.

Cleveland and Joseph (1988) identified eleven major cooperative efforts among nations and the reasons why these efforts worked. The eleven are weather forecasting, fighting infectious diseases, coordinating civil aviation, allocating radio frequencies, building a worldwide agricultural research network, reducing pollution in the Mediterranean, slowing the use of chlorofluorocarbons, suspending territorial claims in Antarctica, suspending territorial claims in outer space, developing a law-of-the-sea treaty, and developing a comprehensive strategy for assisting homeless international refugees. These efforts have been successful for at least ten reasons:

1. There is a consensus on desired outcomes. Folks can agree that smallpox is a threat to all, more accurate weather forecasts are needed, enclosed seas should be cleaned up, civil aircraft shouldn't collide, somebody should help refugees. There's no comparable consensus about armaments, trade, or money.

2. No one loses. We didn't get an INF [Intermediate-Range Nuclear Forces] treaty until each side concluded that its security could actually be enhanced by getting rid of unusable weapons systems.

3. Sovereignty is "pooled." Whenever a nation can't act effectively without combining its resources, imagination and technology with those of other nations, cooperation doesn't mean giv-

ing up sovereignty but *pooling* it—that is, using it together to avoid losing it separately.

4. Cooperation is stimulated by "a cocktail of fear and hope." Fear alone produces irrational, sometimes aggressive behavior. Hope alone produces good-hearted but unrealistic advocacy. Reality-based fear and hope, combined, seem to provide the motivation to cooperate.

5. People, not bureaucratic structures, make things happen. In each of the cases, a crucial role has been played by a few key individuals able to lead, inspire, share knowledge, and generate a climate of trust that brushes off the distrust still prevailing in other domains.

6. Key roles are played by nongovernments—scientific academies, research institutes, women's groups, international companies and "experts" who don't feel the need to act as representatives of their governments.

7. Information technologies are the essence. Needs for complex data processing and rapid, reliable communication seem to be common to the success stories in international cooperation.

8. Flexible, uncentralized systems work best. The more complicated the task and the more diverse the players, the more necessary it is to spread the work around so that many kinds of people are "improvising on an agreed sense of direction."

9. Educated "local talent" is essential. Especially where developing countries play a big part, cooperation works best when they use their own talent to do their own thing. The colonial days are past: imported experts shouldn't plan to stay.

10. The United States is a key player. For better or worse, American initiative, resources, and entrepreneurial bias seem to be indispensable. If the United States is "dead in the water," as Wash-

ington is just now, the international system is
likely to be becalmed as well [p. 33A].

System Savvy

Bryson and Crosby (1992) and Cleveland (1985) suggest specific
strategies authentic action leadership should adopt when framing
issues and resolving problems in complex systems. The overall requirement for leadership in these situations is what I call *system
savvy*. Senge (1990) is also particularly adamant about leadership's
need for systems knowledge, and my colleagues and I have seen this
need illustrated dramatically in our work with rural communities,
although the insight is not limited to those communities. We are
beginning to see what it might mean to lead "through" a system,
rather than to manage a system. As we move among communities
that are experiencing decline, we repeatedly confront people who
know only vaguely how complex organizational systems operate.
To respond to this need for system savvy, the Humphrey Institute
and the Reflective Leadership Center have recently entered into a
two year partnership with the Minnesota Extension Service in a
project entitled "Project Future." The project couples a variety of
visioning processes with systems thinking insights to support rural
communities in their desire to shape their own destinies. System
change manuals will target particular change issues such as getting
and keeping a hospital and consolidating a school system, and each
manual will seek to identify the critical levers of impact for comprehensive system redirection.

   We should begin looking for and expecting leadership from
surprising places and from surprising groups. It will burgeon at
many levels in complex systems and cooperative ventures. It will
become more important in self-directed teams, which are an important component of the quality movement. It will come from political downs, who are culturally savvy. It will appear at the margin,
at points of metaphor shear, not metaphor comfort. And it will no
longer be thought of primarily as a positional responsibility, but
will be seen to exist anywhere people courageously call forth authentic action.

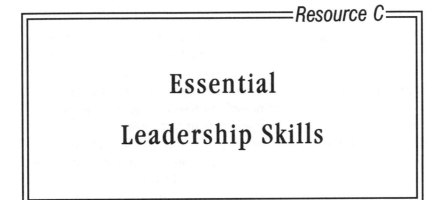

Essential

Leadership Skills

I have stated that leadership is practicing the art of authentic action, that it is not as much skill-driven as a special mode of engagement. Nevertheless, leadership does require skills, and personal type and character do play a role in leadership effectiveness.

Leadership Skills

Earlier, I identified my Myers-Briggs type—Extrovert, Intuitor, Feeler, Perceiver (ENFP). When I look at that fact, I must admit that the good news about me is, *I am who I am.* The bad news is, *I am who I am.* Even though I seek to be inclusive, I recognize the limit and possibility of being an ENFP.

However, being an ENFP or any other type is not an absolute limit. Even though I have a personality preference, I can learn from other preferences, just as I have a preference for right-handedness but I can learn to write left-handed. Skill acquisition and character development, while grounded in type, can transcend type. At the

Reflective Leadership Center, my colleagues and I cluster skills for leaders into six categories, based on the six schools of leadership thought and the Action Wheel.

Leadership School (Feature of Action)	Essential Skills
Personal (existence)	Understanding and using the Myers-Briggs Type Indicator and other tools for knowing oneself and others
Team (resources)	Diagnosing team needs with situational model, understanding small-group management techniques
Positional/Functional (structure)	Strategic planning, leading from the middle, promoting growth, managing retrenchment during organizational change, possessing system savvy
Political (power)	Managing and utilizing conflict, community organizing, encouraging collective leadership in communities
Visionary (mission)	Using intuition, storytelling, understanding and using myths, symbols, and metaphors
Ethical (meaning)	Identifying and defining critical ethical categories, performing ethical analysis, practicing clarity

These six skills come under the overarching skill of issue framing, using the Action Wheel. Like any skill, issue-framing is acquired through continual practice.

Knowledge of History

In addition to these skills, leadership must possess a deep knowledge of history and ecology, the setting (existence) from which all action emanates. Too many of those striving for leadership think that the future must be disconnected from knowledge of the past. They believe that the past only limits action. But our past, like our personality, is limit and possibility. We are not freed from the past by ignoring it. Only by understanding it and understanding ourselves as part of it can we transcend it. There is no vantage point high enough for us to see the whole picture of any issue. Even when we try to dwell in virtual reality, we never totally sever the tether to our true dwelling. I believe that our vision of the future is as profound and expansive as our grasp of the past. The further back we can see, the further forward we can envision. Therefore, I agree with Maccoby (1981), who recommends leaders read biographies and history. Historical illiteracy undermines leadership, depriving it of the experience of a broad section of existence.

The implications of this historical rootedness are humbling. Bumping into others and their ideas and their history is essential. Leadership is not solitary.

Character Building

Crises of meaning take us full circle to our past and the richness of existence for inspiration, courage, and hope. These experiences become the foundation for character building. There is no simple way to go about character building, for it is lifelong. It is *living* authenticity while also *living into* authenticity.

For example, sometimes one learns about leadership from unusual, even tragic events. One event that deepened my understanding of leadership occurred in the context of the murder of the twenty-six-year-old daughter of my best friends. The tragedy was real and excruciatingly painful for anyone who had known this young woman.

The unexpected learning about leadership came when I met the mortician, Roy, and his partner and wife, Pat. What I learned from them penetrated my soul. First, I was struck by Roy's suggestion that funeral directors have, as one of their missions, to help people through the process of grief. However, he said morticians often get in the way. They make people helpless. By doing everything for the mourners, morticians disempower them so that they are victims of the grieving process rather than shapers of it. Pat and Roy's perception of themselves was that they provided opportunities for people to "grab their grief" by making choices about the extent to which they will be involved with the funeral.

Roy and Pat begin with little choices. They ask people, Do you want to read the death certificate, or do you want us to keep it? Do you want to pick the clothes out for the burial, or do you want us to do that? Do you want to help dress the body, or do you want us to do that? The choices are endless. People can do very little, if that seems appropriate, or they can go to the extent of helping embalm the body, build the casket, dig the grave, fill it in, drive the hearse, even activate the switch that ignites the cremation furnace. Roy and Pat were enabling those who were grieving to take charge of the grieving, rather than be passive under its weight.

When Pat and Roy visited the young woman's parents they suggested the parents should take about six months to build a list of all the losses that they could imagine from Molly's death. The losses should be very concrete, very particular. After creating that list, the parents were to build a list of the gifts from Molly's death, reflecting not on the gift of her life, but no, on the gift of her death! Death just is. It's not good. It's not bad. It just is. To work through the meaning of death, we have to finally be able to believe and to say the "gift of death," not just the "gift of life."

Truly, leadership comes from surprising and often painful sources. Roy and Pat were exhibiting leadership by being authentic. They were calling forth authentic action in the commons. They were doing it in the most painful and personal context of life.

REFERENCES

Abilene Paradox. Carlsbad, Calif.: CRM Films, 1991. Videotape.

Adams, J. (ed.). *Transforming Work.* Alexandria, Va.: Miles River Press, 1984.

Adams, J. (ed.). *Transforming Leadership: From Vision to Results.* Alexandria, Va.: Miles River Press, 1986.

Aiken, H. D. *Reason and Conduct.* New York: Knopf Pub., 1962.

Alinsky, S. *Reveille for Radicals.* New York: Random House, 1989.

Anthony, D., Ecker, B., and Wilber, K. *Spiritual Choices: The Problem of Recognizing Authentic Paths to Inner Transformation.* New York: Paragon House, 1987.

Arendt, H. *The Human Condition.* New York: Doubleday, 1959.

Astin, H., and Leland, C. *Women of Influence, Women of Vision: A Cross-Generational Study of Leaders and Social Change.* San Francisco: Jossey-Bass, 1991.

Autry, J. *Love and Profit: The Art of Caring Leadership.* New York: William Morrow, 1991.

Bailey, F. G. *Humbuggery and Manipulation: The Art of Leadership*. Ithaca, N.Y.: Cornell University Press, 1989.

Barker, J. A. *Discovering the Future*. Lake Elmo, Minn.: Infinity Limited, 1985a. Videotape.

Barker, J. A. *Discovering the Future: The Business of Paradigms*. Lake Elmo, Minn.: Infinity Limited, 1985b.

Barker, J. A. *Future Edge: Discovering the New Paradigms of Success*. New York: William Morrow, 1992.

Barndt, J. *Liberating Our White Ghetto*. Minneapolis, Minn.: Augsburg, 1972.

Barrett, W. *Irrational Man: A Study in Existential Philosophy*. New York: Doubleday, 1958.

Bass, B. (ed.). *Stogdill's Handbook of Leadership*. New York: Free Press, 1981.

Bates, C. *Pigs Eat Wolves*. St. Paul, Minn.: Yes International, 1991.

Bennis, W. G., and Nanus, B. *Leaders: The Strategies for Taking Charge*. New York: HarperCollins, 1985.

Bernstein, R. *Beyond Objectionism and Relativism*. Philadelphia: University of Pennsylvania Press, 1985.

Birnbaum, J. "Crybabies: Eternal Victims." *Time,* Aug. 12, 1991, p. 16.

Blanchard, K., and Peale, N. V. *The Power of Ethical Management*. New York: Fossett-Cress, 1988.

Blanchard, K., Zigarmi, P., and Zigarmi, D. *Leadership and the One Minute Manager*. New York: William Morrow, 1985.

Blauner, R. *Racial Conflict*. Boston: Little, Brown, 1971.

Block, P. *The Empowered Manager: Positive Political Skills at Work*. San Francisco: Jossey-Bass, 1987.

Bly, R. *Iron John*. Reading, Mass.: Addison-Wesley, 1990.

Boehme, R. *Leadership for the 21st Century: Changing Nations Through the Power of Serving*. Seattle, Wash.: Frontline Communications, 1989.

Bok, S. *Lying: Moral Choice in Public and Private Life*. New York: Vintage Books, 1978.

Bok, S. *Secrets on the Ethics of Concealment and Revelation*. New York: Vintage Books, 1983.

Bolan, R. "The Professional Phenomenon: The Philosophy of Expertise." Unpublished manuscript, 1985.

Bolman, L. G., and Deal, T. E. *Modern Approaches to Understanding and Managing Organizations.* San Francisco: Jossey-Bass, 1984.

Bolman, L. G., and Deal, T. E. *Reframing Organizations: Artistry, Choice, and Leadership.* San Francisco: Jossey-Bass, 1991.

Bothwell, L. K. *The Art of Leadership: Skill Building Techniques That Produce Results.* Englewood Cliffs, N.J.: Prentice-Hall, 1983.

Boyte, H. C. *The Backyard Revolution.* Philadelphia: Temple University Press, 1980.

Boyte, H. C. *Community Is Possible.* New York: HarperCollins, 1984.

Boyte, H. C. *Commonwealth: A Return to Citizen Politics.* New York: Free Press, 1989.

Boyte, H. C., & Evans, S. *Free Spaces.* New York: HarperCollins, 1986.

Brodsky, J. "Uncommon Visage." *Poets & Writers Magazine,* Mar.-Apr. 1988, pp. 13–24.

Brown, M., and Paolucci, B. *Home Economics: A Definition.* Washington, D.C.: American Home Economics Association, 1979.

Bryson, J. M., and Crosby, B. C. *Leadership for the Common Good: Tackling Public Problems in a Shared-Power World.* San Francisco: Jossey-Bass, 1992.

Burke, J. *The Day the Universe Changed.* Boston: Little, Brown, 1985.

Burns, J. M. *Leadership.* New York: HarperCollins, 1978.

Burns, J. M. Foreword. In B. Kellerman (ed.), *Leadership: Multidisciplinary Perspectives.* Englewood Cliffs, N.J.: Prentice-Hall, 1984.

Burns, J. M. *On Being a Leader.* Reading, Mass.: Addison-Wesley, 1989.

Callahan, K. *Effective Church Leadership: Building on the Twelve Keys.* New York: HarperCollins, 1990.

Cameron, A. *Daughters of Copper Women.* East Haven, Conn.: Inland Publishers, 1988.

Campbell, D. Foreword. In W. Rosenbach and R. Taylor (eds.), *Contemporary Issues in Leadership.* Boulder, Colo.: Westview Press, 1984.

Campbell, J., and Moyers, B. *The Power of Myth.* New York: Doubleday, 1988.

Capra, F. *The Turning Point.* New York: Simon & Schuster, 1982.

Case, J. "Desperately Seeking Leadership." *Inc.,* Dec. 1987, p. 20.

Chancellor, J. *Peril and Promise: A Commentary on America.* New York: HarperCollins, 1990.

Clancy, J. *The Invisible Powers: The Language of Business.* Lexington, Mass.: Lexington Books, 1989.

Clark, K., and Clark, M. (eds.). *Measures of Leadership.* West Orange, N.J.: Leadership Library of America, 1990.

Clement, S., and Ayres, D. "A Matrix of Organizational Leadership Dimensions." U.S. Army Administration Center Leadership Monograph Series, #8. Oct. 1976.

Cleveland, H. *The Future Executive.* New York: HarperCollins, 1972.

Cleveland, H. *Education for Reflective Leadership Prospectus.* Minneapolis, Minn.: Hubert H. Humphrey Institute of Public Affairs, University of Minnesota, 1980.

Cleveland, H. *The Knowledge Executive.* New York: Dutton, 1985.

Cleveland, H., and Joseph, G. "In Affairs Among Nations, Cooperation Is Key." *Minneapolis Star Tribune,* Feb. 14, 1988, p. 33A.

Cohen, H. *You Can Negotiate Anything.* New York: Bantam Books, 1980.

Cohen, M. D., and March, J. G. *Leadership and Ambiguity: The American College President.* Boston, Mass.: Harvard Business School Press, 1986.

Coles, R. *The Spiritual Life of Children.* Boston: Houghton Mifflin, 1990.

Columbus, C. *The Log of Christopher Columbus,* R. H. Fuson (trans.). Camden, Maine: International Marine, 1987.

Conger, J. A. *The Charismatic Leader: Behind the Mystique of Exceptional Leadership.* San Francisco: Jossey-Bass, 1989.

Covey, S. *Principle-Centered Leadership.* New York: Summit Books, 1991.

Covey, S. *The Seven Habits of Highly Effective People.* New York: Simon & Schuster, 1989.

Cribbin, J. *Leadership: Your Competitive Edge.* New York: American Management Association, 1981.

Crosby, P. *Leading: The Art of Becoming an Executive.* New York: McGraw-Hill, 1990.

Deford, F. "America the Beautiful's Team." *Sports Illustrated,* Aug. 3, 1987.

Deming, W. E. *Out of the Crisis.* Cambridge: Massachusetts Institute of Technology Center for Advanced Engineering Study, 1986.

De Pree, M. *Leadership Is an Art.* New York: Doubleday, 1989.

De Pree, M. *Leadership Jazz.* New York: Currency Doubleday, 1992.

Dionne, E. J., Jr. *Why Americans Hate Politics.* New York: Simon & Schuster, 1991.

Eaton, M. *Basic Issues in Aesthetics.* Belmont, Calif.: Wadsworth, 1988.

Etzioni, A. *The Active Society.* New York: Free Press, 1968.

Falvey, J. "Before Spending $3 Million on Leadership, Read This." *Wall Street Journal,* Oct. 3, 1988, p. A22.

Ferguson, M. *The Aquarian Conspiracy.* Los Angeles: Tarcher, 1980.

Fisher, R., and Brown, S. *Getting Together: Building a Relationship As We Negotiate.* New York: Penguin, 1988.

Fisher, R., and Ury, W. *Getting to Yes: Negotiating Agreement Without Giving In.* New York: Penguin, 1983.

Fox, M. *Original Blessing.* Santa Fe, N.Mex.: Bear, 1983.

Frankena, W. *Ethics.* Englewood Cliffs, N.J.: Prentice-Hall, 1983.

Freire, P. *Pedagogy of the Oppressed.* New York: Seabury Press, 1974.

Friedman, M. *Capitalism and Freedom.* Chicago: University of Chicago Press, 1962.

Friedman, M., and Friedman, R. *Free to Choose.* Orlando, Fla.: Harcourt Brace Jovanovich, 1980.

Fritz, R. *The Path of Least Resistance.* Selma, Mass.: DMA, 1984.

Fugard, A. *"Master Harold"—and the Boys.* Yale School of Drama, Winter, 1982.

Gardner, H. "Beyond the IQ: Education and Human Development." *Harvard Education Review,* May 1987, 57(2), 188–189.

Gardner, J. *On Leadership.* New York: Free Press, 1989.

Gardner, J. *Building Community.* Washington, D.C.: The Independent Sector, 1992.

Geertz, C. *The Interpretation of Cultures.* New York: Basic Books, 1973.

Geertz, C. *Local Knowledge: Further Essays in Interpretive Anthropology.* New York: Basic Books, 1983.

Gewirth, A. *Reason and Morality.* Chicago: University of Chicago Press, 1982.

Gilligan, C. *In a Different Voice: Psychological Theory and Women's Development.* Cambridge: Harvard University Press, 1982.

Gleick, J. *Chaos.* New York: Viking Press, 1987.

Goleman, D. *Vital Lies, Simple Truths: The Psychology of Self-Discipline.* New York: Simon & Schuster, 1985.

Goleman, D. "The Dark Side of Charisma." *New York Times,* Apr. 1, 1990, Sec. 3, Part 2, p. 25.

Greenleaf, R. *Servant Leadership.* New York: Paulist Press, 1977.

Hagberg, J. *Real Power.* Minneapolis, Minn.: Winston Press, 1984.

Hagberg, J., and Guelich, R. *The Critical Journey.* Dallas: Word Publishing, 1989.

Hallie, P. *Lest Innocent Blood Be Shed: The Story of the Village of Le Chambon, and How Goodness Happened There.* New York: HarperCollins, 1985.

Hampl, P. *Spillville.* Minneapolis, Minn.: Milkweed Editions, 1987.

Harvey, J. B. *The Abilene Paradox: The Mismanagement of Agreement.* Amacom, N.Y.: Organizational Dynamics, 1974.

Heider, J. *The Tao of Leadership.* Atlanta, Ga.: Humanics New Age, 1985.

Heifetz, R., and Sinder, R. "Political Leadership: Managing the Public's Problem-Solving." In R. Reich (ed.), *The Power of Public Ideas.* New York: Harper Business, 1988.

Hersey, P. *The Situational Leader.* Escondido, Calif.: Warner Books, 1984.

Higham, J. (ed.). *Ethnic Leadership in America.* Baltimore, Md.: Johns Hopkins University Press, 1978.

Hillesum, E. *An Interrupted Life.* New York: Washington Square Press, 1985.

Hodgkinson, C. *The Philosophy of Leadership.* New York: St. Martin's Press, 1983.

Hopcke, R. *A Guided Tour of the Collected Works of C. G. Jung.* Boston, Mass.: Shambhala, 1989.

Hyde, L. *The Gift.* New York: Random House, 1983.

Introduction to Type. Palo Alto, Calif.: Consulting Psychologists Press, 1987.

Johnson, D., and Johnson, F. *Joining Together.* Englewood Cliffs, N.J.: Prentice-Hall, 1975.

Johnson, M. (ed.). *Philosophical Perspectives on Metaphors.* Minneapolis: University of Minnesota, 1980.

Jordan, W. *White over Black: American Attitudes Toward the Negro 1550–1812.* Chapel Hill: University of North Carolina Press, 1968.

Kanter, D. L., and Mirvis, P. H. *The Cynical Americans: Living and Working in an Age of Discontent and Disillusion.* San Francisco: Jossey-Bass, 1989.

Karlsson, J. L. *Inheritance of Creative Intelligence.* Chicago: Nelson-Hall, 1978.

Katz, P., and Taylor, D. (eds.). *Eliminating Racism: Profiles in Controversy.* New York: Plenum Press, 1988.

Keifer, C., and Senge, P. "Metanoic Organizations." In J. Adams (ed.), *Transforming Work.* Alexandria, Va.: Miles River Press, 1984.

Keirsey, D., and Bates, M. *Please Understand Me.* Del Mar, Calif.: Prometheus Nemesis Books, 1978.

Kellerman, B. (ed.). *Leadership: Multidisciplinary Perspectives.* Englewood Cliffs, N.J.: Prentice-Hall, 1984.

Kelley, R. *The Power of Followership: How to Create Leaders People Want.* New York: Doubleday/Currency, 1992.

Kierkegaard, S. *Fear and Trembling* and *Sickness unto Death,* W. Lowrie (trans.). New York: Doubleday Books, 1954.

Kirkpatrick, J. "Private Virtues, Public Vices." In *Ethics and Public Policy Essay, #41,* Washington, D.C.: The Ethics and Public Policy Center, Dec. 1982.

Koestenbaum, P. *Leadership: The Inner Side of Greatness.* San Francisco: Jossey-Bass, 1991.

Kotter, J. *The Leadership Factor.* New York: Free Press, 1988.

Kotter, J. *A Force for Change: How Leadership Differs from Management.* New York: Free Press, 1990a.

Kotter, J. "What Leaders Do." *Harvard Business Review*, May-June 1990b, pp. 104–111.

Kouzes, J. M., and Posner, B. Z. *The Leadership Challenge: How to Get Extraordinary Things Done in Organizations*. San Francisco: Jossey-Bass, 1987.

Kuhn, T. *The Structure of Scientific Revolutions*. Chicago: University of Chicago Press, 1970.

Kupfer, J. *Experience as Art: Aesthetics in Everyday Life*. New York: State University of New York Press, 1984.

Kushner, H. S. *When Bad Things Happen to Good People*. New York: Avon Books, 1992. (Originally published 1981.)

Lakoff, G. *Women, Fire, and Dangerous Things: What Categories Reveal About the Mind*. Chicago, Ill.: University of Chicago Press, 1987.

Lakoff, G., and Johnson, M. *Metaphors We Live By*. Chicago: University of Chicago Press, 1980.

Lebacqz, K. *Six Theories of Justice*. Minneapolis, Minn.: Augsburg, 1986.

Lee, C. "Can Leadership Be Taught?" *Training*, July 1989, p. 20.

Lefkowitz, M. "The Myth of Joseph Campbell." *The American Scholar*, Summer 1990, pp. 429–434.

Levitz, L. *No Fault Negotiating*. New York: Warner Books, 1987.

Lopez, B. *Arctic Dreams*. New York: Charles Scribner's Sons, 1986.

Lukas, J. A. *Common Ground*. New York: Vintage Books, 1986.

Lutz, W. *Doublespeak*. New York: HarperCollins, 1990.

Maccoby, M. *The Gamesman*. New York: Simon & Schuster, 1976.

Maccoby, M. *The Leader*. New York: Ballantine Books, 1981.

McGuffey, W. H. *McGuffey Readers*. 9 vols. New York: Gordon Press, 1973. (Originally published 1844.)

McKeon, R. (ed.). *The Basic Works of Aristotle*. New York: Random House, 1941.

McKeon, R. *Freedom and History and Other Essays*. Chicago: University of Chicago Press, 1990.

Martin, M. *Self-Deception and Morality*. Kansas: University Press of Kansas, 1986.

May, R. *Power and Innocence*. New York: Norton, 1972.

May, R., Angel, E., and Ellenberger, H. (eds.). *Existence*. New York: Basic Books, 1958.

Mintzberg, H. *The Structuring of Organizations.* Englewood Cliffs, N.J.: Prentice-Hall, 1979.

Mitroff, I. I., and Bennis, W. *The Unreality Industry.* New York: Carol, 1989.

Moore, C. *The Mediation Process: Practical Strategies for Resolving Conflict.* San Francisco: Jossey-Bass, 1986.

Morgan, G. *Images and Organizations.* London: Sage, 1986.

Morris, H. *Freedom and Responsibility.* Stanford, Calif.: Stanford University Press, 1961.

Morton, K. "Bookshelf." *Tesseract: University YMCA Book Review.* Minneapolis, Minn., 1987, *188,* p. 2.

Morton, N. *Journey Is Home.* Boston: Beacon Press, 1986.

Munsey, B. (ed.). *Moral Development, Moral Education, and Kohlberg: Basic Issues in Philosophy, Psychology, Religion, and Education.* Birmingham, Ala.: Religious Education Press, 1980.

Myers, I. B. *Gifts Differing.* Palo Alto, Calif.: Consulting Psychologists Press, 1980.

Naisbitt, J. *Megatrends: Ten New Directions Transforming Our Lives.* New York: Warner Books, 1982.

Nanus, B. *Visionary Leadership: Creating a Compelling Sense of Direction for Your Organization.* San Francisco: Jossey-Bass, 1992.

Neihardt, J. *Black Elk Speaks.* Lincoln: University of Nebraska Press, 1961.

Nicoll, D. "Grace Beyond the Rules: A New Paradigm for Lives on a Human Scale." In Adams, J. (ed.), *Transforming Work.* Alexandria, Va.: Miles River Press, 1984.

Niebuhr, H. R. *The Responsible Self.* New York: HarperCollins, 1963.

Niebuhr, R. *Moral Man and Immoral Society.* New York: Charles Scribner's Sons, 1960. (Originally published 1932.)

Nixon, R. *Leaders.* New York: Warner Books, 1982.

Nouwen, H. *Out of Solitude.* Notre Dame, Ind.: Ave Maria Press, 1983.

Nouwen, H. *Lifesigns.* New York: Doubleday, 1986.

Nouwen, H. *In the Name of Jesus: Reflections on Christian Leadership.* New York: Crossroad, 1989.

Oden, T. (ed.). *Parables of Kierkegaard*. Princeton, N.J.: Princeton University Press, 1978.

Orsburn, J., Moran, L., Musselwhite, E., and Zenger, J. (eds.). *Self-Directed Work Teams: The New American Challenge*. Homewood, Ill.: Business One Irwin, 1990.

Parsons, T. *Sociological Theory and Modern Society*. New York: Free Press, 1967.

Pastin, M. *The Hard Problems of Management: Gaining the Ethics Edge*. San Francisco: Jossey-Bass, 1986.

Patterson, J., and Kim, P. *The Day America Told the Truth*. Englewood Cliffs, N.J.: Prentice-Hall, 1991.

Peck, M. S. *The Road Less Traveled*. New York: Simon & Schuster, 1988.

Pepper, S. *World Hypotheses*. Berkeley: University of California Press, 1970.

Peters, T., and Austin, N. *A Passion for Excellence: The Leadership Difference*. New York: Random House, 1985.

Peters, T., and Waterman, R. *In Search of Excellence*. New York: HarperCollins, 1982.

Philp, H. L. *Jung and the Problem of Evil*. New York: McBride, 1958.

Pinkerton, E. C. *Word for Word*. Old Lyme, Conn.: Verbatim Books, 1982.

Powell, C. Remarks in Interview with David Brinkley, NBC, Jan. 14, 1990.

Powell, J. "Scandals, Scoundrels, and Saints—Ethics and Integrity in the Federal Government." Speech presented at conference sponsored by Senior Executive Association, Spring 1987.

Pritchard, M. *On Becoming Responsible*. Lawrence: University Press of Kansas, 1991.

Public Broadcasting System. *A Viewer's Guide to Ethics in America*. New York: CI Systems, Inc., 1989.

Rawls, J. *A Theory of Justice*. Cambridge, Mass.: Harvard University Press, 1971.

Reich, R. *Tales of a New America*. New York: Times Books, 1987.

Rest, J. "Can Ethics Be Taught in Professional School? The Psychological Research." *Ethics, Easier Said Than Done*, Winter 1988, *1*(1), 22–26.

References   **303**

Roberts, W. *Leadership Secrets of Attila the Hun.* New York:
Warner Books, 1985.
Rost, J. *Leadership for the Twenty-First Century.* New York:
Praeger, 1991.
St. Paul Pioneer Press, Sept. 13, 1992, pp. 1, 18.
Sanders, J. O. *Spiritual Leadership.* Chicago: Moody Press, 1980.
Schaef, A. W., and Fassel, D. *The Addictive Organization.* San Francisco: HarperCollins, 1988.
Schneiders, S. "The Effects of Women's Experience on Their Spirituality." In J. Conn (ed.), *Women's Spirituality.* New York:
Paulist Press, 1986.
Schön, D. *The Reflective Practitioner.* New York: Basic Books,
1983.
Schwager, R. *Must There Be Scapegoats?* San Francisco: HarperCollins, 1978.
Schwartz, P. *The Art of the Long View.* New York: Doubleday,
1991.
Senge, P. M. *The Fifth Discipline: The Art and Practice of the
Learning Organization.* New York: Doubleday, 1990.
Shirts, R. G. *BAFA' BAFA'.* Del Mar, Calif.: Simile II, 1977.
Skinner, B. F. *Walden Two.* New York: Macmillan, 1976.
Smith, H. *Beyond the Post-Modern Mind.* New York: Crossroad,
1982.
Smith, H. *The Power Game.* New York: Random House, 1988.
Smith, K., and Clark, R. "Executive Development Center." *Journal
of Extension,* Winter 1987, pp. 19–22.
Stacey, R. *Managing the Unknowable: Strategic Boundaries Between Order and Chaos in Organizations.* San Francisco: Jossey-Bass, 1992.
Steger, W., and Schurke, P. *North to the Pole.* New York: Times
Books, 1987.
Stengel, R. "Whatever Happened to Ethics: Assaulted by Sleaze,
Scandals and Hypocrisy." *Time,* May 25, 1987, p. 20.
Terry, R. *For Whites Only.* Grand Rapids, Mich.: Eerdmans, 1970.
Terry, R. "The Negative Impact on White Values." In B. Bowser
and R. Hunt (eds.). *Impact of Racism on White Americans.* London: Sage, 1981.

Thomas, L. "Man's Role on Earth." *New York Times Magazine,* Apr. 1, 1984, pp. 36–37.

Thompson, K. (ed.). *Political Traditions and Contemporary Problems,* Vol. II. Washington, D.C.: University Press of America, 1982.

Tichy, N., and Devanna, M. A. *The Transformational Leader.* New York: Wiley, 1986.

Tillich, P. *Love, Power and Justice.* Oxford, England: Oxford University Press, 1954.

Time, Jan. 12, 1990, p. 27.

Toffler, B. *Tough Choices: Managers Talk Ethics.* New York: Wiley, 1986.

Tucker, R. *Politics as Leadership.* Columbia: University of Missouri Press, 1981.

Vaill, P. B. *Managing as a Performing Art: New Ideas for a World of Chaotic Change.* San Francisco: Jossey-Bass, 1991.

Webster's Third New International Dictionary, Unabridged. Springfield, Mass.: Merriam-Webster, Inc., 1986.

Welwood, J. "On Spatial Authority: Genuine and Counterfeit." In D. Anthony, B. Ecker, and K. Wilber, *Spiritual Choices: The Problem of Recognizing Authentic Paths to Inner Transformation.* New York: Paragon House, 1987.

Winter, G. *Liberating Creation: Foundations of Religious Social Ethics.* New York: Crossroad, 1981.

Yukl, G. *Leadership in Organizations.* Englewood Cliffs, N.J.: Prentice-Hall, 1981.

Zukav, G. *The Seat of the Soul.* New York: Simon & Schuster, 1989.

INDEX